Svend Robinson: A Life in Politics

Svend Robinson

A Life in Politics

GRAEME TRUELOVE

 NEW STAR BOOKS • VANCOUVER • 2013

NEW STAR BOOKS LTD.

107 – 3477 Commercial Street | Vancouver, BC V5N 4E8 CANADA
1574 Gulf Road, #1517 | Point Roberts, WA 98281 USA
www.NewStarBooks.com | info@NewStarBooks.com

The views expressed in this work are solely those of the author in his private capacity. While all due care was taken, the responsibility for any errors, omissions or views expressed herein remains with the author, and cannot and should not be attributed to the House of Commons, its employees, officers and agents, or the Board of Internal Economy.

The publisher acknowledges the financial support of the Canada Council for the Arts and the Government of Canada through the Canada Book Fund, and the Province of British Columbia through the British Columbia Arts Council and the Book Publishing Tax Credit.

Cataloguing information for this book is available from Library and Archives Canada, www.collectionscanada.gc.ca.

Cover design by Rayola Creative
Printed on 100% post-consumer recycled paper
Printed and bound in Canada by Imprimerie Gauvin, Gatineau, QC
First printing, October 2013

Contents

All the world will be your enemy, Prince with a Thousand Enemies, and whenever they catch you, they will kill you. But first they must catch you . . .

— RICHARD ADAMS, *Watership Down*

Introduction

He has been called Canada's protester-in-chief, the knight of the vanishing left, his name synonymous with an entire political movement for most of the 25 years that he sat in the House of Commons. Such longevity on the battlefields of Parliament Hill is in itself an impressive achievement. In Canadian history, only two other British Columbians and three other New Democrats managed that length of continuous service in Ottawa. But it is not merely for his longevity that Svend Robinson will be remembered.

The lessons of a tumultuous youth instilled a set of principles and a sense of compassion that set him apart from his peers. His transformation — from a brazen kid who stood up for his beliefs to a precocious lawyer with an activist streak — did not alter his purpose, and the same principles that defined him as a child and as a young man drove him in his political career. His resume as a member of Parliament provides a tour of some of the greatest moments in modern Canadian political history. From his involvement with the most significant pieces of justice legislation passed during Pierre Trudeau's final term in office, including the Charter of Rights and Freedoms, to his landmark efforts to ensure equal rights for gay and lesbian Canadians during the governments of

Brian Mulroney, Jean Chrétien and Paul Martin, his impact on our legal landscape is undeniable. His influence also reached beyond the limits of parliamentary jurisdiction and into the realm of international power politics, as he fought for minority self-determination and environmental protection throughout the world.

His name is sprinkled throughout the headlines of a quarter century. As a 27-year-old rookie MP, he learned the value of bold action and dramatic language in drumming up popular support for a cause. In his first days as an MP, he used that support to save the life of a Chilean refugee about to be shipped back to Augusto Pinochet's Chile by Canadian immigration officials. It was a tactic he would repeat again and again, sometimes audaciously but often effectively. It was central to his role in the legendary environmental protests in Haida Gwaii and Clayoquot Sound, to his support for Sue Rodriguez and the right to die with dignity, and to countless other causes that he made his own. Armed with the courage of his convictions, he trekked through jungles and war zones, and stared down riot cops and armed soldiers in the pursuit of justice. His ability to capture the media's attention and galvanize public opinion was also a crucial ingredient in allowing him to do what no other Canadian politician had dared to do before him: affirm that he was gay.

When opponents would not yield, he pushed, hard. He would say what no one else would, often bringing both the public and his own party decades ahead of views commonly held at the time. His commitment to profound socialist change was unabashed. Instead of telling Canadians what they wanted to hear, he bluntly told them the truth, exactly as he saw it. He knew that there were environmental limits to economic growth, for example — that we cannot have our cake and eat it, too. The boldness of his vision was often a direct threat to those who had the most to gain from the status quo, and that ensured fierce resistance. Opponents pushed back, in bitter caucus debates, in vicious barbs flung across the aisle in the House of Commons, in taunting editorials and in anonymous hate mail slipped under his door under cover of night.

Both the vitriol of opponents and his own driven — at times

obsessive — behaviour took their toll, culminating in the baffling theft of a valuable ring, an act that prematurely ended his career. Although he remains a hero to countless Canadians, that disastrous act has been given disproportionate stature, an ugly asterisk on the public memory of a giant in the fields of human rights and environmental protection.

His absence on the federal scene today is palpable. As a Reform MP, Stephen Harper sat only a few seats away from Robinson, and later claimed that there was no politician he disagreed with more often than his formidable NDP opponent. Now, as prime minister, Harper leads a majority government; unsurprisingly, the profound socialist change that Robinson sought is not on the agenda.

Still, modern Canada has been heavily affected by Robinson's work. There has yet to be an exhaustive study of that impact — on the mainstream, on the NDP and on the left. There has yet to be a satisfactory explanation of the factors that led to his fall. There has yet to be closure for his supporters, who lost their hero at the height of his influence. It is hoped that this book will provide what's been missing and, along the way, draw an accurate portrait of a fearless and troubled Canadian who challenged his country to become more forward-thinking, more peaceful and more compassionate. The House of Commons is still waiting for Robinson's replacement, and the task he set for us daunts us still.

ONE

The Year of the Dragon

Svend Robinson would later say that his father Wayne had "a wandering spirit in the blood," but that hardly covered it. Wayne Robinson was born in Portland, Oregon, in 1927. The son of an insurance salesman, Wayne was still a boy when his mother, drunk and passed out, burned to death in a house fire.

Despite the spectre of alcoholism that darkened his childhood and left him with a constant, simmering anger, he became a top student and athlete. He was an Eagle Scout and a competitive swimmer. He spent time in the U.S. Navy, developing a toughness that stayed with him throughout his life. But what was most striking about him was the way he let his fierce and insatiable intellect direct his life. He had already studied at three universities before deciding to set sail for Denmark in 1950 to study the works of Søren Kierkegaard and Henrik Ibsen.

A few months later, he met a beautiful young Danish woman named Edith Jensen. Edith was the youngest of Alfred and Johanne Jensen's 11 children. She inherited a family talent for painting, a deep religious faith and a gentle beauty that captivated the angry young American student. While Wayne's early years were marked by the constant wars that ravage the family of an alcoholic, Edith's adolescence was marked by the war in Europe. Her parents had a secret compartment in their basement where they hid Jews during the Nazi occupation, helping them escape to Sweden. Edith would bring food to the people hiding in the basement, while her older brothers were active in the legendary Danish resistance. The bravery and selflessness of her countrymen in those terrifying years left a deep impression on Edith, as they did on the world.

Wayne and Edith were married in Copenhagen on November 5, 1950. Edith's family didn't get along with Wayne, but there was nothing they could do. She was in love. The young couple moved to Minneapolis, where Wayne continued his studies and worked as a hospital orderly. They lived in student housing in an area of the city known as Dinkytown. On March 4, 1952, Edith gave birth to a son. She named him Svend after her youngest brother, an artist. Family lore has it that Edith's newborn son peed on the doctor, a fitting beginning for a man who would make a career out of challenging authority.

It could have been a commonplace childhood for the little half-Dane, but there was that "wandering spirit" in his father's blood. Wayne had earned a master's degree in English literature, and had become a talented and popular teacher. However, he also had a serious drinking problem, which made it difficult to hold down a job. Angry and frustrated, he had a nervous breakdown while travelling through Grant's Pass, Oregon, that ended with a brief stay in a mental hospital. Edith, who was pregnant with Svend's sister Gretchen at the time, returned to her relieved family in Denmark, taking Svend with her. Discharged from the hospital, Wayne hitch-hiked to Minneapolis and begged Edith to come back.

"I have no doubt that he loved my mother a lot. I have no doubt about that," Gretchen says. "You can still love somebody and mistreat them."

Still in love, Edith agreed to return to Minneapolis, and the young family was reunited. But while Wayne had won Edith back, he still could not control his drinking or keep a job for longer than a year. In 1956 the family moved to California. They were back in Minneapolis the next year. The year after that they were in Columbia, Missouri, where Svend began Grade 1. The next year they were in

Canada. Svend liked living in Victoria, in their house near a field where he loved to play. By this time he had a second sister to play with, Ingrid. But there was no point in getting comfortable.

The pattern was always the same: Wayne would get a great job, perhaps as an English professor at the local college, and the family would start to settle, but sooner or later Wayne's drinking would get him into trouble. Something would happen — like the time he had a car accident on campus — and they'd be on the move again.

Seattle, Washington.

Jamestown, North Dakota.

Lethbridge, Alberta.

At times, Wayne was a wonderful father. He quoted Shakespeare, drew cartoons and took the family camping. "We went on a lot of family drives," recalls Gretchen. "I remember one time in Pennsylvania. It was so beautiful, the trees and everything out there. We had a hamburger fight right in the middle of the car! I don't know how it started, I don't know who was responsible, I have no idea. I just know some of us were slinging hamburgers at each other." Wayne had a mischievous side, and he was happy to see his family having fun.

Wayne and Edith encouraged their children to enjoy learning, too. Svend was an excellent student who could read before Grade 1 and was allowed to skip Grade 2. His parents also had powerful social consciences. Wayne was a determined class warrior, while gentle Edith was a compassionate woman of faith and an ardent admirer of the medical missionary Dr. Albert Schweitzer. There were always political conversations around the dinner table, and the convictions of his parents had an impact on Svend at a young age. When Svend was sent home from his Seattle school in Grade 3 for refusing to recite the Pledge of Allegiance because he felt that the promised "liberty and justice for all" didn't describe the impoverished, mostly black housing project the Robinsons called home, his parents were proud of him. The same was true in Lethbridge, in Grade 6, when Svend refused to shake the hand of the school principal after winning the top student award, having heard the same principal once say he "wouldn't shake an Indian's hand because it would be dirty." Both parents could see a bit of themselves in these little acts of bravery.

But when Wayne drank, he was a different man. The wonderful camping trips turned ugly. Svend recalls Wayne pelting him with rocks until he climbed a tree to escape. Quiet nights at home would be shattered when Wayne flew into a sudden rage. He beat Edith, threw things and once stabbed her in the arm with a fork. When Svend tried to intervene, he'd be beaten, too. Once, at dinner, Wayne hit Svend in the face so hard that his glasses snapped and his nose was broken, giving him the slight hook in the bridge of his nose that would later be exaggerated by political cartoonists. On another occasion, Svend was hog-tied, beaten and locked in a closet. He managed to untie himself and ran out into the street, tears streaming, swearing that he would never return.

School was no better. Scrawny, clumsy, a top student and constantly the new kid, Svend was bullied at every school he attended. Children can be vicious towards those who don't fit in, and the vaguely effeminate kid who hadn't wanted to recite the Pledge of Allegiance was different. He was beaten up and pushed down the stairs at school. On his way home, he was chased by bullies hurling rocks. Books became his friends, and he got used to being alone. He wasn't afraid of the bullies; he came to expect them. Conflict became a way of life.

In Lethbridge, Wayne admitted he had a problem and joined Alcoholics Anonymous. It worked for a while. The beatings continued, now fuelled by the torment of withdrawal instead of by drunken fury, but professionally Wayne thrived. He became head of the faculty association at Lethbridge Junior College, and the family stayed put for three years. For the first time the Robinsons owned their own home, and now there was a third sister to help fill it, Kim. This was the longest Svend had lived anywhere, and at age nine, he began to make friends. In his last year in Alberta, he was elected to his first public office, Grade 7 student rep at Wilson Junior High School. At last, his childhood stood a chance of being a happy one.

But Edith became homesick for Denmark, and Wayne set his

sights on a PhD at the University of Minnesota. They couldn't agree on where to go, so the family split in two. In 1964 Edith took the girls to Copenhagen, and Wayne took Svend, then 12, to Minneapolis. The new kid in school once more, Svend was again the victim of bullies. Wayne was bitterly disappointed, too. He expected to be able to enroll in the doctoral program he'd applied for, but he discovered when he arrived that the university remembered his last stay and didn't want him back. After a short time, Wayne decided that he and Svend would return to Denmark, too. They gave up their beloved German Shepherd, Perle, and in the middle of winter drove to Montreal, sold the car and boarded the Polish ocean liner *Batory* for the nine-day crossing to Denmark.

Svend and his sisters dutifully learned Danish at school, while Edith reconnected with family and worked as a telephone operator. Wayne had more difficulty adjusting. He still didn't get along with Edith's family. Unable to speak Danish, he couldn't find work. With nothing for Wayne to do but rage at Edith and the kids, life in Denmark was worse than ever. "He and my mother fought constantly, sometimes violently. I remember one time, when the fighting got particularly ugly, going into the kitchen and getting a small, sharp paring knife. I took it back into my room and tried to get up enough nerve to kill myself, to slice my wrists," Robinson remembers. After a few hellish months, the family decided they were better off in the United States. They moved to a trailer park in Slippery Rock, Pennsylvania, and Wayne taught at the local college. Two years sober, he started to drink again. As Wayne descended into the old patterns, Svend tried to stop him. He recalls once taking his father's beer and dumping it in a nearby river, and then disconnecting the car battery to stop him from driving into town to buy more. The results were predictable; Wayne flew into a rage and beat him mercilessly.

For Svend, it was a rootless, powerless childhood. Children need to feel a sense of control over their environment, and expect a certain predictability from the world around them, but children of alcoholic parents don't have that security. Instead, they are the victims of the chaotic, miserable life of the parent, who is loving one day, violent and abusive the next. Like many of those children, Svend developed an entrenched yearning for control over his surroundings. "There are certain defined behaviour patterns of a child in that situation," he explained to *Saturday Night* in 1989. "One is repressing one's feelings and emotions as a kind of survival mechanism, and developing a shell to withstand the emotional trauma. The other pattern is control."

Learning how to assert that control as he entered his teenage years was difficult. He mouthed off to his teachers and argued with his sisters. Sometimes he could be a bully. Gretchen remembers him once tormenting her into stealing a chocolate bar and another time throwing rocks at her. He set fires out in the bush, and more than once was caught and brought home by the police. He stole worthless items from shops, and broke into rural cottages with other troubled kids to steal money to play poker.

During his political career, Robinson rarely spoke publicly about his childhood and never spoke about the abuse his father perpetrated on the family. Many of his closest friends had no idea what a difficult childhood he'd had. Even today, while acknowledging it as an important part of his story, he finds it difficult to discuss. "It wasn't a very happy childhood," he observes carefully. His voice belies the understatement. "It's not the kind of thing that you forgive."

He was closest to his mother during those tormented years. "She was about as innocent as they come. A very fine human being. Just a very compassionate, decent human being. Just worshipped my Dad. Would do anything for him," Robinson recalls. If he feels any resentment towards his mother for her role in that dysfunctional family system, it is only for remaining in it. "She shouldn't have stayed with him a day," he says.

•   •   •

By the mid-1960s the Vietnam War had escalated. A little over a decade earlier, Vietnam had been a French colony, but a Vietnamese nationalist and communist movement forced the French from the north, while pro-Western forces consolidated in the south. The

U.S., believing that communism was a threat to western investment and trade, became increasingly entangled in the conflict and eventually entered into a full-scale war against the communists. That war would ultimately cost, by most estimates, at least one million lives. Like many Americans, Wayne and Edith wanted no part of it. To them, the bodies dropping on the other side of the Pacific had drenched their country in blood. They hated seeing their tax dollars finance what they believed was an immoral war, and they hated the idea that their 14-year-old son might one day be subject to the draft if the war continued. Thousands of Americans evading the draft, deserters and conscientious objectors packed up and left for Canada, and the Robinsons were among them. Wayne got a job at the brand-new Simon Fraser University (SFU) in Burnaby, B.C., and in 1966 the family left the U.S. behind.

In many ways Burnaby was the perfect fit. SFU was known for its progressive politics. Capitol Hill, the neighbourhood where the Robinsons rented a brown and white bungalow with a view of Burrard Inlet, was sometimes called "Red Hill" because of the left-leaning tendencies of its residents. In Burnaby, academics and activism, the twin inheritances of Svend's troubled childhood, no longer made him a victim. Instead, they allowed him to flourish. Even though he raised a few eyebrows for bringing a leather briefcase to school, at Burnaby North Secondary he wasn't the strange, bullied kid who wouldn't recite the Pledge of Allegiance. Instead, he was the leader of the opposition in the school's model Parliament, where he was also named Best Debater. He edited the school newspaper and yearbook. He became a cadet leader with St. John's Ambulance and a volunteer in an assisted-living residence, where he helped with chores, called bingo and took residents for outings. He had best friends, and even a girlfriend. He and his mother sang together in a local church choir. For the teenaged American immigrant, childhood finally started to make some sense.

There was a provincial election in B.C. the year the Robinsons arrived in Burnaby. The ruling Social Credit Party, which had significantly limited the power of labour unions and reduced spending on social welfare, seemed to have too much in common with the people who had turned the U.S. into a place where the Robinsons no longer wanted to live. Instead, Edith was drawn to the New Democratic Party (NDP), whose policies more closely resembled the social democracy in her native Denmark. When she invited her teenaged son to join her in handing out leaflets for the local NDP candidate, Eileen Dailly, she ignited a passion that would define him, consume him, and one day change the face of the Canadian left.

TWO

Directions

"The minute I could leave home, I left."

At 17, Svend moved into residence at the University of British Columbia (UBC). His parents agreed to give him $50 a month (about $300 today), but only until his 18th birthday, and he would have to make up the rest of his expenses with entrance scholarships and part-time employment. He found a wide variety of jobs, working as a taxi driver, a driving examiner and a night-time desk clerk at the Sylvia Hotel. He also lifted crates at the Coca-Cola bottling plant. "It was good for my back, if not my spirits," he says. Like many children of alcoholics, he drank too much, but he thought he had it under control. It felt good to know that his days of returning home from school to a family tearing itself apart were over.

A student in the faculty of science, Svend planned to become a pediatrician. His activist bent was growing stronger, and he saw medicine as a good way to contribute to a world in need, perhaps by working for an international health care organization. Edith, who had worked for a time as a nurse, couldn't have been happier. Wayne joked that she'd made incantations over her womb during her pregnancies, hoping one of her children might follow in the footsteps of her hero, Albert Schweitzer. Svend had always been an excellent chemistry and biology student, and at UBC he also showed a strong aptitude for psychology. His social psychology professor, Peter Suedfeld, today recalls him as one of the most outstanding students he'd had in nearly 40 years of teaching.

But UBC in the 1970s could be a distracting place. Like many undergraduate students, exposed to a wider range of possibilities than ever before, Svend began to question his chosen path. The volunteer spirit that had blossomed in Burnaby found further expression at UBC. In the fall of 1970, transient young people hitchhiking across the country occupied the Student Union Building because they had nowhere else to stay. Students voted in a referendum to evict them, and there were some scuffles between students and youths. With the atmosphere on campus tense, Svend pitched the idea of a youth referral centre to Vancouver City Council. The centre would find homestays for travelling youth and then reimburse the host families for their expenses. Council liked the idea, and Svend himself worked at the new centre for two summers. He also spent time protesting U.S. foreign policy and defending Canadian civil liberties after Prime Minister Pierre Trudeau invoked the War Measures Act. In fact, he probably spent more time protesting than he did on his studies, which held less and less interest for him, and he soon began to look for something else.

Frontier College, the respected literacy organization that has sent labourer-teachers to the toughest, most remote parts of Canada since 1899, offered exactly the opportunity he was looking for. In January 1971 he quit UBC. Nine days later, he was in tiny Balmertown, Ontario, working as an underground ditch-digger at the Dickenson gold mine for $2.26 an hour (76 cents above minimum wage at the time), living in a bunkhouse and teaching literacy to his fellow miners in the evenings.

Digging trenches a kilometre underground was the toughest work he had ever done, but the grassroots community work he did in the evenings for Frontier College was deeply satisfying. He taught reading skills and helped the miners write love letters to their girlfriends back home. He volunteered at the Native Friendship Centre, arranged showings of National Film Board movies and started a coffee house for young people. As he had at UBC, he started to spread himself thin (he missed two shifts because he slept in), but his work was satisfactory, and he was well-liked by his fellow miners. After a couple of months, he began to feel as if he'd lived there for years.

As it does today, northern Ontario in the 1970s had a high rate of unemployment and poverty, particularly in areas with large aboriginal populations. There were also thousands of illegal immigrants, many of whom were willing to work 12-hour days for less than minimum wage, and were too afraid of deportation to demand better working conditions. In that context, there wasn't a lot of incentive to hire local aboriginal employees. There was no shortage of workers willing to do what they were told and keep their mouths shut.

Doing what he was told and keeping his mouth shut was not a Svend Robinson specialty. Whether because of the political discussions that had taken place at the dinner table every night of his childhood or the mistreatment he'd faced growing up, Svend already had an extraordinary compassion for the downtrodden. He'd applied to work at the mine through Frontier College, so he hadn't seen the regular application form with its questions about nationality and religion, information that could easily be used to weed out aboriginal applicants. When Svend saw the form, he went straight to the mine manager. Told he was a "smart-aleck bastard kid" who should mind his own business, he wrote to the Ontario Human Rights Commission about what he saw as discriminatory hiring practices, as well as the poor treatment of the aboriginal employees the mine did hire. The mine manager heard what the interfering Frontier College labourer-teacher had done and immediately fired Svend.

That didn't sit well with the miners' union, the United Steelworkers of America. Svend's work had been satisfactory, and there was no cause for dismissal. Not only was it a matter of principle, but there were also financial considerations for Svend. He was planning to return to UBC the following September, and he'd need the money. With the encouragement of the Steelworkers, he filed a grievance and returned to Vancouver to await the outcome.

The mine management pulled out all the stops. They argued that his work had been unsatisfactory, but the union showed that he had been complimented by his shift boss and had only been verbally reprimanded once for a work-related error. Management made undefined allegations of "questionable character," but the union submitted a dozen character references from locals and a petition from the Balmertown Young People. Finally, management argued that, as a student, Robinson wasn't covered by the collective agreement, but the union countered that only summer students were exempt from the agreement. Furthermore, it was a moot point; Robinson had since left UBC and was no longer a student. It was a classic case of an unfair, vindictive dismissal — exactly the situation the miners had joined the union to prevent — and it soon became clear that management had no choice but to settle. They cut Robinson a $325 cheque, which was worth approximately three-and-a-half weeks' wages and would pay a good portion of the next year's tuition.

"It is impossible in a few words to describe the deep gratitude that I feel for all of the time and trouble that has gone into my case, starting from the moment I made a frantic phone call to you, a total stranger, until the time I got a call from you saying that a fair settlement had been reached, from an old friend," Svend wrote to his union president, Gord Prest, after the settlement. "Give my regards to the union friends and brothers — the cheque for $325 was sure useful — and I know how much work went into that piece of paper ... Very sincerely yours, from a union man always," he closed the letter.

"This really had an impact on me and my understanding of the importance of the trade union movement," reflects Robinson. "They went to the wall for me, even though I was only a temporary Frontier College labourer-teacher, and that really did have a formative impact on me, no doubt about it."

Invigorated by the victory and by the grassroots work he'd done up north, Svend returned to UBC more motivated both as a student and as an activist. Still a science student on the path to medicine, he earned outstanding marks, and in 1972 he won UBC's most prestigious award, the Sherwood Lett Memorial Scholarship for "high standards of scholastic achievement, sportsmanship and the ability to serve and lead others."

Politics was never far from his thoughts. When, during the 1972 federal election campaign, local television broadcaster BCTV poked around UBC for a student radical to join a panel discussion with Pierre Trudeau, Svend was the natural choice. The idea was to show Trudeau interacting with a student, but according to an article by Allan Fotheringham in the *Vancouver Sun*, Trudeau appeared "completely bollixed" by Svend's request that Trudeau reveal the donors to the Liberal campaign. "I nailed him in the exchange," Robinson says, smiling as he recalls his first clash with a sitting prime minister.

Although popular with his peers and respected by his professors, Svend was still an outsider. Youth culture in the 1960s was changing the world, but he never felt like the product of the cultural revolution that he was supposed to be. There was a superficiality to his generation that he was never comfortable with; he had the sense that once his contemporaries were faced with the realities of jobs and bills, the rock music might remain, but the counterculture principles wouldn't. While many of his classmates were smitten by "Trudeaumania" and dazzled by their exciting Liberal prime minister, Svend never was. "A lot of it was smoke and mirrors and image. You do a pirouette around the Queen, and somehow that makes you progressive? And he talked a good line," he says, chuckling at the obsession so many Canadians had with Trudeau.

Ever since Edith had introduced him to the NDP, politics had become his greatest passion. The more he became aware of larger-scale social issues, the less medicine appealed to him. He had been attracted to medicine out of a desire to help others, but doctors could only help people one at a time. NDP Leader Tommy Douglas, on the other hand, had achieved far more for health care by instituting the first public hospital insurance in North America as premier of Saskatchewan. If someone like Douglas were to become the prime

minister, how much more could be accomplished? The same compassion that had driven him to want to be a doctor began to drive
him unalterably towards politics.

Svend decided that if he wanted to pursue a career as a politician,
law would be a much better stepping stone than medicine, so in
1973 he switched faculties and redoubled his commitment to activism. By then B.C.'s Social Credit government had been defeated,
and in 1974 NDP Premier Dave Barrett established a commission
to study the governance of post-secondary education in the province. As a well-known student advocate, Svend was appointed to
serve as a commissioner, and his recommendation that students
and non-academic staff be represented on the governing bodies
of post-secondary institutions was accepted by the government.
Fittingly, in 1975 he became one of the first two students elected to
serve on UBC's Board of Governors.

"Academic politics was the bloodiest, most vicious form of politics that I'd ever seen," Robinson says, recalling the battles that gave
him the razor-sharp political skills that would serve him so well in
later years. As a member of the board, he successfully argued that
UBC should join the growing boycott of California grapes in solidarity with the United Farm Workers, who faced poor wages and
working conditions on grape farms. He argued that UBC should
divest itself of shares in companies doing business in apartheid-era
South Africa, and lost. Whether it was a furor over residence fees
or the salaries of UBC support staff, Svend was front and centre.
Professors took notice of the empty chair in their lectures and
dubbed him "The Phantom."

Somehow that phantom kept his grades near the top of the class.
Remarkably, at the same time he was on the board of directors at
the New Vista Senior Citizens' Housing Society and was an active
volunteer with the Burnaby Citizens Association and various other
Burnaby community groups. Of course, as busy as he was, he always
had time for the NDP, and became a ubiquitous presence at meetings for the federal party, the provincial party, and even the Young
New Democrats. Of the hectic schedule he kept as a young man, he
says simply, "I don't know how I did it, but I managed to do it."

"Why don't you leave politics and concentrate on the studies only, until you have your degree?" Edith wrote to her son. "It just seems to me if a person runs in too many directions at one time, he breaks."

• • •

During most of his time at UBC, Svend was a married man. Patricia Fraser was an artist, a musician and a fellow UBC student, and she and Svend had been in love since high school. Svend and Patricia were married in St. Anselm's Anglican Church, the little chapel at UBC, in 1972. They held the reception on campus, too, at International House, and spent their wedding night at the Sylvia Hotel, where Svend still worked part-time, and their honeymoon in a cabin by the ocean on Pender Island.

"It was bliss," remembers Robinson.

But it wasn't to last. Even before they were married, Svend had wondered if he might be gay. He'd see an attractive man — a lifeguard, perhaps — and joke about it to Patricia. They'd laugh, but he wasn't really joking. The dissociation between who he was and who he was forced to pretend to be was confusing and painful. The more he tried to have that "normal" life, to force his identity into the slot the world had carved out for him, the more it hurt. Longing for an escape, he began to drink even more. Burying himself in school and volunteer work and drowning himself in alcohol worked for a while, but eventually the denial caught up to him. When he met Vince, a student politician from another university in town for a student conference, they hit it off immediately. His new friend invited him back to his hotel room, and they got drunk. There was no more ambiguity about his sexual orientation after that.

"It was frightening and exhilarating at the same time. I knew I'd had sexual attraction to guys, but to actually do it was different," Robinson recalls of his first homosexual experience.

He'd heard what everyone had heard about homosexuals: that they were depraved, sick, predatory. He knew he wasn't those things. What he couldn't fathom was how to reconcile his feelings with how society felt. Hiding his homosexuality from Patricia made him feel dishonest, but he knew how much pain it would cause her if she knew the truth. One night he drove her to a beautiful spot at UBC overlooking the ocean and told her there was something she needed to know. At first she blamed herself. They tried counselling, but their marriage was over, and in 1975 they separated. "The extent to which I was prepared to become involved in politics affected the relationship," Svend explained to the *Vancouver Sun* in 1981 when asked about his personal life.

He felt awful about hurting Patricia, but even more powerful was Svend's feeling that he was now a new man. At first he'd visit gay bars tentatively, using a fake name. (In those days, gay bars were private clubs, and customers had to sign in at the entrance.) Soon, though, he grew bolder. He'd honk at men from his car or try to flirt with straight men in bars, sometimes risking a beating for his audacity. He had a relationship with another young NDP activist, an experience that he found even more liberating. He even signed up to audition as a go-go dancer at a gay bar, but got cold feet, abandoning the attempt as soon as the first funky notes of "Little Green Bag" began to play.

The easiest and safest way to meet other gay men was in bars, and that didn't help his drinking. "I was drinking absolutely to excess. I would get drunk, I would pass out, I would pee my pants sometimes. It was terrible," he admits. There is an awful reproductive quality to alcoholism, and the disease that had taken control of Wayne Robinson seemed to have infected Svend, too. Edith was worried and wrote to her son that he didn't seem like the Svend she used to know.

It was a difficult time for Edith, too. She'd had rheumatic fever as a child and, as a result, had a weak heart. In 1974, shortly after she and Wayne moved to Kamloops, and as Svend's marriage was falling apart, Edith had a massive heart attack. Doctors expected her to die. She didn't, but she wasn't the same woman: she became paranoid and often hallucinated. Painting, the love of her life since her childhood in Denmark, was no longer possible, and she became deeply depressed. Wayne handled it poorly. He quit his job and forced Edith to move with him to Alberta, first to Edmonton and then to Fort McMurray. He belittled her and called her useless. He threatened to sell her paintings so that they could afford to move to New Zealand. It was a heartless and vindictive threat; earlier, Edith had tried to sell some of her paintings at a fundraiser for aboriginal children and was heartbroken when not one had sold. The prospect of yet another pointless move to the other side of the world, with a husband who said he loved her and acted like he hated her, was too much for Edith. She tried to overdose on heart pills during a family camping trip, but her stomach was pumped and her life was saved. Still quietly determined to end her life, in 1976 she stopped taking her pills altogether. She died of heart failure at age 47 while playing Scrabble with her youngest daughter, Kim. Svend, then 24, scattered her ashes at Crescent Beach in White Rock, south of Vancouver. "She was the most decent person I've ever known," he would say later, recalling his beloved mother.

Without Edith, the family fell apart. Gretchen retreated into her own private world. Her relationship with her father became distant. Although she and Svend were never close, Svend paid for Gretchen's wedding and was the only member of the family to attend. "The only one in my family. That says a lot about Svend, too. He brought me a dozen roses," she remembers.

It is common for children of alcoholic parents to grow up to be relentlessly driven achievers like Svend; it is also common for them to follow in their parents' footsteps. Ingrid, the sister Svend was closest to growing up, was drinking and doing drugs by age 12. Her relationship with Wayne, like Svend's, was fraught with tension. "There was no wavering in what she thought about him," explains Jason Richter, Ingrid's son. Jason never met Wayne, and based on what he heard from his mom, he never wanted to. Ingrid left home at 15 and moved to Prince George with her abusive partner a few years later. After one year of living there, she looked as though she'd aged a decade.

Wayne was devastated after Edith's death, but he dealt with the trauma of losing his wife the same way he dealt with the other setbacks in his life: he just kept moving. He took Kim to live with him in a 17-foot trailer and started making plans to become a park ranger.

•   •   •

In the same year that he lost his mother, Svend lost his articling position. His status as classroom ghost notwithstanding, in 1976 he graduated from the faculty of law with top marks and was offered articling positions with several law firms and with the B.C. Attorney-General's office. He chose the firm of Dohm Russell. The senior partner was former B.C. Supreme Court justice Thomas Dohm, who, as chair of UBC's Board of Governors, had seen Svend at work first-hand. However, with just one month left in his term on the board, Svend attended a rally in support of a campus workers' strike and released a confidential memo concerning the administration's plans to break the strike. He then resigned from the board. He felt he'd performed a public duty, but some of the partners at Dohm Russell felt that by breaching UBC confidentiality, he'd shown himself to be untrustworthy. They summoned him to appear before them at the exclusive University Club, but because the club didn't allow women, Svend refused to set foot in the place. The meeting was held at the law office instead, where the partners voted to withdraw their offer of an articling position by a one-vote margin. (Dohm himself voted in support of Svend.)

Still devastated by his mother's death, still drinking to excess and firmly on the other end of a burned bridge with Dohm Russell, Svend again began looking for a way to get out. When a friend was accepted to the London School of Economics, the iconic school that counted John F. Kennedy, Pierre Trudeau and Mick Jagger as former students, Svend sent in a late application and was accepted.

After the turmoil of the previous year, a year in London was the perfect antidote. His studies in economics, law and political science were stimulating, and he enjoyed meeting the bright young students from around the world. His favourite classes were the labour law classes offered by professor Bill Wedderburn, with whom he remained in contact for many years. Although he quickly got up to speed on Labour Party politics, and even attended the party's conference in Blackpool, he was over 7,000 kilometres away from the lure of the B.C. NDP. With his newfound free time, he attended theatre and ballet, and explored London's parks and pubs. It was, he felt at the time, the best year of his life.

THREE

The Giant-Killer

Even in the midst of the bright lights of London, Robinson knew he'd be back in Burnaby before the next election. Burnaby was, after all, the perfect training ground for a young activist who hoped to become a politician. The city hasn't been called the People's Republic of Burnaby for nothing. Home to a collective farm colony in the 1920s, Burnaby elected a socialist city council in the 1930s and became the rare community in Canada in which the Communist Party was a legitimate feature of the political landscape. The NDP's roots in Burnaby are deep. Ernie Winch represented the provincial riding for the Co-operative Commonwealth Federation, the forerunner to the NDP, for decades, and federal NDP Leader Tommy Douglas represented Burnaby–Coquitlam from 1962, when he won a by-election after being defeated in Regina, until 1968, when he was narrowly defeated by his Liberal opponent in the wave of Trudeaumania. Successive Burnaby city councils showed that left-wing governance could work in Canada, and work well. "It was always a legitimate option to be left-wing in Burnaby, and to be left-wing and successful," explains former NDP MP Bill Siksay, who would go on to represent the riding after Robinson.

Opportunities to be involved with the NDP seemed limitless, and even while he was still a teenager, Robinson took full advantage.

He attended every convention and every local meeting he could. He knocked on doors in federal and provincial elections, tasting the bitterness of defeat (he and Edith campaigned for Tommy Douglas in his unsuccessful 1968 run) and the thrill of victory (he was proud to see the NDP elected to government for the first time in B.C. after winning the 1972 election, finally toppling the Social Credit government). He became a member of the Provincial Executive and the Federal Council, the bodies of volunteers that oversee the administration of the party, and in 1974 he was elected president of the B.C. Young New Democrats. As committed as he was, he made no effort to endear himself to the party establishment, and in everything he did he positioned himself firmly on the party's left flank. "The more we co-operate with the Liberals, and the more liberal we become, the more we lose credibility, votes and integrity. The NDP must be pushed to the left," he wrote to his family, who had by then moved to Victoria.

And push he did. With the rest of the Provincial Executive, he co-wrote a letter warning Premier Dave Barrett and the B.C. NDP government that it risked alienating supporters if it didn't move more forcefully towards socialism. Robinson felt that Barrett was ignoring key aims of party policy, such as establishing social ownership of housing and food distribution, a universal child care program, and ministries of the environment and women's equality. Later he proposed a motion at a Provincial Council meeting calling for the resignation of the NDP's Minister of Education, Eileen Dailly — the same candidate for whom he and his mother had delivered campaign leaflets in 1966 — for failing to fully implement the party's resolutions on post-secondary education. The party, however, feared alienating the mainstream if it was too radical during its first term. Robinson remembers being called an "enemy of the party" by two of Barrett's ministers, Dave Stupich and Dennis Cocke. He recalls tangling with Barrett's supporters again when Barrett lost his seat in the 1975 election. Sitting NDP MLA Bob Williams stepped down in Vancouver East so that Barrett could run in a by-election, an arrangement Robinson was the only member of the Provincial Executive to vote against.

Some of his NDP friends warned him that he would have to break his habit of criticizing the party if he ever expected to achieve a position of real influence in the NDP, but others were proud that he had the guts to stand up for his beliefs. His preferred candidate in the 1975 federal leadership race, John Harney, came in fourth, far behind winner Ed Broadbent, but still managed nearly 20 per cent of the vote on the first ballot. The left flank of the party was sizeable, and regardless of Robinson's relationship with the establishment, the left flank liked him. He remained a key figure among the youth of the party, and in 1976 he was one of the party's representatives at the Congress of the Socialist International in Geneva.

More importantly, Robinson was well-liked by the volunteers who ran the Burnaby NDP, and they would be the ones to decide who would run as the local candidate in the next federal election. The summer of 1977 would be three years since the previous election, and with local NDP MP Stuart Leggatt planning to make the jump to provincial politics, the team would need a new candidate. While in London, Svend, then 25 years old, decided that the time was right. He wrote to the Burnaby riding association, asking them to postpone their nomination meeting until he had returned from his year abroad.

He had only to ask. "You were a hometown boy, articulate and full of enthusiasm. How could we not support you?" explained Del Carrell, one of the most active members of the riding association, years later. Leggatt liked him, too. "The kind of energy, enthusiasm and new approaches to old problems that you display would clearly be an asset to us," Leggatt wrote to Robinson after hearing of his interest in the nomination. All of the volunteer time Robinson had devoted to the local NDP had earned him the members' goodwill, and they agreed to wait until he was back.

But before Svend could dream of any success as an elected politician, there was an incompatible element of his lifestyle that needed to be addressed. By the time he returned to the doorsteps of Burnaby, Svend had quit drinking for good.

•   •   •

Pierre Trudeau's first terms in office are often remembered today for his efforts to foster a greater sense of national unity: the introduction of official bilingualism, the promotion of multiculturalism and early efforts to amend the Constitution. However, for most Canadians, the number one issue in 1977 was the economy. Canada suffered from a case of "stagflation," in which unemployment, inflation and prices were high, while wages were low. Rents were high, too, but so were interest rates, and banks were reluctant to hand out even short-term mortgages during such an uncertain economy. Strikes were common. The government was running a deficit. The Trudeaumania of 1968 had ebbed, and Joe Clark, the new Progressive Conservative (PC) leader of the Official Opposition, hammered the government on the economic front. Clark, a Red Tory from Alberta, was young, inexperienced and lacked Trudeau's panache, but his campaign nevertheless drew support from middle-class voters who resented rising taxes and increased state intervention.

The new NDP leader, Ed Broadbent, also assailed the government on the economy, arguing in favour of lower interest rates and Canadian ownership of natural resources in order to create jobs. His personal popularity at times exceeded Trudeau's; however, while Canadians may have liked Broadbent personally, they didn't necessarily feel the same way about his party. In the eyes of most Canadians, the choice for prime minister was still between a Liberal and a PC. The federal NDP hadn't achieved anything like the success of the B.C. NDP, which had formed the government in 1972 and remained in a strong position as Official Opposition after losing power to Social Credit in 1975. The federal party, on the other hand, had never finished higher than third, and had only been able to exercise power indirectly, from the far corner of the opposition benches. The NDP's greatest successes had come during the minority parliaments of the 1960s and 1970s, in which they held the balance of power, helping to pass legislation creating Medicare, Petro-Canada, public pensions and a national affordable housing strategy, and reforming the rules governing election expenses. But Broadbent had inherited a caucus of only 16 MPs, tucked away in

the far corner of the House and drowned out by the Liberal majority and the confident PC Official Opposition. Broadbent's popularity was edging upwards, particularly in B.C., but he had to make
up a lot of ground if he hoped to lift the party out of its perennial
third-place status.

If the NDP was safe anywhere, it was usually Burnaby. But in 1976
the riding boundaries were redrawn, and the new Burnaby riding
consisted of parts of three previous ridings: one held by the NDP,
one by the Liberals and one by the PCs. Polls in the new riding
showed inconsistent results. Some predicted an NDP win. Others,
including some internal polling carried out by the NDP itself, had
the party in third place. What could have been an NDP stronghold
was probably now, at best, a three-way race. With only one week
to go before the NDP nomination meeting, Robinson, back from
London, was still the party's only candidate. "I didn't expect people to be lining up to run in this new Burnaby riding, because the
numbers were not encouraging at all," Robinson recalls. "Part of
me thought it was a chance to run and get some experience, and
maybe later run where I had an actual shot at winning."

But while Stuart Leggatt and Del Carrell were excited that Robinson wanted the nomination, not everyone in the NDP was. Some
of the local New Democrats felt that if the party had even the
slightest chance at winning the riding, they should choose someone other than this young radical who had so often butted heads
with the Barrett government. Suddenly Dr. Pauline Jewett — the
54-year-old president of SFU who had served as a Liberal MP from
Ontario in the early 1960s — offered that choice. She had become
disillusioned with the Trudeau Liberals and had quit the party in
1970. She ran unsuccessfully for the NDP in Ottawa in 1972, but
had since let her membership in the NDP lapse. When, just before
the deadline for entering the race, she announced she was running
for the Burnaby nomination, some of the local NDP establishment
breathed a collective sigh of relief. But Robinson had a decision to
make.

"Hey, kiddo," Jewett greeted Robinson, calling to inform him that
she was running and asking him for his support. She had, after all,

already lined up the support of an impressive array of local NDP MLAs, as well as provincial leader Dave Barrett. Robinson should be proud of the work he'd done so far, she told him, and she hoped he would be an active campaigner on her behalf. He replied that he'd need to consult his team. The team met at Del Carrell's house, and they unanimously encouraged him to stay in the race.

"I'm probably toast, but I'll give it everything I've got," Robinson thought at the time, and he informed the surprised Jewett that she still had a race on her hands. "She assumed she was going to win. I was a nuisance. She was going to have to bat this fly away. It would be unthinkable that she would not defeat me," he recalls.

But Robinson had a dedicated, well-organized team, and for that last, crucial week he worked hard, running as though he were only one vote behind. He took every opportunity to remind people of his local connections. He also had another serious advantage: his record as a New Democrat was unblemished by a torn-up Liberal Party membership card. "There was suspicion, probably in retrospect unfair, about Pauline being a former Liberal MP. And I played on that for all it was worth," Robinson smiles, recalling campaign literature that referred to him as "not a part-time socialist."

Many in the riding association didn't like the idea of a new candidate parachuting in at the last minute to take on their hometown boy. On October 2, 1977, they chose the 25-year-old articling student and former student leader over the accomplished university president and former MP by a vote of 176–129. According to journalist Allan Fotheringham, the Jewett team had demonstrated "an astonishing miscalculation of the 'unknown' Svend Robinson . . . The boy is well-known in the party. Unknown he ain't." Nevertheless, baffled that the membership would throw away whatever shot at winning the riding they had by picking Robinson over Jewett, a third of the riding association executive, including the president, immediately resigned. That stung Robinson badly. "It really spurred me to show them I would throw everything I had into this. I didn't want them to be able to say we lost the riding because of Svend Robinson. I just went flat-out. Every spare hour."

The monumental capacity for hard work that Robinson had

already demonstrated as a student went into high gear. Along with the standard coffee parties at supporters' homes where people could come and meet the new candidate, the team organized dances, pub nights, bake sales and raffles. Robinson spent Saturdays holding open houses at his campaign office beside the Astor Hotel in south Burnaby. He put his home phone number on the 40,000 leaflets his team was distributing. Most importantly, he began a door-knocking odyssey that would take him to over 12,000 Burnaby doorsteps, wear out two pairs of shoes and take the better part of two years to finish. It was a good move. He was occasionally mistaken for the paper-boy, especially when, in a helpful but misinterpreted manoeuvre, he handed residents the newspapers they hadn't yet picked up from their front doorsteps. But those visits helped him develop a genuine understanding of local concerns, and soon he knew Burnaby better than anyone else.

However, the election call expected for the spring or summer of 1978 never came. The uncertain economy had continued to hurt the Liberals' popularity, and Trudeau appeared to have decided to wait the full five years of his mandate, hoping Liberal fortunes would improve before he had to call an election.

For Robinson, who was balancing his door-knocking with articling, the delayed election call was a blessing. A young lawyer named Robert Gardner had left an established firm to set up his own and had offered Robinson an articling position after Dohm Russell had withdrawn their offer two years earlier. Robinson had accepted but told Gardner that he would only be able to start after his year in London was over. Gardner had agreed, promising Robinson he would have a job when he returned. Robinson remembers Gardner as a brilliant, iconoclastic lawyer and a good teacher. More importantly, Gardner understood that politics could be a passion and law just a day job. After Robinson won the Burnaby nomination, Gardner promised his young articling student that he would get the time he needed to campaign. Still, he had to get his work done, and colleagues were quickly impressed.

Called to the Bar in September 1978, Robinson developed an expertise in litigation, labour law and criminal law, and enjoyed his work immensely. He won his first major case, *Warner v. Kiniak*, in which an international union imposed a trusteeship on a local in violation of its constitution. As the lawyer for the local, he showed an early propensity for direct action, at one point advising his clients to occupy union offices. The decision was appealed to the B.C. Court of Appeal and later the Supreme Court of Canada, and Robinson won both appeals as well. "He could have made far more money and been just as famous if he had decided to remain as a trial lawyer," one of his former colleagues told the *Globe and Mail* years later.

Still waiting for an election call, Robinson kept practising law by day and door-knocking on evenings and weekends. He only ever had one client hauled off to jail, when the presiding judge was ill and his replacement rejected a plea deal — not a bad track record for a young lawyer who got his dress shirts at the Burnaby Hospital Thrift Shop.

FOUR

Tomorrow Starts Today

On March 26, 1979, Trudeau dissolved Parliament, and the race for Burnaby was on. The PC candidate was Hugh Mawby, a personable elementary school principal with interests in a dry-cleaning business. Nominating their candidate just a few weeks before the campaign began, the Liberals offered Doreen Lawson, a Burnaby alderman with deep local roots.

"In front of a crowd Robinson is easily the most impressive of the three candidates. He's polite, cool, reasoned and well-researched. He oozes sincerity and seems reasonably intelligent. He knows the party line on every issue that is ever brought up and is seldom caught off guard," wrote Roy Wood in *The Columbian*. Furthermore, Wood added cheekily, "the elderly ladies just love his cute little smile."

Appearing clean-cut and serious in his campaign materials, wearing the huge glasses popular at the time, the young candidate was certainly winning on the doorsteps. His focus on unemployment and wages, and his new ideas about alternative energy sources and local conservation projects resonated with Burnaby voters, who were alienated by Trudeau's preoccupation with national unity, constitutional questions and Quebec. Robinson called those issues a "phoney, diversionary, propaganda war" designed to distract Canadians from the country's economic problems. His personal campaign slogan, "Tomorrow starts today," sounded less like a commercial and more like a promise.

In addition to the personal contact that he had established with residents in over 12,000 homes since winning the Burnaby nomination, Robinson had several other important factors working in his favour. The Canadian Labour Congress endorsed the NDP and used its organizational strength to run a supportive parallel campaign. Federal NDP Leader Ed Broadbent was far more popular in the west than Trudeau was, and the NDP was picking up steam in B.C. And, in a political rarity, the federal election campaign coincided with the provincial election in B.C.; the provincial election was scheduled for May 10 and the federal election for May 22. The federal NDP, far more closely tied to its provincial counterpart than the other parties were, used the opportunity for some joint campaigning and ran the Burnaby campaigns from the same headquarters on Kingsway. Robinson attended B.C. NDP events, at one point flipping pancakes with Dave Barrett, both men smiling for the cameras despite their tense relationship. Meanwhile, Robinson tried to use criticism of the right-wing Social Credit government in B.C. to discredit the federal PCs, alleging that the local Social Credit candidates were members of the federal Tories. The B.C. NDP lost the provincial election but gained eight seats, and the Social Credit majority was now razor-thin. Furthermore, Rosemary Brown's win in Burnaby–Edmonds, one of the provincial ridings encompassed by the federal riding, had the Robinson team in an upbeat mood. Buoyed by their improved results, the B.C. NDP volunteers joined the federal team full-time for the rest of the campaign.

Robinson also used his socialist credentials to gain an advantage. He'd met former Swedish prime minister Olof Palme at the Congress of the Socialist International he'd attended in Europe, and when Palme happened to be in Vancouver for the 1978 Congress, Robinson invited him to a Swedish seniors' home in Burnaby. For years after, the polling station at the home recorded his strongest support in the riding. Robinson also used his socialist background to personally convince the Burnaby Club of the Communist Party not to run a candidate against him, assuring him a handful of votes that could make the difference in a close race.

Election day revealed a divided nation. The economy remained the number one issue, but no one leader could claim the full confidence of Canadians. The Liberals dominated Quebec, but they came in second in Ontario, the most populous province, and were nearly shut out of the west, where they trailed both the PCs and the NDP. The PCs, on the other hand, had strong support everywhere but Quebec. The NDP followed in third, and the federal Social Credit Party was a distant fourth. The final results were something of an oddity. The Liberals won the overall popular vote on the strength of their votes in Quebec and second-place showing in Ontario, but because their support was more concentrated, the PCs won more seats and were elected with a minority government, returning to power for the first time in 16 years. Joe Clark, who had never before held a cabinet post, became the youngest prime minister in Canadian history. The NDP, meanwhile, jumped from 17 seats to 26, and their best results were in B.C. On May 22, 1979, Robinson was elected in Burnaby with just under 40 per cent of the vote.

Svend Robinson was going to Ottawa.

•　　•　　•

Perched above the massive cliffs along the Ottawa River, Parliament Hill dominates its surroundings from almost every vantage point. The buildings themselves are stunning neo-Gothic masterpieces, designed to convey a sense of majesty and evoke a powerful national pride in the Canadians who visit. The architects did their work well. The Hill is beautiful in every season and adapts itself to any imagination. In the deep blue Ottawa midnight, the buildings are the eerie edifices of Dickensian London. Against a fiery orange and red autumn sunset, they are medieval castles with turrets piercing the sky. Against the grey winter clouds that seem to obliterate the world behind it, Parliament Hill seems like the last structure standing at the edge of the world. In the summer months, this austere centrepiece of power morphs into one of Canada's top tourist attractions. Centre Block is mobbed by visitors from around the world eager for the free tours offered by parliamentary staff. The lawn comes alive with tourists snapping photos, families enjoying picnics and off-duty employees tossing a Frisbee or playing soccer. It was on a hot July day, the oppressive Ottawa humidity soaking his T-shirt in minutes, that Robinson first approached the imposing sandstone wall separating Wellington Street from the parliamentary precinct.

"I was in total awe," he recalls. "I almost had to pinch myself to believe this was actually happening. It was an incredible experience, an incredible sensation."

Robinson arrived at the private members' entrance, eager to get down to business, and was immediately sent back to the public entrance by a gruff security guard. Robinson's powers of negotiation were still in their infancy, and the experienced guard was certainly not going to be taken in by any silly story from this kid in sandals and shorts about being a member of Parliament.

He may have looked like an overgrown teenager, but it wasn't long before Robinson began to be taken seriously. Broadbent took advantage of his rookie MP's legal training and named him the official NDP critic for the Solicitor-General. Although in recent years the responsibilities of the Solicitor-General have been absorbed by the Minister of Justice, in 1979 the minister had a prominent role in cabinet and was responsible for prisons and the RCMP, among other duties. As critic, it was Robinson's job to monitor government policy in those areas, make proposals for improvement and hold the government to account when it slipped up. He was assigned to the high-profile justice and legal affairs committee, which traditionally studied some of the most important legislation proposed to the House. As was often the case in the small NDP caucus, where too few MPs had to balance too many responsibilities, he was also given a second official critic responsibility: consumer and corporate affairs.

Almost within his first week in the House, Robinson found a story that made him a star in Question Period. A transport association had allegedly been illegally using anti-competitive price schedules.

The Justice Department laid charges, but there were suggestions that Transport Minister Don Mazankowski had attempted to interfere in the Justice Department's decision. Robinson was the first to raise the issue in the House, and his insistent questioning elicited inconsistent and contradictory responses from Clark's ministers and from Clark himself. First, they said Robinson's allegations were "completely and totally erroneous"; then they admitted that the Justice Minister had indeed met with Mazankowski, but it was only an "information-giving briefing." Finally, they admitted that Mazankowski had given advice. Smelling blood, some of Trudeau's former ministers started asking questions about it, too. It was the first criticism to stain the new government, and the media took notice. "Clearly, the NDP in young and slight Svend Robinson from Burnaby have a rookie who needs hardly any seasoning," wrote Douglas Fisher in the *Vancouver Sun*. "He commands the floor when on his feet."

He was quickly involved in the types of social issues that became the hallmarks of his career. When Liberal MP Harold Herbert presented a private member's bill that would narrow the grounds upon which a woman could seek an abortion, it was Robinson and his NDP colleague Margaret Mitchell who killed it by "talking it out" — a common procedural tactic in those days, similar to a filibuster, in which members opposed to a bill would continue to speak on it until the time allotted for debate ran out, and the bill was dropped from the agenda.

Robinson's first private member's bill also dealt with abortion. Had it been adopted, it would have taken the opposite approach and removed abortion from the Criminal Code, leaving the decision to the woman and her doctor. Continuing the work of his friend and predecessor Stuart Leggatt, he also closely followed conditions in prisons, which appeared to be approaching a crisis due to violence and overcrowding. In his first private member's motion (which provides a direction to the House but does not create an actual law), he called for the establishment of a special parliamentary committee to oversee penitentiary reform. Both of these early legislative efforts met the standard fate for private members' business in those days; his motion was talked out, and before it was his bill's turn to be debated, Parliament was prorogued, which wipes the legislative slate clean. However, his bill and motion both helped raise awareness and helped Robinson establish credibility in two areas he would closely monitor throughout his career.

But it was the case of a 22-year-old Chilean refugee named Galindo Madrid that provided the most lasting impression of the rookie MP during the Clark administration. Late to return from shore leave from the freighter *Star Pride*, Madrid was confined to quarters and told by the captain that he'd be returned to Chile at the nearest opportunity. Madrid was scared. As a student leader in Chile, he'd been vocal in his criticism of dictator Augusto Pinochet and had fled the country on a black market passport. Return could mean torture, imprisonment or worse. The longshoremen's union in Squamish, B.C., where the *Star Pride* was docked, heard of the young Chilean trapped on board and refused to unload the freighter's cargo until Madrid was allowed ashore. The captain had no choice but to comply with the union's demand. Madrid came ashore and immediately went to the RCMP to ask for asylum.

As Madrid's case meandered unsuccessfully through the various immigration courts and appeal boards, he worked as a dishwasher in Vancouver and looked for friends in the Chilean-Canadian community. He found many. Joining forces with churches and labour groups, Madrid's allies formed the Galindo Madrid Defense Committee and set about making the case to the Canadian public that Madrid should be allowed to stay. Madrid's chilling stories of his time in the Chilean army, and of the mass executions of dissidents ordered by Pinochet, captured the media's attention. His condemnations of the Pinochet regime were scathing. If Madrid wasn't a legitimate refugee before, he was now. When Chile issued him a new passport, it bore the dreaded "L" — the mark of an undesirable person.

On July 23, 1979, Robinson received word that the RCMP were looking for Madrid, about to enact the long-standing deportation order against him. Immigration Minister Ron Atkey had previously delayed the order due to the public outcry that Madrid's story had generated, but now the fatal moment was just hours away. Robinson took a gamble. Inviting Madrid to his home in the Norman Bethune Housing Co-operative in Burnaby, he called a press conference and announced that he was offering his home as a sanctuary to Madrid until Atkey agreed to let him stay in Canada.

"I don't think the RCMP are going to break down my door," he told the assembled media. "I'm sure the government is well aware of the political implications of violating the sanctity of a member of Parliament's house."

The dramatic gesture of an MP taking the law into his own hands was front-page news the next day. Of course, Robinson had no authority to grant legal sanctuary to anyone. It has been hundreds of years since even churches had that authority. However, he hoped that his action would contribute to a groundswell of support from the public that might convince the government to at least postpone the deportation again. "It was all symbols. So much of it is symbolism," he explains. "It told the public what was happening with this guy, and that helped generate support for him."

"The world-improvers, meanwhile, were busy playing their Silly Symphony full blast under the baton of Sir Svend," wrote far-right journalist Doug Collins derisively in an editorial for *The Columbian*, in which he expressed his doubt about Madrid's claims, but his cynicism wasn't shared by most. With the public largely onside, Robinson and Madrid flew to Ottawa and sat outside Atkey's office until he agreed to meet with them. Meanwhile, the Galindo Madrid Defense Committee kept pushing. Atkey's office was deluged with letters and telegrams. Supportive editorials appeared in major newspapers. Robinson raised Madrid's case in the House. Finally, Atkey had had enough. Although the government's position was still that Madrid did not qualify as a refugee, the minister issued a special permit allowing him to stay. Madrid became a landed immigrant in 1982 and eventually a Canadian citizen.

The Galindo Madrid formula — injustice, dramatic action, media attention, result — had a profound impact on Robinson. "I am absolutely certain that we saved his life," Robinson states confidently. "I remember feeling such a sense of awe and empowerment that I was now in a position where I could actually effect change. Even though I was an opposition member of Parliament, I had that incredibly precious access to the media, and if I could use that effectively, I could make a difference. Galindo Madrid was my baptism by fire in the use of that approach."

• • •

Under the Clark government, the economy continued to struggle, and both the Liberals and NDP climbed in the polls. The PCs survived several confidence votes with the support of the tiny Social Credit caucus, but in December 1979 the government proposed a budget that included an 18-cent-per-gallon gas tax that none of the opposition parties would accept. When the NDP introduced a motion of non-confidence in the government, the Liberals voted in favour while Social Credit abstained, and the motion passed. Clark informed the Governor-General that he'd lost the confidence of the House, and Parliament was dissolved for a general election.

In caucus, Robinson was one of the hawks calling for the government to be brought down, but now that meant he'd have to fight to keep his job. In Burnaby, Hugh Mawby and Doreen Lawson were back as his PC and Liberal opponents. Anti-abortion activists hadn't forgiven Robinson for blocking Liberal MP Harold Herbert's abortion bill, and they campaigned hard against him. Making re-election even more difficult, Robinson himself had to leave the campaign for three days, at a crucial juncture in the race, in order to appear before the B.C. Court of Appeal on behalf of a union he'd represented in one of his first cases as a lawyer. But episodes like the attempted deportation of Galindo Madrid had given Robinson a strong public profile, and the NDP's popularity was still increasing in B.C. Nationally, the 1980 election produced similar results to the 1979 election; the Liberals were popular in Quebec but not in the west, and the NDP continued its incremental gains. Ontario proved the difference, swinging from the PCs back to the Liberals and handing them a majority government. Robinson was re-elected with an increased share of the popular vote, and he returned to Ottawa to take his seat in the House, this time two sword-lengths away from a rejuvenated Prime Minister Pierre Trudeau.

• • •

"Politics is like an addiction after a while. It gets in your blood," Robinson told the *Burnaby Times* after a few months on the job, in an article they called "All work and no play." The addiction was all-consuming. "In terms of being able to spend time with other people relaxing, I haven't got that kind of time," he continued. "Your phone is always ringing, and I mean always. Six o'clock, seven o'clock in the morning through to midnight. That's the price one has to be prepared to pay."

He was prepared to pay it. He lived for a while in Del Carrell's basement, and she doesn't recall him taking any time off, apart from a single ski trip. "His whole life was working," she says.

It is the rare member of Parliament who has reasonable expectations of his or her staff. Unlike their American counterparts, who employ small armies of staff, Canadian MPs usually have to make do with just four or five assistants, divided between those who work on Parliament Hill on policy and political matters, and those who work in the constituency doing less-partisan casework on behalf of residents. It is fair to say that assistants of MPs of all parties are overworked and surprisingly underpaid. Passionate supporters of their MPs, even their private lives are filled with volunteer work on behalf of their party. Robinson quickly developed a reputation for being as demanding of his staff as he was of himself. For some members of the team, there was nothing strange in this. They hadn't been attracted to politics for the work-life balance and were as driven as he was. Others found it more difficult to live up to his expectations, and Robinson's office became known as the sort of place where you either left after a few weeks, or stayed for years.

"I used to come to work some mornings to find him asleep on his couch because he had been up the entire night dictating dozens of letters, and there could be six one-foot-high piles of files with two or three dictation tapes on top of each one," recalls Sandra Loewen, who moved to Ottawa to work for Robinson in 1979. "After a couple of hours of me working on them — between answering phones and many other tasks — he would come out of his office and ask if I had come to such and such a letter that could have been somewhere in pile four. My reaction was not good."

He could be a relentless micromanager, and he could be disorganized. There was always one more task, one more assignment. "I can still see him, coat flapping, briefcase trailing. He would be late because he insisted on making just one more phone call or leaving yet more instructions for the staff. We knew there would be the inevitable phone call to us from the airport as we could hear the last boarding call on the speakers," recounts Loewen. Like many of Robinson's former staff, she describes a boss who could be both endearing and exasperating. "We all breathed a sigh of relief when we knew his plane was finally in the air, and we would have a few hours' peace. Thank goodness this was before cell phones!"

Somehow, Robinson made it all worth it. He had a surprising sense of humour (staff recall a great Joe Clark impersonation), and if staff faced challenges in their personal lives, they knew they could count on him for support. "The depth of his caring and compassion was a side of Svend that he shared with a certain few, and which bred strong and deep loyalty amongst those close to him," says Coro Strandberg, a former assistant who developed a lasting friendship with Robinson.

Most of all, there was a sense among the staff of being part of something bigger, a sense that by helping him do what he did, his achievements were their achievements, too. "He drove me crazy. But on the other hand, he'd turn around and he'd do something in the House, or he'd stand up for our union in caucus, and you'd be like, 'Aw, now I have to like you again! And I just want to be mad at you right now!'" laughs long-time assistant Jane Pepper. "So relentless, yes, but despite the fact that you went home thinking, 'Oh, God, I really should just quit. I can't do this anymore,' you'd get up the next day and he'd do something like that, and you'd think, 'God, I've got a good job.'"

FIVE

The Just Society

"It's hard to believe I've only been in Ottawa a year and a half. It feels like about 20 years," Robinson told the *Vancouver Sun* in 1981. "My job has totally dominated my life. I'm working from first thing in the morning until late at night. I suppose in some ways it's a lonely life." Whenever he did see friends, he was always a little late and always had somewhere else to go. Many dropped by the wayside. "I knew it was going to be bad, but I didn't realize it would be as bad as this."

But Robinson's stock on Parliament Hill was only just beginning to rise. Ed Broadbent had been pleased with his work in the previous parliament, so after the 1980 election he promoted him to the high-profile role of justice critic. Robinson felt that this was an area in which Trudeau was weak. The Liberals had won a majority government, but the Trudeaumania that had swept the nation in the late 1960s and early 1970s had abated, and Robinson hoped progressive Canadians were ready to see what he saw: that Trudeau was not one of them. "Ever since the War Measures Act — this was the great defender of civil liberties?" he asks, referring to the October Crisis of 1970. Trudeau had invoked the War Measures Act and imposed martial law in response to a series of bombings and two high-profile kidnappings carried out by Quebec nationalists. More than 450 people were arrested, most were never charged with any offence, and the act played little if any role in apprehending the real perpetrators. "He smashed civil liberties in one of the most massive and repressive ways possible," Robinson says, still incredulous at Trudeau's enduring reputation as a progressive.

One of Robinson's first targets was Trudeau's approach to Nazi war criminals who had escaped to Canada from post-war Europe. By the time Robinson was appointed justice critic, not one Nazi had faced legal proceedings in Canada for crimes committed during the Holocaust. There was simply no legislative framework allowing it. In 1972, for example, West German police informed Canadian authorities that Helmut Rauca, an SS Master Sergeant implicated in the murder of more than 11,000 Lithuanian Jews, was living in Canada, but Canadian authorities were fettered by legal restrictions and could not assist the West German police. Robinson asked questions in the House and pressured Justice Minister Jean Chrétien in committee, demanding legislation allowing the prosecution of Nazi war criminals. Chrétien responded that the Charter of Rights and Freedoms, then still being negotiated, needed to be finalized first. Later, Chrétien told the justice committee that, in fact, no such legislation would be coming. "I do not intend to introduce a piece of legislation in Canada to deal with crimes committed in other nations some 35 years ago," he said, and Robinson's motion calling on the government to do so failed.

Although the government finally did extradite Rauca to West Germany in 1983, no other extraditions, or legislation to prosecute the other Nazis suspected of being in Canada, were approved during the Trudeau years. It's a part of Canadian history that still enrages Robinson. "If there was a mass murderer in a Canadian community who managed to escape justice by moving to a South American community, for example, and we discovered where that person was, would we just throw up our hands and say, 'He's an old man now, a lot of time has passed, we don't need to worry about that'? Of course not! We would demand that justice be done. And we were dealing with people who were responsible for the most barbarous acts of inhumanity imaginable. Not only — and this is what I find so offensive — not only did we close the doors to Jews who were trying to flee from that terror, from that genocide, but we also allowed the people who were responsible for it to come to Canada and to live in our communities without any kind of serious effort to bring them to justice. I just thought that was an outrage. It is an outrage," Robinson says. "Anybody who knows anything about history couldn't possibly accept that those who were the perpetrators of those crimes should have impunity, and yet Trudeau did."

Robinson was active on women's issues as well. In 1980 the Supreme Court ruled that an accused rapist could be acquitted if he honestly believed that his victim had consented to her rape, even if there were no reasonable grounds whatsoever for that belief. Robinson called the decision a "rapist's Charter" and pressured Chrétien to take action. As the months went by, Robinson suggested that Chrétien was too preoccupied with constitutional questions to resolve other important justice issues. "We need a full-time Minister of Justice in this country," he said. He launched a petition campaign and spoke across the country. The law was eventually changed.

The prison system was another of Robinson's regular targets. The Canadian prison system in the early 1980s was tearing itself apart, with unrest at institutions across the country. He would visit prisons and hear horrific stories of abuse perpetrated by guards. Prisoners complained of being sprayed in the face with mace. One prisoner alleged he'd been left in his cell naked and without a mattress for a week. Another recounted men in his unit being made to lie on the floor, arms outstretched through the cell bars into the hallway beyond. They were handcuffed through the bars, and then guards stomped on their hands. Suicides were common. There were penitentiary riots at Kent, Dorchester and Laval. Each time there was an incident, Robinson would be up on his feet in the House, demanding that the government take action to improve the under-funded and under-monitored system. In June 1981 there was a massive riot at Matsqui Institution in B.C., and the army had to use a helicopter to rescue prison staff from the roof. "I do not think this incident can be characterized as being a crisis," Solicitor-General Bob Kaplan told Robinson the next day in the House. Conditions worsened. Prisons grew so crowded that many inmates had to be double-bunked in single-inmate cells. Riots continued. One hostage-taking at Archambault Institution left three guards and two prisoners dead. In 1983 Kaplan cancelled the post-secondary education program for federal prisoners. Rehabilitation no longer seemed to be a priority for the government. Prisoners felt warehoused, often with guards they felt needed rehabilitation as badly as they did. "The longer I'm here, the further I go backwards," one prisoner wrote to Robinson.

In that context, Robinson was incensed to learn of a senior prison official in B.C. who was buying carved violin chin rests from an inmate, and then improving and reselling them at a personal profit. Robinson called a press conference to expose what he saw as the exploitation of inmate labour and successfully prompted regulatory changes in the institution. However, Robinson also found himself in court being sued for defamation. He lost and had to pay $20,000 to the official in question. He appealed to the B.C. Court of Appeal, which ruled in his favour. The decision confirmed that, as an MP, Robinson had a public duty to call attention to wrongdoing. Since then, the case has frequently been cited as a precedent in cases concerning defamation and the role of public officials, including in the United Kingdom.

Robinson's filing cabinets were soon stuffed with correspondence from inmates. One of his most frequent correspondents was a murderer whose death sentence had been commuted only when capital punishment had been abolished in 1976. Not every politician would be quick to help such a man, but when the desperate prisoner wrote to Robinson about the inhumane conditions at the institution in which he was housed, Robinson took on the case. "My punishment is supposed to be the loss of my freedom, not perpetual hell, and hell is all I've seen so far," wrote the inmate, who said he'd spent 19 months in segregation and described unprovoked beatings at the hands of guards. According to him, he'd also been constantly ridiculed, denied meals and arbitrarily sprayed with tear gas. He asked to be allowed to continue his studies in order to complete Grades 11 and 12, but permission for this important step in rehabilitation was denied. Robinson wrote to the Commissioner of Corrections on the inmate's behalf and helped secure a transfer to another institution. "I must say that this institution is very much different than what I'm used to," the inmate wrote later, thanking Robinson for his help. "I have spoken to [name removed for privacy reasons] in regards to the better living conditions at this institution. He also mentioned you, and said you had been instrumental in arranging that the community have some input into what's happening in this prison. It's unfortunate that other prisons across Canada cannot be run on a similar basis."

To that inmate and many others, Robinson's personal attention to their cause when no one else would listen meant the world. But it wasn't what got him the headlines. Accusing Jean Chrétien of lying, however, did. In 1982, Thomas Berger, a respected judge, criticized the weakness of the aboriginal rights provisions in the Charter of Rights and Freedoms. Trudeau thought it inappropriate for a judge to publicly criticize the Charter, and urged judicial authorities to conduct an inquiry and consider removing Berger from the bench. In Question Period, Robinson defended Berger, pointing out that Trudeau had had no such objections when another judge made public statements supporting Trudeau's invocation of the War Measures Act. "I do not know if the judge is as much of a cry baby as the honourable member," Trudeau replied dismissively. The Canadian Judicial Council ruled that although Berger had perhaps been indiscreet, his comments would not justify his removal from the bench. However, when speaking to reporters, Chrétien seemed to indicate that the council had recommended that Berger be fired. In the House, Robinson said that Chrétien had lied. According to parliamentary tradition, accusing another

MP of lying, whether the accusation is true or not, is considered a serious breach of protocol, and Robinson was promptly ejected by the Speaker. Pierre Trudeau caught Robinson's eye from across the aisle, smirked and jerked his thumb toward the door like a Major League umpire calling an out, while Robinson rose from his seat and left to be interviewed by the waiting media.

Robinson had adapted quickly to the rhetorical tone of the House and its sometimes archaic procedures governing debate; he knew the rules and he used them, raising points of order if he thought an opponent was trying to pull a fast one. But he had also learned to jettison the rules when it suited his purpose. Less than half a year after committing the parliamentary sin of accusing an MP of lying, he was thrown out a second time for another breach of protocol. He suggested that the ostensibly neutral Speaker, Jeanne Sauvé, was taking her marching orders from the government when she allowed a time limit for the debate on a bill to abolish the Crow Rate, legislation which had guaranteed lower freight rates to western farmers since 1897. "What has taken place in this House is a travesty. If I did not know better, I would say that the Speaker was in cahoots with the government," he said. Questioning the impartiality of the Speaker is only permitted through a formal motion of censure, something that has happened only a handful of times in Canadian history, and Robinson was ejected once again.

He also found other creative ways to break the rules to get his point across. In the early 1980s there was a serious problem with faulty 750-millilitre glass pop bottles. Hundreds of the bottles had exploded and caused injuries, including to a Burnaby letter carrier who got glass in his eye and had to spend a week in hospital. In Question Period, Robinson tried the usual tactics. He compared the bottles to the 1.5-litre bottles, which had been banned several years earlier after similar problems. He suggested compromise options, such as plastic coating, and even identified a plant in Ontario that could do the work. He responded to complaints about industry costs with emotive imagery — "What is the cost of an eye or an arm to a family whose child is hurt by these bottles?" — but the *coup de grâce* added a theatricality rarely seen in the House.

In a flagrant violation of the rule against using props, prompting shouts from offended members and entreaties from the Speaker to sit down, Robinson brandished one of the offending pop bottles. "I will certainly send a sample bottle to the Prime Minister," he said.

•   •   •

The chattering classes of Parliament Hill were thrown into a tizzy by such unparliamentary behaviour, but Robinson faced no real consequences. "Ed Broadbent probably rolled his eyes a few times and got a few more grey hairs," he laughs. That he wasn't struck by lightning for flouting the ancient conventions of Parliament wasn't lost on him. However, it was his work within the traditional parliamentary structure on three significant pieces of Trudeau legislation — the Young Offenders Act, the Freedom of Information Act and the establishment of the Canadian Security Intelligence Service (CSIS) — that established him as a major player in the justice realm.

The Juvenile Delinquents Act of 1908 had become woefully out of date, so in 1981 the Trudeau government proposed the new Young Offenders Act to modernize the approach to youth justice. It wasn't a bad bill, but it failed to impose a standard maximum age at which a young person in conflict with the law could be considered a young offender, instead allowing the provinces to apply whatever maximum ages they wished. The result was a patchwork of different ages across the country. The bill also allowed accused youth to be excluded from their own trials, and there were a variety of other technical deficiencies. The NDP opposed it at second reading, but the Liberal majority sent it to committee nevertheless, and Robinson got to work. "One of the differences between Mr. Robinson and us is that we want young people to be convicted sometimes," grumbled Kaplan in the justice committee, but he agreed to a half-dozen of Robinson's technical amendments. He also agreed to impose a nationwide maximum age of 18 in response to complaints from Robinson and others, and removed the provision allowing youth to be excluded from their trials after Robinson put

forward a motion to do the same. The atmosphere in the committee was collegial, and Robinson felt comfortable supporting the
bill at third reading.

That atmosphere of collegiality was in short supply when the
committee considered Communications Minister Francis Fox's
Freedom of Information bill. Robinson was strongly in favour
of a bill guaranteeing Canadians the right to information about
their government. "It is only if Canadians have access to information that they will be able to fully exercise their other rights,
such as freedom to vote, freedom to be candidates and freedom
of the press," he argued in the House. What Robinson didn't like
was a provision in the bill that allowed government departments
to withhold the results of product safety tests and environmental
tests if they found them "misleading." Robinson called that vague
justification the "Mack Truck clause" because it was a hole you
could drive a truck through, and he launched a filibuster in the
committee. After an excruciating month, only a dozen of the 150
clauses had been passed, and Liberal patience was wearing thin.
The glacial pace forced the committee to continue sitting in July,
when most members count on returning to their constituencies to
spend time with their families. None of them wanted to be wearing
suits in the stifling Ottawa heat, listening to Robinson talk about
environmental tests. "They were attacking me personally," Robinson remembers. "It was really tough. I remember the minister sitting at the other end of the table glaring at me." Eventually Fox had
had enough and agreed to remove the offending provision and add
several other amendments that Robinson had been demanding.

With the improved bill back in the House, Robinson became a
fervent supporter and urged the government to pass it right away.
Fox couldn't believe his ears. "Madam Speaker, I am pleased to see
that the honourable member shows so much diligence in hurry-
ing to get the bill through. If it had not been for him, it would have
been passed last summer," an exasperated Fox told the House. "The
bill is not through the House at the moment, and the honourable
member must bear most of the responsibility for that."

Robinson made no apologies. He felt the bill was better as a result of his work. But once the bill was out of the committee, the government amended it in the House. The new amendment allowed the government to exclude a wide variety of documents not only from being made public but also from judicial review. While most critics of the bill begrudgingly accepted the amended version, believing it to be better than nothing, Robinson became an opponent again. He voted against it, but the bill passed anyway. Looking back, he concedes that the bill was indeed better than nothing. "It took a lot to satisfy me in those days," he says, laughing.

Of the three pieces of Trudeau legislation previously mentioned, the establishment of CSIS provoked Robinson's strongest opposition. At the time, the RCMP was responsible for investigating threats to national security. However, the force had been getting bad press for years over troubling reports that members were opening mail and committing break-ins, forgery and theft during national security investigations, so in 1983 the government decided to remove responsibility for security intelligence from RCMP jurisdiction, and turn it over to a brand new spy agency. When Robinson saw the bill creating the new agency, he was deeply concerned. It seemed that instead of prosecuting the Mounties who had committed illegal acts, the government simply intended to change the law, so that what had been illegally done by Mounties could be legally done by CSIS agents. Most worrisome were the broad powers being proposed for CSIS, including the authority to share information about Canadians with security services in foreign countries. There was also a startling lack of oversight. In the U.S. a congressional body monitored the FBI, but there would be no such parliamentary body in Canada. Instead, CSIS would only be supervised by the government-appointed Security Intelligence Review Committee. "It would be ironic if, in seeking to achieve the objective of guarding Canada against totalitarian influences, we should adopt the very tools of those totalitarian governments themselves," Robinson warned the House.

The bill reached the justice committee in the spring of 1984, a marvellous opportunity for Orwellian references that Robinson didn't waste. By June it still hadn't made any progress, as he and other opponents of the bill, such as left-leaning Liberal MP Warren Allmand and PC MPs loyal to the RCMP, continued to raise objections at every stage of debate. On June 5 Liberal MP Gaston Gourde proposed a motion to cut off further debate in the committee. However, that new motion had to be debated, too, and Robinson proceeded to filibuster until the meeting finally ended. "The question now is how long one single member of this House can prevent the parliamentary process from working," complained Kaplan. The next day it happened again. MPs drank two urns of coffee, ate 36 pastries and eventually traded newspapers with each other as Robinson continued to filibuster, his vocal chords straining painfully. NDP MP Dan Heap provided chocolate milk and bananas to help Robinson keep up his energy, but eventually the Liberals had had enough. In a violation of committee procedure, Chairman Claude-André Lachance unilaterally imposed time limits on any further debate. The Liberal Whip removed Allmand from the committee and replaced him with a more compliant Liberal MP, and the bill was passed by the committee and returned to the House. Lachance then resigned as chair, sensing that his leadership of the committee had been tainted by his controversial ruling and by the acrimonious debate on the bill.

The filibuster was over, but Robinson kept fighting in the House, proposing 96 amendments, most of them to delete individual clauses of the bill. The voting began at 9 p.m. and finally ended at 5 a.m. the next bleary-eyed morning. When Robinson stood to vote, he was booed by the Liberal benches. "This represents one of the darkest days for democracy in the history of this country. I remind members of this Chamber, and those Canadians who are observing our proceedings, that it is the same government that brought forward the War Measures Act in 1970 that now brings forward legislation which constitutes nothing less than a massive assault on the fundamental civil liberties and privacy of all Canadians and anyone visiting our country. In the guise of protecting our national security, the government would take a sledge-hammer to our civil liberties," Robinson stated.

The debate was largely ignored by a media distracted by the 1984 Liberal leadership race, but the role of CSIS has been scrutinized far more carefully in recent years. Lawyer and civil rights expert Clayton Ruby actually views Robinson's dire warnings in 1984 as conservative. "CSIS operates like a true secret police, like a law unto itself," Ruby explains. "Governments don't like hearing it, so they choose not to hear it." The years since the September 11, 2001, terrorist attacks in the U.S. have given a chilling resonance to Robinson's concern that sharing information about Canadians with foreign security services could have dangerous consequences. In 2002 Maher Arar, a Syrian-born Canadian citizen, was apprehended by U.S. authorities during a stopover in New York City on his way home from a family vacation. Acting on information supplied by Canadian officials who believed Arar was linked to terrorists, U.S. authorities had him deported to Syria, where he was held in a tiny cell and tortured for nearly a year. A later commission of inquiry showed there was no evidence that Arar posed a security risk of any kind, and the Canadian government formally apologized. However, what had happened to Arar was illegal only because in this case the Canadian officials involved had not followed proper procedures, not because the government had become opposed to sharing "suspicious" names with U.S. authorities. In 2011, documents released by the WikiLeaks website showed that, even after what happened to Arar became public, CSIS continued to give U.S. officials information about dozens of Canadians without proof that they were involved in any wrongdoing.

Despite his filibuster and his amendments, Robinson lost the fight in 1984. He had pulled out all the stops, except one. He reveals that he was offered a shockingly underhanded opportunity to challenge the bill — an opportunity he did not take. While the bill was still being debated, two grim-looking men insisted upon meeting with Robinson in his office. They claimed they had information that could help him kill the bill and allow the RCMP to maintain its jurisdiction over national security. Judging by their demeanour, Robinson wondered if they were Mounties themselves. The two men refused to identify themselves but opened a briefcase to reveal glossy, 8-by-10 photos of a key Liberal minister in compromising sexual positions with another man.

Robinson was appalled and quickly told the two men to leave. He immediately went to the minister in question to warn him that the photos existed and that someone was trying to use them against him. Shaken, the minister thanked him for his discretion.

The unsettling encounter with the two men deeply disturbed Robinson. That the minister's very private sexual identity could be used against him to subvert the exercise of his democratic duties was infuriating, horrifying and wrong.

SIX

Love Without Fear

His aborted audition as a go-go dancer notwithstanding, Robinson was quiet about his sexuality. There were, of course, no openly homosexual elected politicians anywhere in Canada, at the federal, provincial or municipal level. Some of his colleagues in the NDP knew that he was gay, but the general public didn't. Athletic, forceful and with an indifferent fashion sense, he didn't conform to the homophobic stereotypes of how a gay man looked and acted. He looked forward to one day being open about his sexuality, but first he knew he needed an ironclad reputation in his constituency so that when he eventually did come out, the positive perception people had of him as an MP would help them overcome whatever prejudices they might have about homosexuality. But that would take time. When he first raised issues of homosexual rights, in the eyes of many he did so as a straight man.

The late 1970s and early 1980s were still frightening years to be homosexual in Canada. Homosexual acts themselves had only been decriminalized a decade earlier (while Robinson was a high school student, homosexual acts had been punishable by up to 14 years in prison), and police still regularly conducted raids of gay bars and bathhouses, confiscating membership lists and sometimes violently beating the customers. There was a series of raids in Montreal in 1975 in an effort to "clean up" the city before the 1976 Olympics. Similar raids occurred in other major Canadian cities in the next years. In February 1981 the Toronto Police simultaneously raided four bathhouses in "Operation Soap," conducting the largest mass arrest in Canada since the October Crisis. When protesters gathered the next day to march on Queen's Park, there were violent attacks not only from the 20 or 30 gay-bashers who had turned up, but from Toronto Police officers as well. In one incident, witnesses reported seeing a fallen man being kicked by half a dozen officers. Other witnesses reported seeing officers removing their identification badges.

Despite such a hostile environment, Robinson was already on record supporting the inclusion of sexual orientation in the Human Rights Act. He'd raised it with Trudeau in Question Period, and as a member of the Special Joint Committee on the Constitution of Canada he had proposed including sexual orientation in the draft Charter of Rights and Freedoms. There was a political cost; Robinson had already begun receiving calls in his office from citizens saying they were disgusted and expressing irrational, homophobic panic that he'd "have it in the schools next." However, Robinson's willingness to address the issue anyway meant that when activists in Toronto planned the Gay Freedom Rally in response to Operation Soap, Robinson was already on their radar. They invited him to attend, along with Margaret Atwood and other speakers. (Robinson still remembers Atwood's speech, punctuated by her wry sense of humour: "What have the Toronto Police got against cleanliness?")

Robinson's speech condemning the actions of the Toronto Police caused some tension in the NDP caucus. The NDP had been the only party to support his bid to include sexual orientation in the Charter, but some of the caucus felt that participating in the Toronto rally was going too far. They felt it was an unnecessary political risk that could hurt the party in the Ontario election, which was in full swing at the time. Robinson recalls some of the

Ontario MPPs and MPs, including future premier Bob Rae, angrily telling him not to attend. Robinson didn't care. He had only just begun speaking out.

The first MP to propose a bill adding sexual orientation to the Human Rights Act had been PC MP Pat Carney in May 1980, although her bill didn't come up for debate until a year later, after the protests in Toronto. Carney, too, was something of an outsider within her caucus. "I was a Red Tory, sort of viewed by some in my caucus as an NDP pinko Tory," she says. As the MP for Vancouver Centre, even then a neighbourhood with a substantial gay population, Carney learned of the discrimination faced by homosexuals, who could be legally fired, evicted or otherwise persecuted simply because they were gay. Police raided their bars and bathhouses in Vancouver, too. "I was struck by the fact that they lived in fear," she recollects. Robinson felt that her bill had some flaws, but they were flaws that could be corrected in committee, and he spoke passionately in favour. "What we are talking about here is a fundamental question of human rights, of the right to live and the right to love without fear," he said.

The Liberals killed Carney's bill by running down the clock, the same way Robinson had killed the abortion bill in the previous parliament. It was the standard fate for private members' bills in those days, but Robinson nevertheless brought forward a similar bill of his own. Like Carney, Robinson had to contend with complaints from opponents who thought that his bill to add sexual orientation to the Human Rights Act would create "special rights" for homosexuals. "I emphasize, Mr. Speaker, that the bill does not in any way seek any special or preferential treatment whatsoever," Robinson insisted when his bill came up for debate in 1983. "It seeks equality."

Carney supported the bill, noting that several prominent PCs were also in favour, including Joe Clark. The Liberals remained opposed, but agreed this time that the bill could at least be studied in committee. However, when debate concluded and Robinson asked the House for the unanimous consent needed to send the bill to the justice committee, several PC backbenchers refused to give consent, and his bill, like Carney's, was dead.

Simply addressing the topic of homosexuality had provoked angry calls to the constituency office in Burnaby, some tense moments in caucus and occasional snickers from political opponents, but Robinson survived his first forays into the issue relatively unscathed.

Surviving a crusading Los Angeles Police Department (LAPD) officer named Mike Brambles was another matter. In late 1982, Vancouver police officers with a warrant to search for drugs entered the apartment of John Lewis, an American citizen living in Canada. They didn't find any drugs in his apartment, but they did confiscate a photo album filled with pictures of naked men, some of whom looked like they might be teenagers. The officers carefully tracked down each of the men in the photographs and started asking them questions about their sexual practices. In some cases they even informed startled families that their sons might be gay.

When Lewis happened to meet NDP MP Ian Waddell at the Vancouver Playhouse theatre, he described the grossly inappropriate investigative technique. Waddell, then the critic for economic development, gave Lewis his business card but suggested that he contact the party's justice critic instead. Lewis wrote "Svend Robinson — NDP — invading privacy/slander" in his address book and paid the Burnaby MP a visit. When Lewis described what the police were doing, Robinson was concerned and phoned the police for further details. The superior officer he spoke to agreed that what the investigators were doing wasn't proper police procedure and promised that it would be stopped immediately. But the investigation had already yielded the results the officers were looking for. Two boys, a 15-year-old and a 16-year-old, each admitted to having had sex with the then 29-year-old Lewis. While the age of consent for vaginal sex was 14, it was 18 for anal sex, and Lewis was going to jail.

LAPD Officer Mike Brambles had become aware of Lewis several years earlier when his name came up in connection with an underage sex case in California. When he heard that Lewis was in a Canadian prison on similar charges, he called Vancouver to see what the local police had on him. The Vancouver Police sent Brambles copies of what they'd confiscated from Lewis's apartment, including the address book with Robinson's name in it. Brambles was delighted, and on August 26, 1983, he held a press conference in which he announced that he'd uncovered an international kiddie porn and child prostitution ring, which included two Canadian MPs as clients. He had proof, he declared: a ledger listing sexual acts, prices and clients. The media bought it, and the existence of the infamous "Chicken Book" — so named because "chicken" was a common slang term for a young gay man at the time — was widely reported. "Reports Link Politicians to Sex Ring," read the headline in the *Vancouver Sun*. The Vancouver Police Department denied that Brambles had any such document, and two days later so did the LAPD, but the story didn't die.

Robinson was heading home after visiting a friend when he heard the news about Brambles's press conference on the radio. There was something familiar about the name John Lewis. He pulled over, shaking.

This is not the way it's supposed to happen. Not like this.

The ludicrous charges could easily be refuted. But it was only a matter of time before he'd be asked the inevitable question. "I had always been so careful to never affirm or deny being gay, and being forced to confront the issue in this sordid context would have been a nightmare," Robinson explains. He'd either have to come out — and in the context of having assisted the convicted Lewis — or lie. Neither was acceptable. Unsure of what to do, he went home, packed and left for his cabin in Sechelt. On the ferry, he stayed in his car listening to the radio as the story developed. As he drove the rest of the way, a BCTV helicopter circled overhead. The cabin was his little-used retreat from the stresses of public life, but this was a stress unlike any of the others he'd had in his career thus far. Finally alone in the cabin, a distraught Robinson tried to focus and plan his next move.

His name hadn't appeared in any of the news stories yet, but the media was sniffing. They called his office. They called Broadbent. Some of Robinson's colleagues asked him to stay away from NDP events, a request that hurt him deeply. He retained a respected defamation lawyer, Peter Butler, and they issued an ultimatum to the media: if journalists identified Robinson, either directly or indirectly, they'd be sued. Butler also met with the police, who still appeared to be actively investigating the case, and warned them that they would face a major libel action if they didn't back off. Such threats were bluffs — the question of Robinson's sexuality would surely have come up in any court proceeding, and that would have been no better — but they worked. Coverage continued and speculation abounded, but the names of Robinson and Waddell were never revealed.

The legacy of the Chicken Book witch hunt was not forged by the headlines of Vancouver newspapers, but off the record, in the winks and quiet murmurs of connected media and the political elite. Rumours that Robinson couldn't respond to without addressing his sexuality trickled from Parliament Hill to Burnaby, and he began to receive his first gay-related hate mail. "For some four years I would be fighting this terrible phantom of being involved in a kiddie porn and child prostitution scandal, yet never able to reveal the true story," Robinson laments. "How many friends, neighbours and political colleagues heard and believed the story, I will never know."

In 1987, at Robinson's request, the so-called Chicken Book was finally released to the *Vancouver Sun*'s Terry Glavin, and he reported that it was nothing more than a simple address book. Robinson's name was in it, but there was no story there. His accuser, Brambles, was arrested in 1994 on a total of 26 charges, including armed robbery and sexual assault, and was sentenced to 102 years in state prison. The scandal that never was eventually faded from memory, but the whisper campaign had just begun.

•   •   •

Around the time Robinson met Lewis, the sexual issue that pre-occupied most of Vancouver was prostitution. The visibility of the sex trade had people angry. "We are not dealing with the age-old problem here of street prostitution in red-light districts or street prostitution in downtown areas," Pat Carney said in the House. "We are dealing with the problem of prostitution on people's lawns, by their paper boxes, right in front of their grocery stores, in their churches, and in their daycare centres. It is an infestation of a quiet and beautiful neighbourhood." Many residents felt that the government and the police weren't dealing with the problem, and some, such as Carney, feared the next step would be frustrated citizens forming vigilante groups and using violence and intimidation to force the prostitutes out of their neighbourhoods. Politicians of all stripes seemed to feel that prostitutes were victims, but at the same time, even on the left, there were many who believed that the police needed new powers they could use against customers but also against prostitutes. The mayor of Vancouver, for example, future NDP premier Mike Harcourt, appeared before a parliamentary committee and urged the government to strengthen the laws against solicitation to remove the qualification that it be persistent.

In that context, in December 1982, Robinson was invited to appear on the BCTV program *Webster!* The host, Jack Webster, was as influential as a journalist gets. Once called "the information impresario to an entire generation of British Columbians," Webster had a devoted following. He also had a gruff, abrasive style. The segment was supposed to be about airline charter cancellations — Robinson believed that Canada's major airlines were overcharging customers for cancelling flights, in violation of government guidelines — but in his thick Scots brogue, Webster kept asking Robinson about the prostitution problem. Even though it was not the interview he'd expected, Robinson felt he had a duty to respond to the direct questioning. He replied that he favoured the decriminalization of solicitation and the repeal of bawdy house laws.

Webster was shocked. He demanded to know what neighbourhoods Robinson thought bawdy houses belonged in, a trap his

guest refused to be drawn into. The veteran journalist was so outraged that he crossed his arms and turned his back on Robinson on
the air.

Robinson's comments made headlines. Opponents salivated at
what they saw as his first giant misstep and were quick to reframe
his support for the decriminalization of solicitation as support
for legalization of prostitution. The next day in the House, PC MP
Benno Friesen demanded that Robinson "explain whether his party
also favours government grants and loans to assist those wishing
to open business in human flesh," and asked if Robinson planned
to make such business transactions tax-deductible. "Don't you
wish you were the PC candidate in Burnaby right now?" crowed a
speaker at the next PC convention. For the first time, news media
began regularly referring to Robinson as the "controversial" Burnaby MP. It happened so often that it sometimes seemed as if it were
not Robinson's views that were controversial, but Robinson himself — as if the acceptability of his existence were up for debate.

In Robinson's view, decriminalization was just NDP policy.
The NDP constitution bound the caucus to the policies passed at
convention, and in 1981 grassroots New Democrats had passed a
motion in favour of decriminalizing solicitation. Laws preventing
open solicitation meant prostitutes had to make split-second decisions about potential customers, which could end up jeopardizing
their safety if, for example, they got into a car with the wrong person.

When Robinson made his comments on camera, though, Ed
Broadbent was furious. Certain NDP policies were vote-losers,
and at the time, decriminalization was one of them. Those policies
were mostly ignored by a media that didn't usually cover NDP convention resolutions in great detail. Members of caucus, meanwhile,
used the airtime they did get to focus on the elements of their platform that were more palatable to everyday Canadians. Earlier that
year, caucus had discussed decriminalization of solicitation and
had decided not to make it a focus of the NDP platform. If there
was a vote in the House, they would have to respect convention
policy, but in the meantime they didn't need to voluntarily draw

attention to their most controversial policy positions. In the eyes
of some of the B.C. caucus, Robinson should have done what politicians normally do when asked to comment on something politically awkward: deflect the question. They worried that Robinson's
comments might put their seats in jeopardy, and they accused him
of placing his own ideological purity over the needs of the party.

Robinson was disappointed in what he saw as a lack of courage
on the part of his colleagues, but at first he was conciliatory, even
apologetic. He admitted that he could have stated his position more
clearly and prevented the kind of misinformation now spreading
that portrayed the NDP as being on some kind of public sex crusade. If he were kept on as justice critic, he promised he'd be more
careful in the future. "I do ask for this opportunity. This past week
has been perhaps the most trying of my political life. The lessons
learned from it will not be lost on me," he wrote to Broadbent. But
in January 1983 he was fired as justice critic and demoted back to
consumer and corporate affairs, with continuing responsibility for
the Solicitor-General. When he heard the news, it was Robinson's
turn to be angry.

Broadbent didn't publicly state that Robinson was being dropped
as justice critic as punishment for his comments, choosing instead
to describe the shuffle as a routine re-assignment of responsibilities, but the media quickly made the connection.

"Tell people you wanted an economic portfolio," suggested one
of Broadbent's staffers, offering Robinson an opportunity to save
face.

I'm not going to lie.

"We're compromising by letting you stay on the justice committee. You're lucky to get even that."

*Make me critic of the Parliamentary Restaurant for all I care. I'm not going
anywhere.*

The episode severely strained his relationship with Broadbent
and with many of his NDP colleagues. Robinson accused them of
political fear and continued to insist that he had a duty to articulate convention policy, even when it wasn't one of the issues caucus had chosen as a focus. His was a loyalty shaped by a decade of

work in riding associations, on councils and on convention floors as a Young New Democrat. The policies so carefully crafted and debated there had to mean something. If those policies involved a political risk, so be it. Somebody had to be the first to take the risk or nothing would ever change. "To the best of my knowledge, I did not defy the grassroots will of the party at any point in my career on anything substantive," Robinson states with a measure of pride.

But Bill Blaikie, one of Robinson's longest-serving caucus colleagues, presents another perspective. "It would be his own reading of convention policy," Blaikie says. "Convention policy doesn't dictate how you handle things. The rest of us felt that there was a certain amount of judgement that had to be exercised. We didn't always feel that everything that got passed at a convention had to be highlighted. There was a time and a place to advance things that were decided at convention, and that would be decided by the leader or by the caucus." In the meantime, the NDP was trying to use its limited airtime for other issues. "None of this ever happens out of context," Blaikie adds. "If you've collectively decided, this fall we're going to hammer the government on this, you don't need somebody individually doing something else, taking all the attention away."

It's an assessment Broadbent agrees with. There were mechanisms to ensure that caucus respected the wishes of the grassroots. Accountability sessions at convention, for example, allowed party members to raise grievances with caucus if they thought caucus had ignored or misinterpreted NDP policy. "But in the meantime, caucus members are supposed to act according to caucus solidarity," Broadbent says. "It's not up to each individual member of the caucus to go back and interpret what should or should not be done in terms of a resolution passed by the council or convention of the party." In his view, the duty of individual MPs is to make your point in caucus and try to persuade your colleagues. If you can't, you accept the majority position. Robinson had had that chance, but the majority in caucus wanted to keep quiet on solicitation. "All MPs, on a number of issues, sacrifice what they think is important to the common view of caucus colleagues," Broadbent says, and he'd expected Robinson to do the same. If Robinson was allowed to stake an independent position, perhaps other members would want to do the same in other areas, and what the NDP stood for would become unclear in the minds of Canadians.

Despite predictions of his political demise, Robinson survived the prostitution debacle, and so did the NDP. The NDP's B.C. seat count dipped slightly in the next election, held nearly a year later, but it seems unlikely that Robinson's comments were a factor. "One caucus member in one or two speeches is not likely to cause people to shift their voting attitudes, to be quite candid," Broadbent acknowledges. The passage of time has further blunted the audacity of Robinson's comments. Over the ensuing decades, support for decriminalization of solicitation gradually passed from the fringes to the mainstream. At the 2005 Liberal convention, party members adopted a motion encouraging the government to propose new legislation that would protect sex workers better than the ham-fisted Criminal Code. In 2006 a subcommittee of the justice committee wrote a report that presented decriminalization of solicitation as worthy of serious discussion. In 2012 the Ontario Court of Appeal struck down Canada's bawdy house laws as unconstitutional. Time has vindicated Robinson's position, but Broadbent has no regrets about firing him as justice critic in 1983. "I don't believe in rewriting history," he says. "At the time, it required a decision. I thought that was inappropriate, and even though I now support decriminalization myself, it wasn't appropriate at the time."

Robinson had clearly staked his position on the party's left flank. More cautious — Robinson might say fearful — NDP MPs may have been frustrated, but there was nothing they could do about it. Justice critic or not, he promised he'd continue to speak out.

That is, as long as Burnaby kept sending him to Ottawa.

•　　•　　•

It became a familiar refrain in the coffee shops and living rooms of Burnaby: Svend Robinson might say some outrageous things, but he always went to the wall for his constituents. Burnaby residents may not have realized that those two distinguishing features of their MP were closely related. "I had to build a security blanket in my constituency to be able to stick my neck out so far on the many controversial issues that I took a stand on," Robinson reveals. "And my constituents had to believe, and by and large they did believe — and I think, modestly, with considerable validity — that they had one of the hardest-working local constituency members in the country."

He flew back from Ottawa every weekend. Any time he was invited to anything, he was there, sometimes appearing at a dozen events in a single day. No one understood how he found the time. "Whenever he saw something that he thought would be good for Burnaby, he'd be on it like *that*," says former assistant Jane Pepper, snapping her fingers. When Robinson saw how readily cabinet ministers rubber-stamped proposals recommended to them by their bureaucrats, he turned that process to his advantage. He learned how to lobby key bureaucrats to earmark funds for Burnaby programs long before the proposals ever reached a minister's desk. At first Robinson's staff would cringe, overhearing him relentlessly hounding bureaucrats until he had convinced them to recommend Burnaby programs for funding, but soon his staff learned to do it, too. Burnaby did well in the deal, and in gratitude the Burnaby Chamber of Commerce named Robinson their first-ever Honorary Member of Distinction. He presented reams of bills to the House on almost anything a community group asked for. He took on provincial casework, much to the annoyance of his overworked staff, who continually reminded him that he had no obligation to do the work of an MLA on top of the work of an MP.

When members of Parliament were given a pay increase in 1982, Robinson took a portion of that increase and created an annual bursary for outstanding Burnaby high-school students. He named it the Tommy Douglas Memorial Scholarship in honour of his political hero (and a former Burnaby MP), and the scholarship included a biography of Douglas. Robinson continued to award it until the end of his career. The riding association chipped in, too, and when MPs were given another pay increase in 1991, Robinson added some of that as well. Not only was it a generous gesture, but it was also a great way to advertise, and the tradition was carried on by his successor, Bill Siksay.

Surprised constituents would call the constituency office at 10 o'clock on a Sunday night and find Robinson himself answering the phone. No matter what he was doing, the constituent became the priority. "He had great empathy for those who had been beaten down by the system. The harder the case, the more he considered it a personal challenge," remembers former assistant Sandra Loewen — and stories of the impossible conundrums Robinson solved for constituents struggling with an unyielding bureaucracy became legendary. In one case, an elderly Burnaby man dying of cancer was having difficulty applying for a passport so he could travel to the U.K. for one last visit with his son. Born into a travelling carnival family, the man had no birth certificate. He was getting nowhere with the bureaucracy, but Robinson took up the fight and got him his passport.

Another of the cases that brought Robinson great personal satisfaction involved a Burnaby resident who approached him in 1980 about her late husband's pension. Her husband had been a Mountie who'd died in a plane crash while transporting a prisoner in the Yukon Territory. His RCMP pension provided only $10,000 a year to his wife and children. What struck Robinson as unfair was that if the Mountie had been murdered on duty, the pension would be much higher. He didn't see why a plane crash should be treated any differently. Robinson went to work lobbying the RCMP and the Solicitor-General, and raised it in the House and in the justice committee. It took years, but eventually the government agreed to increase the widow's pension to $36,000 per year. Best of all, the new policy would be applied to everyone else in her position. She never forgot Robinson's help, and years later she invited him to her son's wedding.

Results like that made Robinson feel good about the work he was doing. But all that good work wouldn't get him re-elected if nobody knew about it, and he was aggressive in his self-promotion. His "householders" (pamphlets mailed by MPs to their constituents) regularly detailed every federal dollar spent in Burnaby and what Robinson had done to get it there. Most of the time his influence had been very real. At other times it was an exaggeration. "I wanted my constituents to believe that I was personally responsible for every dollar that flowed into Burnaby," Robinson admits. "When Burnaby would get funding for a particular employment centre or something like that, even though I didn't have anything to do with it, I would blaze the headlines across my householder."

It wasn't completely honest, he concedes, but it helped solidify his reputation with constituents and kept him in Ottawa. "In order to be able to do the good work that I did in so many other areas, there had to be a little bit of creativity," he says, smiling.

•   •   •

The five-hour flight back to Ottawa was leaving at 8 a.m. Robinson checked his watch. That was only six hours away.

Is there any real point in going to bed?

He checked his agenda again. He'd already done what he'd set out to do for the day. The speech was ready. The mail was read. The newspapers were read, too.

I could have done that on the plane. I should have just gone with them to the movie. A break wouldn't have killed me.

Actually, he hadn't read all of his mail yet. He reached across his desk for the folder he reserved for hate mail. He took the first letter from the pile and read it. He already knew what it would say — like so many of the others, it would be an illiterate mishmash of references to abortion, prostitution and that damned Chicken Book — but it still hurt. No matter how many times he heard words like the ones in those obscene letters, they never sounded any less poisonous. He fed a blank sheet of paper into the typewriter.

"Thank you for your missive of hatred and prejudice," he wrote. "I do hope you will see the light one day and repent. Please write me when you do."

That felt better. Robinson addressed the envelope, sealed it and set it aside. He reached again for the folder.

SEVEN

Barnacles and Eavestroughs

Svend Robinson doesn't usually get a lot of credit for the creation of the Canadian Charter of Rights and Freedoms. The Charter is, after all, the enduring highlight of Pierre Trudeau's legacy, and understandably so. It was a remarkable achievement. Before Trudeau embarked on his constitutional odyssey, the British Parliament still had the final say over Canadian constitutional amendments, and the document protecting the rights and freedoms of Canadians was the Bill of Rights, a safeguard so ineffective that it had been used to strike down only one piece of legislation since its passage in 1960. Without the fullness of Trudeau's passion, vision, persistence and even guile, what are now cornerstones of our modern Constitution might never have been achieved.

As a legal document, the Charter revolutionized both politics and the judiciary, and today neither operates without an ever-present awareness of its relationship with the other. Politicians speak of "Charter-proofing" legislation to ensure it can withstand potential court challenges, and it would be naive to think that Supreme Court justices are not intimately aware of political realities when they render their decisions. Through hundreds of thousands of briefs, facta and billable hours, the Charter's strengths and weaknesses have been painstakingly debated, triumphantly vindicated and crushingly lamented. Over 30 years later, it remains a cherished national symbol, displayed in elementary school class-rooms across the country, and distributed to proud immigrants at citizenship ceremonies.

To alter the fabric of Canada so dramatically, Trudeau needed sub-stantial public and political support. He faced a labyrinth of oppo-sition, particularly from provincial premiers like Quebec's René Lévesque, who believed the federal government was encroaching on provincial rights. Nevertheless, in late 1980 Trudeau had a draft that he thought was good enough to send to a special committee of MPs and senators who would study it in further detail. Most of the premiers were still opposed, but Trudeau hoped that if he could get it through the House with the support of all the major political par-ties, it would send a strong signal to the premiers to get on board. However, Joe Clark's PCs also feared a weakening of provincial rights and sided with the premiers. The NDP had similar reserva-tions, but Ed Broadbent pledged to support the draft after wringing an assurance from Trudeau that the final document would at least strengthen provincial control over natural resources, an essential source of wealth for cash-starved provinces. After a bitter cau-cus debate, when the motion to send the draft to the Special Joint Committee on the Constitution of Canada came up for a vote in the House, the NDP voted in favour — all except for one tall, bespecta-cled MP.

It was an odd sensation for Robinson to be applauded by the PC MPs as he stood to vote against the motion, especially since he had always welcomed the principle of an entrenched charter of rights. It was clear to him that the existing parliamentary system, which could be so easily manipulated by majority governments, was an inadequate safeguard against civil rights abuses, like the intern-ment of Japanese Canadians during World War II or the arrest of hundreds of innocent Québécois during the October Crisis in 1970. However, the draft Charter proposed by Trudeau fell far short of what Robinson felt it should achieve. Provisions for aboriginal rights were too weak. There was no guarantee of equal rights for men and women, no right to trial by jury, and no protection from discrimination based on sexual orientation, physical or mental disability, political belief or marital status. Much of what he'd hoped to see in terms of economic, social and legal rights was nowhere to be found. After so much promise, it was a deeply disappointing result.

In an hour-long meeting, Robinson was reprimanded by his colleagues for breaking caucus solidarity, but Broadbent still wanted him to be one of the NDP's chief spokespeople on the file. The NDP was given two spots on the committee, and Broadbent chose Saskatchewan MP Lorne Nystrom and Robinson to fill them. The Burnaby MP was still young and inexperienced, but he was a lawyer and had proven himself an effective parliamentarian. "I was a leader who tended to give high levels of responsibility to people I thought could do it," Broadbent recalls. "I saw him as a young, smart guy. Intellectually able. He would be careful on that file."

Judging from the bilingual notes scrawled in Robinson's distinctively poor handwriting on his copy of the draft Charter, he understood French well enough to compare the subtle nuances of the wording in each official language; most of the NDP caucus at that time didn't. Furthermore, this was the first time in Canadian history that the work of a parliamentary committee would be televised, and Robinson excelled in that medium. With his prominent glasses and shaggy haircut, at first glance he appeared better suited to a university chess club than the bright lights of television, but on camera, Robinson shone. In less telegenic subjects, any hint of nervousness or uncertainty is magnified tenfold. As he articulated difficult legal principles, Robinson projected nothing but passion, competence and confidence.

Clause-by-clause consideration of the draft Charter began in January 1981. At one of the first meetings, PC MP Jake Epp put forward a motion that the Charter begin with a clause recognizing the supremacy of God. He had the full support of the committee — almost. In Robinson's view, not only would such a clause be legally meaningless, but it would also contradict the freedom of religion promised by Section 2 of the Charter. When he informed caucus of his intention to oppose the clause, his leader was furious. "We're not going to be on record voting against God!" Robinson recalls Broadbent saying. On the day that Epp's motion was scheduled for debate, Broadbent temporarily replaced Robinson on the committee with Father Bob Ogle, a Catholic priest. Undeterred, Robinson attended the hearing anyway. Although he was no longer entitled to a vote, he approached the co-chair, Serge Joyal, and arranged to be allowed to speak. His brief comments suggesting that the proposal was disrespectful of Canadian religious and cultural plurality failed to sway the committee, and God made it into the very first sentence of the Charter. Since then, the clause stating that Canada "is founded upon principles that recognize the supremacy of God" has had about as much legal weight as the page numbers. It has never been cited by government lawyers in any legal proceeding, not even in 1985 when the Supreme Court considered the legality of the 1906 Lord's Day Act, which banned Sunday shopping.

After divine supremacy was assured, the serious legal work began. Many of the amendments moved by Robinson, now back as a voting member of the committee, envisioned a much more robust and far-reaching Charter than his fellow MPs were willing to accept. The following are some of the rights he was unsuccessful in getting guaranteed in the Charter:

- that workers have the right to organize and bargain collectively
- that legally acquired Canadian citizenship be inalienable
- that individuals be protected from arbitrary or unreasonable interference with privacy
- that an accused person be provided with free legal counsel if unable to pay for it
- that individuals be protected from discrimination on the basis of sexual orientation, political belief or marital status
- that the multicultural heritage referred to in the Charter specifically include the distinct cultural, economic and linguistic identities of aboriginal peoples

More radically, he proposed an amendment to strike the word "peaceful" from the right to peaceful assembly, the memory of which causes him to chuckle. Most radically of all, Robinson's Charter would have entrenched the rights to a clean and healthy environment, and safe and healthy working conditions. If that amendment had passed, it would have been the only mention of the environment in the Charter. Instead of Canada taking that bold step, it was left to other countries, such as South Africa, to become the first jurisdictions in the world to recognize a constitutional right to environmental protection.

One can only wonder what character our nation would have today had the Liberals and PCs shared Robinson's vision in 1981 and adopted any of the above amendments. However, Robinson's contribution to the debate still greatly impacted the document, earning him high praise. "He, perhaps more than any other opposition MP, has been the architect of the Charter of Rights," wrote Michael Valpy in the *Vancouver Sun*. "No MP worked harder or more effectively to improve the constitutional proposals."

With the encouragement of the NDP caucus, the first amendment he proposed to the committee guaranteed the equal rights of men and women. It was defeated, but lobbying from women's groups continued, and in response the Liberals eventually changed their position and added a clause guaranteeing equal rights themselves.

The draft Charter stipulated that all of its rights were subject to "reasonable limits as are generally accepted in a free and democratic society with a parliamentary system of government." The clause was designed to permit necessary violations of Charter rights, such as violating the Section 2 right to freedom of expression by criminalizing hate literature. However, the clause used vague wording that didn't appear anywhere else in Canadian or international jurisprudence, and Robinson vigorously opposed it. The government changed the wording to "reasonable limits prescribed by law as can be demonstrably justified in a free and democratic society," which Robinson felt was an improvement, though he still argued that the limits could be interpreted too broadly. In his view, certain rights — freedom from cruel and unusual punishment, for example — should never be abrogated with limits of any kind.

The first drafts of the Charter didn't include the right to trial by jury. Robinson, who had written a paper on the importance of the right while at the London School of Economics, argued strenuously in the committee for its inclusion. "Mr. Robinson, member for Burnaby, British Columbia, has made strong representation to guarantee the right in serious criminal matters to trial by jury," Justice Minister Jean Chrétien acknowledged to the committee. "I welcome his representations as being very constructive and would be prepared to accept the following amendment," he said, adding what would become Section 11. Robinson smiled. He hadn't thought it was Chrétien's style to give credit to a member of the opposition.

Section 15 of the draft Charter guaranteed protection from discrimination on the basis of race, national or ethnic origin, colour, religion, sex and age. That list didn't include sexual orientation, physical or mental disability, political belief or marital status. Chrétien had conceded that the list would not be set in stone. "I want to make clear that the listing of specific grounds where discrimination is most prohibited does not mean that there are not other grounds where discrimination is prohibited," Chrétien informed the committee. "Indeed, as society evolves, values change, and new grounds of discrimination become apparent." Robinson recalls speaking with Chrétien prior to the meeting, urging him to make such a statement. Chrétien's statement provided a crucial caveat. If the amendment Robinson had in mind failed, at least future courts would be empowered to take evolving social mores into account and expand the list themselves.

But Robinson hoped Canadian society had already evolved. The United Church, the B.C. Civil Liberties Association, the Canadian Teachers Federation and, most importantly, the Canadian Human Rights Commission had already recommended including sexual orientation in the list. On January 28, 1981, Robinson moved an amendment to add sexual orientation, physical or mental disability, political belief and marital status to the prohibited grounds of discrimination listed in Section 15.

"We cannot include every barnacle and eavestrough in the Constitution of Canada," grumbled Jake Epp, and he seemed to speak for the room. Neither Robinson's legal analysis nor his telegenic appeal swayed the stony faces sharing the table with him. His motion was defeated by a vote of 22–2, with only his NDP colleague Nystrom joining him in favour. However, there was wide support for one element of Robinson's amendment: the provision on physical and mental disability. It later found its way into the Charter through an amendment by PC MP David Crombie.

Although Robinson was disappointed that the Charter didn't provide the broad guarantee of rights he had hoped for, he felt that the version passed by the committee, after 267 hours of deliberations on national television, was a vast improvement over the original. He was pleased to see entrenched the equal rights of the sexes and the disabled. He was proud of the role he'd played in getting the guarantee of the right to trial by jury. He felt more comfortable with the Charter's impact on aboriginal peoples, thanks to a successful motion championed by NDP MP Peter Ittinuar that affirmed aboriginal rights. Most of all, Robinson was convinced that if the Charter wasn't passed then, it might never be passed at all. The maelstrom of provincial opposition still swirling around Trudeau's proposal might discourage any future attempts at a charter of rights. Further improvements to the Charter were battles that could wait for another time. Some accused Robinson of flip-flopping — the cynical term often used by the media when legislators change their minds after hours of legal analysis — but he was unrepentant. "I say we should move on this Charter today, and move with pride," he told the House.

Most of the provinces were still opposed on the basis that the Charter infringed upon their jurisdiction. After the Supreme Court ruled that "substantial" provincial consent was required before the Constitution could be amended, Trudeau held a conference with the premiers in Ottawa. There, Chrétien and the English-speaking premiers cut a deal. The new "notwithstanding clause" agreed to by Chrétien and the premiers dramatically altered the document. It would allow federal or provincial governments to override the core elements of the Charter for five-year periods which could be re-enacted indefinitely. If the government passed a law that infringed upon Charter rights, but argued that it was allowable under the reasonable limits to Charter rights referred to in Section 1, the law could be challenged in the courts and overturned if it was unjustified; however, no legal justification at all would be necessary for use of the notwithstanding clause. It would be totally unchallengeable.

The deal with the premiers assured the support of the PCs, and the NDP remained in favour of the draft Charter, but Robinson was disgusted. This Charter wouldn't stop abuses like the internment of the Japanese Canadians or the October Crisis arrests from happening again, he reasoned. When these actions occurred, the majority of Canadians hadn't even recognized them as human rights abuses and had, in fact, supported them enthusiastically. If the government ever again enacted a law that violated legitimate Charter rights but was nevertheless overwhelmingly popular with Canadians, the courts might find it unconstitutional, but the government would be able to use the notwithstanding clause to ignore the courts and do whatever it liked.

The notwithstanding clause wasn't the only problem. Peter Ittinuar's motion affirming aboriginal rights was modified to refer only to "existing" rights, which Robinson was concerned would make it more difficult for aboriginal people to claim further rights. There was also the matter of Quebec. That a deal had been reached without the consent of Premier René Lévesque caused bitter resentment in that province, and Robinson feared that proceeding without the consent of Quebec (which Trudeau eventually did) could be devastating for national unity. When the House voted on the final version of the Charter, Robinson was among the handful of members, from disparate parties and regions and with disparate reasons, who voted against it. The only other New Democrat to vote against it was Jim Manly, spokesperson on aboriginal issues. Following the stormy debate, Robinson was deeply touched to receive a deerskin scroll from the Assembly of First Nations. "When we looked around for help, you offered yourself. When our hearts were on the ground, you gave of your courage. When we spoke in our own defence, your voice was joined with ours. Our words are soft with gratitude and praise as we call you Brother," it read.

When the results of the vote were announced (246–24), members spontaneously burst into "O Canada." Glowing MPs milled about Trudeau's front-row desk, heartily slapping one another on the back and booming their congratulations to the prime minister. Clark and Broadbent were similarly surrounded by their rejoicing teams. Robinson gathered his notes from his desk, pushed aside the orange curtains separating the Chamber from the Opposition Lobby, and left.

"I recognize the understandable resentment, and indeed anger, on the part of some of my caucus colleagues resulting from my response to the very difficult issues which arose during the course of the constitutional debate," Robinson wrote to Broadbent following the vote. "As one who strongly supports the principle of caucus solidarity, I found it extremely painful to dissent at some points from the position taken by the caucus on the Constitution."

Not all of his colleagues accepted Robinson's explanation. The constitutional debate had been extremely divisive for the NDP. Caucus meetings during that period were tempestuous, with MPs routinely storming out of the room in fury. "I'd never seen a caucus under such pressure," Nystrom remembers. "One MP was literally crying. You know? Crying. A grown man in his 50s." That they had finally achieved a measure of unanimity prior to the final vote was no easy feat. But throughout the debate, Robinson had always maintained the same line in the sand. If the Charter wouldn't unequivocally prevent abuses like the internment of the Japanese Canadians or the War Measures arrests from being repeated, he wouldn't support it.

Robinson maintains that we don't have the protection we think we do, and that so far we've dodged a bullet. "There hasn't been a decision of the courts which really put the gun to the head of politicians," he says. "If the courts had ruled in a way that politicians didn't feel reflected the public mood, then they would have used that overriding clause in a heartbeat. It's precisely at those points that you need to have safeguards against strong tides of public opinion. We haven't had a Japanese-Canadians scenario, so far, since the adoption of the Charter, in which that notwithstanding clause could actually be invoked. So far, so good. But it's still wrong."

•　　•　　•

When Queen Elizabeth sat down at a small wooden table for two to sign what the beaming colonial prime minister presented to her, the development of the Charter didn't end. Successive court decisions interpreting clauses have significantly refined the Charter, and on occasion new rights have been "read in," meaning that although the right was not expressly included in the original document, courts proceed as though it is there. What is not often appreciated is that three of the most crucial modern refinements were proposed by Robinson to deaf ears in an Ottawa committee room years earlier.

Robinson had spoken against the clause allowing "reasonable limits" to certain Charter rights and freedoms, arguing that such undefined limits would be open to abuse, and that if Parliament didn't take steps to define them, the courts would. The Supreme Court was indeed forced to examine just how far the limits could go in the Oakes case, a 1986 challenge to the Narcotic Control Act. David Oakes, who had been caught with a quantity of drugs, claimed that the legal presumption that he intended to traffic the drugs violated his presumption of innocence, guaranteed by Section 11. The government replied that such a violation was necessary to fight drug trafficking and was therefore a reasonable limit. In its decision, the court carefully defined reasonable limits, and today the "Oakes Test" is applied by the justices every time they examine whether a law qualifies as a reasonable limit to a Charter right. Fortunately, the landmark decision has been lauded by legal scholars as one of the wisest decisions ever made by a Canadian court (although it's probably not as lauded by David Oakes, who lost his case). Applying the Oakes Test would likely prevent the abuses Robinson feared could result if certain rights were not exempt from limitations, but it is fair to say that Parliament gambled by leaving the matter to the Supreme Court rather than making the decision itself.

More satisfying still was when the Supreme Court ruled in 1995 that discrimination on the basis of sexual orientation was prohibited by the Charter. Robinson was vindicated yet again. He had never forgotten the sting of losing the fight to have sexual orientation included in the draft in 1981. "We cannot include every barnacle and eavestrough in the Constitution of Canada" still rang in his head. Later in his career he reminded others of the dismissive attitude he encountered in his early attempts to advance the rights of gays and lesbians. "We've moved a long way from the days of barnacles and eavestroughs," Robinson stated proudly in 2003, the night Canadian Alliance Leader Stephen Harper's motion to preserve the ban on same-sex marriage was defeated by the House.

The image of the barnacle took on a special resonance for Robinson. Luckless opponents in Burnaby certainly saw him that way; one frustrated rival candidate told him he was like a barnacle on the bottom of a boat, impossible to get rid of. He grew to like that image of toughness and resilience. It reminded him that it was his own stubborn, hard-headed persistence that had helped him change the world. He joked that if he ever got around to writing his autobiography, he would consider calling it *Barnacles and Eavestroughs*.

The third time the courts affirmed Robinson's point of view involved economic rights, rather than social ones. Believing the Charter should guarantee both, in 1981 he had sought the addition of the right to organize and bargain collectively. In his view, the "fundamental freedoms" promised by Section 2 could reasonably include the freedom to unionize. Both the Liberals and PCs voted against his motion. The Berlin Wall would fall, the World Wide Web would be invented, and the 20-year-old Edmonton Oilers star electrifying the NHL in 1981 would be long retired before Robinson was finally vindicated. In 2007 the Supreme Court ruled that excluding the right to unionize "did not withstand principled scrutiny" and was inconsistent with the values underlying the Charter. The right has now been read in to Section 2.

The Charter of Rights and Freedoms remains awash in Liberal red in the minds of many Canadians. However, an examination of Robinson's contributions to the debate at the time, and of the ways in which the courts have embraced his point of view in the years since repatriation, suggests that his name deserves mention among the movers and shakers who crafted this defining feature of the Canadian legal landscape.

• • •

The Liberals have been on record supporting the entrenchment of property rights in the Constitution since 1968. Provincial opposition kept Trudeau from including property rights in the original constitutional package, but during debate in the Special Joint Committee on the Constitution of Canada in 1981, he was offered another opportunity. When PC MP Perrin Beatty proposed that a right to the "enjoyment of property" be added to the draft Charter, Solicitor-General Bob Kaplan pledged Liberal support. In his battle against the entrenchment of property rights, Robinson revealed just what a multi-faceted politician he had become. Needing neither rhetorical flair nor media-friendly showmanship, he demonstrated foresight, commitment to principle, an adroit understanding of parliamentary procedure, the ability to forge crucial partnerships and the strength to stand alone. In doing so, he may have dramatically impacted the future balance of power between corporations and ordinary citizens in Canada.

The NDP's representatives on the committee, Robinson and Nystrom, had major reservations about Beatty's proposed amendment. They didn't have a problem with the Charter guaranteeing certain property rights, such as the right to own a house, farm or small business. But it was unclear what effect a constitutional right to enjoy property would have on the government's ability to regulate business properties. Measures like minimum wages, rent controls, or environmental, health and safety regulations could be at risk if the government couldn't interfere with the enjoyment of property. How would it affect the government's ability to preserve parks and farmland if citizens had an incontrovertible constitutional right to buy and sell property? How would aboriginal land claims be affected? And what was property, anyway? Beatty's amendment was broad and undefined, leaving it to the courts to decide. Did property include information? What about pensions or government benefits? Would foreign owners of Canadian property have these constitutional rights, too? There were a lot of unanswered questions.

But it wasn't just about unclear wording. Robinson and Nystrom also feared that property rights provisions would be used to enrich corporations at the expense of ordinary citizens. In the U.S., property rights are entrenched in the Constitution, albeit with different wording than that proposed by Beatty, and successive decisions of American courts have used those provisions to grant substantial rights to corporations. For example, among other things, the Fourteenth Amendment guarantees property rights and equal protection under the law for all Americans. In 1886 the court in *Santa Clara County v. Southern Pacific Railroad* ruled that, in certain circumstances, corporations were to be considered persons, and therefore had the same property rights as individuals. In the 50 years that followed that decision, more than 50 per cent of the cases in which the courts applied the Fourteenth Amendment resulted in corporations escaping governmental regulation.

Property rights are also guaranteed in the U.S. by the Fifth Amendment, with the provision that property can be appropriated, with compensation, for public benefit. But even this limitation has been abused. In the widely criticized *Kelo v. City of New London* decision, the courts affirmed the rights of a municipal government that had condemned the homes of residents who refused to sell their properties. The city intended to rezone a residential neighbourhood so that the pharmaceutical giant Pfizer could expand its facilities; in return, the company had promised economic benefits for the community. The dissenting justices lamented the dubious interpretation of public benefit and the apparent legality of taking private property away from citizens for the benefit of a corporation. "The beneficiaries are likely to be those citizens with disproportionate influence and power in the political process, including large corporations and development firms. As for the victims, the government now has license to transfer property from those with fewer resources to those with more. The Founders cannot have intended this perverse result," they stated.

Anxious to avoid creating such a situation in Canada, Robinson and Nystrom were ready for a fight. The filibuster that followed Beatty's amendment was gruelling. "We kept watching the clock," Nystrom remembers. He and Robinson had to keep talking until the end of the meeting; then they'd have the weekend to muster public opposition to Beatty's proposal. There were points of order and repeated attempts to force the vote, but Robinson and Nystrom were within their rights, and they kept talking until the committee co-chair reluctantly struck the gavel, signalling the end of the meeting. Over the weekend, Saskatchewan and other provinces reaffirmed their opposition to the inclusion of property rights, and there were suggestions the NDP might withdraw its support for the entire piece of legislation if property rights were included. By Monday, the Liberals had backed down. The PCs were indignant, feeling they had been betrayed, but their protests were to no avail, and Beatty's motion was defeated. When the Charter was passed in 1982, it made no mention of property rights. For Robinson and Nystrom, defeating the property rights amendment was an NDP badge of honour.

A year later, Robinson played a decisive role in quashing a second attempt at an amendment. At the First Ministers' Conference in 1983, Trudeau tentatively broached the topic of property rights with several of the premiers. This time he found them more open to the concept. In April of that year, Trudeau announced to a startled House that if the opposition parties agreed to limit debate to one day, he would bring forward a bill to amend the Charter to include property rights. The PCs, led at the time by interim leader Erik Nielsen (Joe Clark had stepped down to defend his leadership in a leadership race), provided their consent immediately, but the NDP needed time to consult as a caucus. The NDP MPs still had the same concerns that had been voiced by Robinson and Nystrom in committee two years earlier, but the changed position of the premiers complicated matters. Even B.C. NDP Leader Dave Barrett, in the midst of a provincial election campaign, was now publicly in favour of entrenching property rights. For the next week the PCs begged Trudeau to introduce the legislation with or without NDP consent. Perhaps tired of the constitutional wrangling of the previous years, Trudeau refused. It would be a one-day debate with all-party consent or nothing at all.

Finally, the leaderless PCs took a colossal gamble. On April 29, 1983, they introduced a motion to add property rights to the Charter, but specified that this also amounted to a motion of non-confidence in the government. The Liberals were being forced into a trap: they could either vote for property rights and vote themselves out of office, or they could vote against it, alienating supporters of what had now become a popular cause. What the PCs hoped was that the Liberals would simply step out of the trap by introducing the property rights bill Trudeau had promised. Then the PCs would withdraw their confidence motion and let the Liberal bill pass, whether or not the NDP supported it.

The clean, one-day debate Trudeau had imagined was becoming yet another constitutional headache, and the Liberals refused to put forward a bill. As the brinkmanship continued, Broadbent rose in the House and offered a compromise. The one-day, four-hour debate that Trudeau thought would suffice for a major constitutional change was unacceptable. However, the NDP would agree to have the matter sent to committee, allowing a more detailed study than what had taken place when the PCs sprang their sudden property rights motion on the Special Joint Committee in 1981.

The Liberals and PCs appeared ready to agree, but there was one technicality. The rules regarding the sequence of motions in the House were quite clear: in order to set aside the PC motion and proceed immediately to a vote on Broadbent's compromise, the unanimous consent of the House was necessary. Since the Liberals, PCs and NDP seemed to be in agreement about sending property rights to committee, that consent wasn't expected to be a problem. Suddenly there was a flurry of activity in the NDP corner of the House.

Heated exchanges appeared to be taking place behind the orange curtains. Finally, red-faced, NDP MP Rod Murphy rose to inform the House that the NDP MPs themselves weren't yet ready to provide consent to their own leader's suggestion and needed to meet in caucus first.

That made the PCs nervous. The trap they had laid now appeared to be a major tactical blunder. Because they had made their property rights motion a confidence motion, if it was adopted, it would dissolve Parliament and plunge the nation into an ill-timed election in the midst of the PC leadership campaign. If the motion was defeated, a procedural rule preventing the House from considering the same question twice would prevent their bringing forward another property rights motion for the rest of the session. (This was the opinion of Justice Minister Mark MacGuigan, who warned the House of this possibility.) Their own motion had become the roadblock preventing the property rights they so desired. The only way out was to withdraw it, but once moved, motions become the property of the whole House. That meant they couldn't withdraw their motion without unanimous consent. All it would take to prevent them from getting property rights in the Constitution would be for one member to say no. If the raised voices among the New Democrats were any indication, there was a serious risk that might happen. Hoping to buy time, the PCs asked for the unanimous consent necessary to at least postpone the vote on the PC motion until an agreement on how to proceed could be reached.

"Yay!" the House thundered.

"Nay!" replied a lone voice, as every head in the House swivelled in Robinson's direction. For supporters of property rights, the events following the PC motion pointed to the most disastrous conclusion possible. As long as that damned Burnaby MP remained in his seat, refusing to consent to any measure to bring the motion back from the precipice, there was no way out but over the edge.

The House rose for the weekend, and the vote on the PC motion was scheduled for Monday afternoon. Robinson immediately understood the opportunity he'd been given, but the prospect of physically remaining in his seat in the House until the vote was problematic. Bladders have a finite capacity, after all, and Robinson knew he'd need an ally when the House resumed on Monday. That weekend, he met with his NDP colleague Ian Waddell at the Bino's Restaurant across the street from Waddell's constituency office, and the two B.C. MPs made a deal. "Svend and I agreed that one of us, at least, would be [there] during this period, to make sure our caucus had the guts to resist attempts to persuade us to agree to property rights," Waddell confirms, describing the agreement they called the "Bino's Accord."

The following Monday, either Robinson or Waddell was in the House at any given time (allowing the other to respond to the call of nature), ready to scuttle any last-ditch requests for unanimous consent to postpone or to withdraw the PC confidence motion before the vote that afternoon. Caucus colleagues harangued them, embarrassed that the NDP had agreed to allow property rights to be studied in committee only to have two of their members prevent a motion to do so. Barrett took time out of the B.C. campaign to phone Ottawa and demanded to speak to them. But they wouldn't budge, and eventually the Speaker had to call the vote. The NDP ended up voting in favour of the motion, mainly because they didn't want to vote against a motion of non-confidence in the unpopular Liberal government. Since the Liberals still held a majority, the NDP knew the motion would be defeated. The Charter contains no reference to the enjoyment of property to this day. Whether the consequences of a clause in the Charter guaranteeing property rights would have included those feared by Robinson — limitations on the government's ability to impose a minimum wage, rent controls, or environmental, health and safety regulations — or something else entirely, Canadians have never had to find out.

The incident has been largely lost to history. Even some of the people who were there don't remember that it happened. But in the dusty pages of the Hansard transcripts, the permanent record of everything that is said in the House, it's there. "When you look at the impact of decisions that I made in real terms, keeping that property rights amendment out of the Constitution may have had a more significant impact than almost anything else I did," Robinson reflects today. "No question about it. I think the implications of that were huge. I look back on my 25 years — it's not one I got any headlines for, particularly, but in terms of the impact on the future of the country, I think it was profound."

As in several previous political battles, Robinson had to be unbending in the face of opposition, including that of his own party. Subverting caucus tactics yet again didn't earn Robinson any more friends in the NDP, and he was punished for the next two weeks by not being given any of the NDP's slots in Question Period. "Broadbent was apoplectic, because he had promised to deliver, and he couldn't," Robinson recalls. "But I didn't care." As the election campaign in B.C. continued, Barrett held a rally in Burnaby. Despite being the local MP, Robinson was told he was not welcome on the platform with Barrett. Organizers simply refused to set a place for him. The relationship between Barrett and Robinson, turbulent and challenging at the best of times, had hit a new low over the property rights dispute.

Undeterred, Robinson took a chair from the floor, stuck it up on the platform and sat down anyway. No doubt Barrett clenched his teeth as he grinned to the crowd that day. That didn't bother Robinson. He had a job to do.

EIGHT

Whatever Measures are Necessary

When Pierre Trudeau won the 1980 election, he promised that it would be his last. Early in 1984 he took his famous walk in the snow and announced that he would be resigning. The Liberals chose former finance minister John Turner as his replacement, but Turner didn't hold the job for long. With the country mired in a recession, Canadians were ready for a change. The new PC leader, Brian Mulroney, promised to create jobs and reduce the deficit without cutting social programs, and although it is not often remembered today, a perusal of newspaper articles published during Mulroney's rise to power reveals repeated use of the term "Mulroneymania."

"Youth and experience — that's a hard combination to beat!" promised Svend Robinson's campaign literature in 1984. Only 32, he had already become one of the best-known MPs in the country. He still door-knocked enthusiastically, but he didn't need to introduce himself anymore. Everyone in Burnaby seemed to have heard a story from a friend, family member or neighbour of the incredible lengths he'd gone to helping a constituent. Fundraising was easier than it had ever been. The anti-abortion activists who had tried to defeat him in the previous election were incensed at his enduring popularity and stormed his constituency office at one point during the campaign, but most people didn't share their views. Robinson's hard work in Burnaby was paying off, and in the 1984 election, voters returned him to Ottawa with 48 per cent of the vote, 13 per cent higher than his nearest challenger. NDP support held relatively steady across the country, Quebec abandoned the Liberals, and the PCs led in every region of Canada and swept to power with a record 211 MPs.

The Chicken Book rumours had spurred homophobic innuendo in Burnaby throughout the campaign. Playing on the homophobic fallacy linking homosexuality to child molestation, a Tsawwassen anti-abortion group circulated a pamphlet suggesting that it was not only "unborn" children who needed protecting from Robinson, but "born" children as well. Robinson wondered how many members of Brian Mulroney's huge PC caucus held similar views.

Most, it turned out, didn't really want to talk about homosexuality. Their views were complex and tended to represent the broad spectrum of attitudes in Canadian society. If there was a prevailing attitude in the PC caucus, it was probably one of quiet discomfort and a general hope that the issue would just go away. A sizeable minority, however, was zealously opposed to homosexuality and eager to crusade against it. Most of the time, these MPs were content to hurl snide comments about hairdressers at Robinson, the suspected homosexual, as he made his speeches. ("Why aren't you at Rock Hudson's funeral?" PC MP Dan McKenzie shouted on the day of the gay actor's cremation after his death from AIDS.) Other times, they went out of their way to feature fiery condemnations of homosexuality in their own speeches. Hansard transcripts provide a taste of some of the remarks Robinson was exposed to over the next years. Canadians today might be shocked to hear such language from their neighbours, let alone their representatives in Parliament:

> Mr. Speaker, the New Democratic Party is urging the government to compel the Royal Canadian Mounted Police to accept lesbians and gays. Can you feature a fairy RCMP constable trying to arrest a lumberjack with a powder puff? Can you imagine a lesbian RCMP fairy at the scene of an armed robbery screaming, "Stop, surrender, or I will

hit you over the head with my purse?" If fairies were not hired, they would cry discrimination. [Gordon Taylor, PC MP for Bow River, Alberta, on October 20, 1986]

Sure, let sodomites, pederasts and proponents of bestiality become the custodians of our children. Why not? We are modern. We aren't afraid of taboos. Go right ahead! Let any idiot indulging in his unbridled sexuality get into the police force — we saw that in Quebec — and have fun with our children. [Charles Hamelin, PC MP for Charlevoix, Quebec, on December 1, 1986]

Homosexuality is anti-biological. It is anti-medical, anti-biblical and I quote, "Go ye forth and multiply." It is anti-family, and it is anti-social. It is pro-deviate, and it is absolutely disgusting to most Canadians . . . it is hygienic insanity. It is a crime against humanity. [Ron Stewart, PC MP for Simcoe South, Ontario, on December 1, 1986]

In this context, it was hard to imagine imminent progress on gay and lesbian issues. As former PC MP Patrick Boyer acknowledges, "Parliament in 1985 was stony soil in which to plant such a fragile seed." Nevertheless, for a second time Robinson brought forward his bill to include sexual orientation in the Human Rights Act. "Such changes are an essential first step toward the creation of a society in which each individual is recognized for his or her inherent worth and dignity as a human being," he told the House. "Such changes in the law will hopefully also hasten the day when no man or woman and no young student in Sudbury [where a gay teen had been beaten] or anywhere else in the country will be the victim of fear, violence and intolerance because he or she happens to be gay or lesbian. That day cannot come too soon."

Robinson found he had an unexpected ally in Prime Minister Mulroney. "One of the first caucuses I ever held when I became leader of the Progressive Conservative Party was to tell the Progressive Conservative caucus that I had no time whatsoever for any discrimination of any kind against gays, lesbians, people of any religion, anything," Mulroney recalls. "I can remember saying to them, 'I have 211 members of Parliament here and 40 senators. That's over 250 people. Chances are that in here, if the statistics are right . . . either there are some people right in here, or our children, who are gay. Now, if you want me to discriminate or legitimize discrimination against a member of your family, your own son, your own daughter — I'm telling you right now, if you ask me to do it, I'm not going to do it. I wouldn't discriminate against your children any more than I would discriminate against the children of other families. So it's not going to happen while I'm the leader of the party. So let's all get used to that.' And they did," Mulroney recounts today with evident pride.

As a result, when Robinson proposed his bill, the PCs already had their marching orders, and the government allowed the subject matter of Robinson's bill (although not the bill itself) to be referred to the subcommittee on equality rights.

This was the chance he had been waiting for. Since the passage of the Charter in 1982, the government had been given three years to ensure that legislation conformed to the equality rights that the Charter affirmed. The three years were up, and the government established the subcommittee to evaluate the progress that had been made. Robinson had to ensure that the subcommittee hearings did not become a mouthpiece for intolerance, but instead were an opportunity for the members to learn about the pain and discrimination faced by colleagues, friends and relatives who were gay. Methodically, he contacted supportive witnesses across the country and ensured that everywhere the subcommittee travelled in its cross-country hearings, its members would hear passionate and eye-opening submissions. It was no coincidence that the first stop on the tour was Burnaby, where a group of lesbian mothers shared photographs of their children.

"We had barely begun our work as a committee when a surge of submissions from groups across Canada advocating for gay and lesbian rights made it clear to me that either this had been an untapped vein of public opinion waiting to express itself, or some- one had been orchestrating a widespread campaign to our com- mittee, or both," recalls Boyer, who chaired the subcommittee. "After a couple of public hearings, given the close similarity I saw in the wording of many presentations and written submissions, and what I witnessed of Svend's tight rapport with these groups appearing before us, it was clear he was making sure spokespeople for Canada's homosexual communities would flood the committee's time and attention."

Stacking the witness list is a common tactic used across the political spectrum, but it's worth noting that in 1985 it took tremendous bravery for gay and lesbian witnesses to open their hearts at a public hearing. Nevertheless, Robinson convinced them that the time had come. According to University of Toronto political science professor and gay rights expert David Rayside, it was the first large-scale mobilization of gay activists in pursuit of federal policy.

"Personal stories made the difference," Robinson submits. "It really transformed the members of the committee." Boyer agrees, recalling the photographs shown by the lesbian mothers in Burnaby. "Most politicians, like most people in Canada, are touched by human reality more quickly and deeply than by theoretic discussion," Boyer says. "Ideas flow from emotions."

"For many of us, this was our first contact with people who professed this kind of lifestyle. In all honesty and all candour, we were a bit shocked. First, we were shocked by the number of people we met. In every city we went to, in all the towns and villages, there were people who had chosen a lifestyle that we had not chosen," Liberal MP Sheila Finestone, a member of the subcommittee, would later say of the experience. "We heard details about the physical abuse and psychological oppression from which they have suffered. We heard about the hate propaganda which had been targeted toward them, and how they had been demonized in many ways. We heard about the outright discrimination they faced in employment, in housing and in services."

For many of the members, it wasn't easy handling that political hot potato. "I felt at times that, in dealing with human sexuality, made so complicated by centuries of religious prohibitions and social repression — not to mention more recent medical advances up to and including sex-change operations — I would have found it more satisfying to just spend my time shovelling fog in the dark," says Boyer. Gradually, though, a consensus began to form on the subcommittee. Although the five PCs and one Liberal who joined Robinson on the subcommittee represented a wide range of views, none were overtly reactionary, and as the hearings progressed, party lines began to disappear. When one witness in New Brunswick made negative remarks about homosexuals, it was the PCs, not Robinson, who were the most aggressive in attacking him.

The subcommittee released its report, "Equality for All," in October 1985. Along with 84 other recommendations to eliminate various forms of discrimination from Canadian law, the subcommittee recommended that the government end discrimination on the basis of sexual orientation. Robinson was proud that the subcommittee had made its recommendations unanimously. Privately, though, he expected the report to end up sitting on a shelf. Convincing six other subcommittee members with hours of passionate, personal testimony was one thing, but convincing an entire government with a wordy report that many members would be unlikely to read, let alone consider carefully, was something else entirely. Rather, it was a small victory he could use to harass the government into taking action. Judging from the negative reaction the subcommittee chair, Boyer, was getting from some of his caucus colleagues, Robinson didn't dare hope for much more than that.

"I became a lightning rod for their attacks," Boyer recalls, "just as in my constituency, and across the country, I was the recipient of harsh anger, sometimes displayed in truly unpleasant ways." When PC MP John Reimer hosted a special caucus meeting to discuss how the government should respond to the subcommittee recommendations, he forbade Boyer from participating. "I don't think you should come to this meeting, Patrick," Reimer said. He'd been waiting at the door for Boyer to enter. "You have a conflict of interest."

However, Mulroney hadn't weighed in on the subcommittee report yet. When he did, in a meeting all caucus members were welcome to attend, he masterfully shifted the caucus towards his point of view. In his own words, Boyer reveals for the first time the passionate speech given by Mulroney in the privacy of the caucus room:

"Who can say what God's plan is?" the Prime Minister asked, gazing quizzically over his eye-glasses around the vast assembly of Tory MPs and senators. "Here, look at me . . . married to Mila . . . blessed with children . . . just like God intended." He paused to let that sink in. The ardent Christians, John Reimer especially, were beaming. "And before I was married," he then continued in a confidential, almost conspiratorial tone of voice, "as some of you probably know . . . I was pretty robust as a heterosexual male." The room relaxes with laughter and chuckles, all the straight men on-side, happily identifying with their leader. The evangelicals, for their part, are aglow at Brian's acknowledgement of God's Plan. Everyone's in the palm of his hand. He looks around the vast chamber, alive with good vibes.

"But then there's my brother, another son of the same Christian parents, carrying the very same genes as me. Why did God make him gay, but not me?"

Stunned silence fills the room. The Prime Minister lets the hush take its toll. The changing atmosphere is palpable. Who knew that Brian's younger brother, bachelor Gary, a fine arts teacher in Montreal who excelled at redecorating homes, was one of those whom some in this very caucus had been virulently attacking? The PM's very own brother, for heaven's sake!

That settled it. "There was no great debate ever in caucus on sexual orientation. There was far greater debate on the metric system, which was going to destroy the world, than there ever was on sexual orientation," former PC MP Pat Carney says. "When the prime minister is supportive of something, the others, in self-interest, will kind of shut up."

On March 4, 1986, Robinson got a birthday present he would never forget. Justice Minister John Crosbie ordered his department to release the official government response to the subcommittee report. "The government believes that one's sexual orientation is irrelevant to whether one can perform a job or use a service or facility," it read. "The Department of Justice is of the view that the courts will find that sexual orientation is encompassed by the guarantees in Section 15 of the Charter. The government will take whatever measures are necessary to ensure that sexual orientation is a prohibited ground of discrimination in relation to all areas of federal jurisdiction."

Robinson can still recite the Crosbie response verbatim, a smile creeping involuntarily across his face as he does. The sense of pride and accomplishment he feels as he reflects on it is evident. "That was what was really, absolutely revolutionary," he says. "That's what really made the difference. That's what really changed things."

Crosbie's promise alone didn't change the law, and until the government brought forward new legislation, laws would continue to be administered as they always had been. Robinson knew it would take time for any bills to reach the floor of the House. Crosbie had also committed to expanding the Court Challenges Program, which assisted claimants needing to go to court to challenge discriminatory laws. After Robinson urged further expansion for the program, Crosbie responded, "You are a bleeding heart with a mouth." Robinson would have to be patient as he waited for further changes. But meanwhile, if Canadians were to challenge discriminatory laws in the courts, government lawyers would no longer argue against them. It was unacceptable that Canadian citizens should have to go to court to affirm their fundamental rights, but it was progress.

He had been in the House for seven years, through three governments and four prime ministers, but he hadn't achieved a victory on sexual orientation — until now.

• • •

Robinson still hadn't been forgiven for supporting the decriminalization of solicitation on *Webster!* but now, nearly two years later, Ed Broadbent wanted his old justice critic back. "Thinking it might happen again? Sure. Having faith, I hoped it would not!" Broadbent says, laughing as he describes bringing Robinson back into the fold.

Reappointed justice critic after the 1984 election, Robinson didn't miss a beat. He proposed more bills to strike down the severe restrictions on eligibility for abortions that were still in place in the early 1980s. He worked closely with pro-choice advocate Dr. Henry Morgentaler (one pamphlet circulated by opponents in Burnaby called him Morgentaler's "best friend" in Parliament) and accompanied him to the Supreme Court in 1988 as Morgentaler appealed his conviction for performing illegal abortions. The Supreme Court ruled in his favour, striking down the Criminal Code restrictions. When the judge said, "Acquittal is restored," the Polish-born Morgentaler turned to his lawyer and asked, "Does that mean we won?" When told that it did, he then turned to Robinson and said, "Are you *sure* we won?"

As justice critic, Robinson also kept hammering the government to improve prison conditions and create rehabilitative, community-based alternatives to imprisonment. He successfully filibustered a committee motion sponsored by PC MP Bill Domm to reinstate the death penalty, and led the charge for the NDP when Deputy Prime Minister Don Mazankowski put forward another death penalty motion in the House. "Vengeance as the foundation for punishment must be rejected in any civilized society," Robinson said. "We know as well that it is not the rich and powerful who hang. It is the poor, the illiterate, the uneducated, native people and blacks." The death penalty motion ultimately failed — Mulroney was personally opposed and made a passionate speech in the House — but Robinson also played a role, forming a strategic alliance with Liberal MP Warren Allmand and PC MP Marcel Danis, and working to convince enough PCers to vote with the opposition so that the motion could be defeated. "I was very proud to be a Canadian that day," he says.

Robinson didn't shy away from the prostitution issue, either. In Vancouver, the problem had worsened. In east Vancouver's Mount Pleasant neighbourhood, the city had recommended erecting barricades each night to force prostitutes into a nearby warehouse district, where they would have to work in even more isolated and unsafe conditions. The PC government, meanwhile, proposed more legal restrictions on communicating for the purposes of prostitution. It was already illegal to communicate in public; they sought to make it illegal to communicate in cars, too. "The bill is dangerous and will merely drive prostitution underground in the short run. It will make prostitutes more subject to violence, more dependent on pimps," Robinson said. "This is fundamentally an economic and social problem. To deal with an economic and social problem using harsh and repressive criminal measures is a profound mistake."

By now he had a widespread reputation as an MP willing to raise issues no one else would. When a young lawyer named John Syrtash, working as pro bono counsel for the Jewish advocacy group B'nai Brith, needed an MP to fight for the rights of Jewish women to be granted "gets" from their husbands in divorce proceedings, most of the MPs Syrtash talked to responded with blank stares. "People thought I was crazy," Syrtash recalls. "Initially, I was all alone. Nobody took me very seriously. People didn't know what this was."

A "get" is a document a woman requires from her husband in order to be considered divorced in the Jewish faith. Unfortunately, some men were withholding their gets in order to force more concessions from their wives in divorce proceedings. It was a human rights issue that could be dealt with through changes to the Divorce Act, and Syrtash eventually went to Robinson. "He was the first public figure to actually raise the issue in Canada, and that's something I will always be eternally grateful for," Syrtash says. "Now we have the most effective law in the world, and Svend was instrumental in bringing this to public consciousness."

As Robinson focused on domestic human rights, his attention was inevitably drawn to the hardships faced by people in less fortunate parts of the world as well. He knew there were many places so stained by violence, terror and oppression that it was — and still is — scarcely believable they share the same planet with the parks, malls and coffee shops of Burnaby, British Columbia. As he had already proven so many times in his career, when he learned of an injustice, he was compelled to act.

In his first forays into foreign affairs, he did what was expected of an NDP MP. He attacked the government for not doing enough to help the fight against apartheid in South Africa. He attacked it for flirting with U.S. President Ronald Reagan's "Star Wars" missile defence scheme, an ambitious and expensive plan to create a missile shield that would protect the U.S. from its enemies. He condemned the 1986 American bombing of Libya (a campaign mounted in retaliation for a terrorist attack in West Berlin) and mourned the deaths of civilians. He visited Cuba and proposed establishing a Canada–Cuba Parliamentary Friendship Group. But it was a trip to Chile that gave the first hints of the unique brand of international engagement that would later define him in the eyes of many Canadians.

When the prospect of socialism in Chile threatened U.S. interests in South America, the Americans used more sophisticated tools than in their bungled military operations that characterized their efforts to contain communism in Vietnam. The CIA spent over $3-million on propaganda to prevent socialist candidate Salvador Allende being elected president in 1964. In the 1970 elections it spent more than triple that amount, but Allende won. The CIA continued its anti-Allende propaganda, and U.S. President Richard Nixon personally ordered the spy agency to find a way to "make the economy scream," turn Chileans against their government, and foment a military coup. In 1973 Allende was overthrown by General Augusto Pinochet. Immediately after the coup, Pinochet ordered the creation of what has become known as the "Caravan of Death," a loyal squad that travelled the country conducting summary executions of Pinochet's opponents. Over 40,000 Chileans were arrested during Pinochet's 17-year reign simply for speaking critically about their dictator. Thousands of those arrested were tortured, and at least 3,000 were executed.

When Robinson and two prominent Canadian human rights lawyers, Barbara Jackman and Robert Milen, were invited to Santiago to participate in an inter-parliamentary conference in 1987, the Chilean-Canadian community warned them that they weren't likely to meet any of Pinochet's real opposition in a conference openly monitored by the military. What they needed to do was talk to the hundreds of civilians still behind bars awaiting military tribunals.

What Robinson and his colleagues saw when they visited a Santiago prison confirmed their worst fears: horrific conditions, evidence of torture, and even more death sentences being handed down by Pinochet's hand-picked military judges. The Canadians were appalled, and said so. Not surprisingly, their request to visit a second prison was flatly refused. When a succession of meetings with Chilean Justice Department officials proved useless, the small delegation called a press conference.

The nervous Chilean interpreter hired to convey Robinson's remarks to the assembled media didn't really want to translate everything the brash Canadian politician was saying. He was pretty sure he wasn't going to get into any trouble himself — he'd been hired to translate, and he was just doing his job — but he wasn't at all sure what would happen to the gringo. You just didn't *say* things like that about Pinochet.

Still, the MP was insisting.

"The only terrorism in Chile is state terrorism, and Pinochet is the greatest terrorist of them all," the translator said in Spanish to a shocked room.

Robinson's remarks didn't get any gentler. He recommended that the international community place economic sanctions on Chile. He accused the CIA-funded newspaper *El Mercurio*, influential in the overthrow of Allende, of having blood on its hands. Asked if he was justifying violence against the Pinochet regime, Robinson — often mistaken for a pacifist even though he isn't one — replied that all methods of resistance were necessary, and that the Chilean people had the right to defend themselves.

After the press conference, a reporter quietly took Robinson aside. In a hushed tone, he advised him to leave the country — immediately. The Canadian embassy staff who were present agreed, suggesting he go directly to the airport. Robinson asked if he could get his luggage first. He was told it wasn't a very good idea.

He returned to Canada without incident, but the experience was unnerving. While it is debatable whether the Chilean government would have harmed a Canadian MP, it is certainly true that many Chileans had been targeted for saying less than what Robinson had said. His strongest statements were predictably left out of the media coverage in Chile, but elsewhere his comments were reported in their entirety. Back in Canada, he spoke at rallies organized by Chilean Canadians in Vancouver, Edmonton and Montreal, his remarks becoming part of a growing international condemnation of the Pinochet regime. In the next years, Pinochet gradually eased restrictions on political involvement, and Chile eventually became a democracy again. In a visit to London in 1998, Pinochet was arrested on an international warrant, and he died in 2006 while under house arrest. Robinson's press conference was a mere drop in the bucket, but in a small way it was the Galindo Madrid formula all over again. In quintessential Svend Robinson fashion, he'd used his privileged position as a member of Parliament and dramatic, fearless language to help draw attention to an injustice, hoping to influence change. It didn't matter that he was on the opposition benches; it only mattered that he had a voice.

Svend with his mother, Edith, and sister Gretchen.

Robinson volunteered with St. John's Ambulance as a teenager.

Working underground at Dickenson Mine as a Frontier College labourer-teacher, 1971.

Robinson and Patricia Fraser on their wedding day in June 1972 with Svend's parents, Wayne and Edith.

Robinson faced off against Pauline Jewett for the Burnaby nomination in 1977.

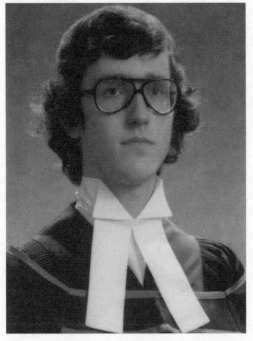

Robinson was called to the British Columbia Bar in 1978.

During his first election campaign, Robinson brought former Swedish prime minister Olof Palme to visit the Swedish Old People's Home in Burnaby. For years after, residents of the home were among Robinson's most loyal supporters.

Robinson with NDP Leader Ed Broadbent at the Socialist International conference in Vancouver, 1978. François Mitterrand, later the president of France, is in the background.

Robinson holding a press conference with Chilean refugee Galindo Madrid in 1979. PHOTO BY SEAN GRIFFIN – PACIFIC TRIBUNE ARCHIVE

Robinson's work on the Special Joint Committee on the Constitution of Canada was a defining moment of his career.

With one of his political heroes, former NDP leader Tommy Douglas.

Robinson with fellow Grand Marshall Karen Andrews during Lesbian and Gay Pride Day in Toronto, 1988. Robinson had come out only a few months earlier. PHOTO BY PHILIP HANNAN

Robinson was a key supporter of Audrey McLaughlin's successful bid to become the first female leader of a federal political party in Canada.

With Palestinian Authority President Yasser Arafat.

Robinson with Penan indigenous people in Sarawak, Malaysia, 1992.

Meeting the Dalai Lama.

NINE

White Swan

Your entire body feels different as you explore the palatial rainforest of Gwaii Haanas National Park. In the depths of the green silence surrounding you, there is a new fluidity to your movements. You feel an alertness and a physical power that you don't feel in the city. As the forest breathes around you, you realize that you have stepped back in time, and that the tangled vines drooping above and the damp moss underfoot are what you would have seen if you had been here during your grandparents' childhoods, or during the childhoods of Shakespeare, Erik the Red or Caesar.

European cartographers called the British Columbian coastal archipelago the Queen Charlotte Islands; the people born there called it Haida Gwaii. They were superb artists and seamen, feared slave traders and fierce warriors. The Europeans brought the ravages of smallpox and the prohibition of the most sacred Haida traditions, but a powerful sense of resistance remained in the Haida Nation. No treaty ceding their territory was ever signed with the newcomers. And as Haida land was carved up by loggers, the dense forests reduced to barren moonscapes, that resistance swelled; in 1985 on Lyell Island, the Haida people took a stand.

Their first choice would have been to negotiate with the B.C. government and with Western Forest Products, the company that claimed logging rights in 38 per cent of the South Moresby region of Haida Gwaii, including Lyell Island. But that would mean negotiating with people who didn't acknowledge that Haida Gwaii belonged to the Haida. "It has to be made clear that the claim that they own the Queen Charlotte Islands or other parts of B.C. is not something that they expect to be on the table," stated B.C. Attorney-General Brian Smith. "If you debate that issue, discuss it or negotiate it, then we're saying that other British Columbians are second-class." It appeared that, in the eyes of the government, the fact that the islands had never been ceded in any treaty and still included the bones of Haida ancestors and an environmental diversity so precious that the area had been called the "Galapagos of the North" was irrelevant.

Without the opportunity for good-faith negotiation, a group of Haida elders set up a blockade on a logging road on Lyell Island, determined to end the clear-cutting of old-growth rainforest in their ancestral lands. Younger Haida wanted to help, too, but the elders were determined that only they should bear the legal risk. Drumming, singing and wearing red and black face paint, younger Haida stood near the blockade in support. Western Forest Products alleged that the protesters let air out of tires, ruined radios, stole lunches, emptied gasoline from chainsaws and, worst of all, "circulated through the woods howling like wolves," but by most accounts the blockade was a completely peaceful act of civil disobedience.

After nine days of protests generating significant media attention and criticism of the provincial government, the B.C. Supreme Court ruled against the Haida and ordered them to dismantle the blockade. It was a setback, but the Haida were undeterred. "Our people were totally committed," affirms Miles Richardson, then-president of the Council of the Haida Nation. "Inside ourselves, we knew we were going to prevail. We just didn't know what the price was going to be."

The blockade remained. After a court hearing in Vancouver, Richardson was approached by Robinson. "He asked if he could help out by coming up to Lyell Island, with the understanding that it was just Haidas involved in the blockade. I invited him to come up there, thinking that having an MP supportive, on-site, speaking to the issues could be helpful," Richardson remembers. Robinson flew to Haida Gwaii and joined the young Haida supporting the elders on the line.

Since Robinson was there in a supportive capacity only, he wasn't invited to the planning sessions held by the elders. But he developed an immediate rapport with Haida elder Ada Yovanovich and was quickly accepted by the community. "He established some strong contacts with the people there and developed some trust with some of the elders," Richardson explains. "People thought they might be comfortable with him doing more."

Robinson and Yovanovich became so close during his stay on Lyell Island that she adopted him into the eagle clan as her son. She named him Tethunadas — White Swan. "It was really one of the most powerful periods of my life, to be welcomed as a family member in the Haida Nation, particularly during that critical point," Robinson recalls, growing quiet. His mother had died when he was just 24, and her absence had left a painful void in his life. In Yovanovich, he found a comforting maternal presence that helped ease that deep-rooted grief. "She was a hero to me. To have her wrap her arms around me and say 'You're my son' was incredibly empowering and moving, and it meant so much to me."

Now an honorary member of the Haida Nation, White Swan was allowed to participate in the planning sessions. He helped develop strategy and took part in role-playing exercises, taking on the role of a police officer. But the most effective way for him to help would be to attract more attention to the Haida cause. To do that, he needed to do something more visible, and more dramatic. On November 15, 1985, with the permission of the elders, Robinson joined the Haida on the blockade. "It was an overpowering kind of experience," he later told *Burnaby Now*, when a reporter asked him how it felt as a lawmaker to break the law. "For me, as both a lawyer and an MP, it was a very traumatic experience to stand on the line blocking trucks, but I didn't want to show my support from the sidelines."

But there was a price to be paid for defending aboriginal title and the future of the local ecosystem. On November 23, Robinson and 17 Haida were charged with contempt of court for defying the B.C. Supreme Court injunction against the blockade. Jail was a serious possibility. However, realizing a court appearance was a valuable public forum in which to raise Haida grievances, Robinson arrived at his hearing dressed in a ceremonial Haida blanket given to him by the elders. "My actions arose from my continuing strong belief in the rightness and justice, both moral and legal, of the Haida people's land claim, and a desire to express my fullest personal support for their cause," he told the court, refusing its request that he apologize for his actions. "It is the Attorney-General of British Columbia who displays contempt for the fundamental law of this land — the Constitution of Canada."

"It is unfortunate that Mr. Robinson chose to make a political speech in his statement to the Court," Justice A.E. McEachern chided, sparing him jail time and fining him $750 instead. Despite this admonishment, Robinson's speech was quoted widely in media coverage of the blockade and had the desired effect. The actions of the Haida elders (and now the law-breaking MP) at Lyell Island made environmental protection in Haida Gwaii a popular cause, and accounts of their struggle were splashed across the front pages of B.C. papers. As public pressure mounted, the B.C. government had no choice but to negotiate, and in 1987, Canada, B.C. and the Haida Nation signed an agreement ending logging in the South Moresby area. "It was the first time in modern Haida history that our people stood up for our fundamental title successfully," Richardson states proudly.

Robinson returned to Haida Gwaii often over the years. He and Yovanovich remained close, and his adopted family grew: David Suzuki was later adopted by Yovanovich, and the legendary environmentalist became the younger Robinson's "little brother." Robinson still collects eagle feathers, a symbol of his clan, and the sense of honour he felt when he was adopted into his second family still remains with him. "This is a nation with an incredibly rich history, and to be honoured in that way meant . . ." He pauses, at a rare loss for words. "It's really impossible to put into words what it meant to me," he says finally. "On both the personal level and the political level it was quite extraordinary."

South Moresby has been officially protected as Gwaii Haanas National Park Reserve and Haida Heritage Site. The rainforest has gradually reclaimed the old whaling station and the mine sites that used to dot the island coastlines. Jagged bits of rusted iron have been engulfed by the green, growing magnificence. There is hope that even the devastation of the clear-cuts will one day completely fade away, replaced by vibrant new growth. The hardiness of the Haida people, who survived the encroachment of the Europeans and the banishment of their language and religion, is matched by the resilience of the scarred, beautiful land as it slowly heals.

•   •   •

"I have never felt as right in anything I have done," Robinson told his constituency association after returning from Haida Gwaii, but many of his NDP colleagues didn't feel the same way. He wasn't the MP for Skeena, the riding that included Haida Gwaii. Neither was he the environment critic, forestry critic or aboriginal affairs critic. Jim Fulton, Skeena MP and forestry critic, was a committed environmentalist who had been working hard behind the scenes with Richardson and other Haida leaders to negotiate a resolution. According to Bill Blaikie, both a good friend of Fulton and the NDP environment critic at the time, Fulton had understood that the protests were being organized by and for Haida only. Blaikie insists that, on that basis, Fulton told caucus not to attend, while Robinson is certain that no such request was made. Richardson, in any case, confirms that he invited Robinson to Haida Gwaii, and in Robinson's eyes the permission of the local aboriginal leadership carried more weight than the permission of the local NDP MP. However, it is clear that there was a breakdown in communication somewhere in caucus. "I don't know what happened in the NDP caucus," Richardson says. "We were very busy on the island. I made the assumption that they would work out their protocols among themselves and had very little concern about relationships within the NDP caucus."

Robinson had tried to contact Fulton before flying up to Haida Gwaii but had been unable to reach him. This was before cell phones, after all. But the two men had never gotten along particularly well, having already clashed on the issue of gun control (with Robinson in favour and Fulton opposed), and Robinson's failure to reach Fulton before arriving in Haida Gwaii exacerbated the tension between them. Most of the caucus seemed to blame Robinson for the breakdown in communication. In their eyes, it fit in with what they already believed about him. Like his comments on the decriminalization of solicitation in 1983, the incident was portrayed in some NDP circles as an example of Robinson ignoring a caucus decision and refusing to be a team player.

"I don't think Svend ever really recognized the hurt that they felt," says Broadbent, but it would have been hard to miss. MPs with bitter memories of the solicitation debacle immediately related to Fulton's frustration. In a colourful, oft-repeated reference to Robinson's actions on Haida Gwaii, NDP MP Nelson Riis once said: "The word 'team' is not in Svend's vocabulary. As long as it is within his ideological framework, Svend will go to unbelievable lengths to be helpful. Two hours later he will drive a knife into your neck with no remorse. He epitomizes the old Mafia expression, 'Nothing personal, Nelson, just business.'"

The criticism that Robinson was not a "team player" followed him throughout his career. Some of his colleagues felt Robinson owed the NDP caucus a little more loyalty. He wouldn't have been elected as an independent, and he'd probably have been expelled from the Liberals or PCs. "If he hadn't been a member of the NDP caucus, forget it," Broadbent contends. "So he had a reciprocal obligation, in my view, to that caucus because of that status that I don't think he ever really recognized."

At its heart, however, the question of whether or not Robinson was a good team player may be a matter of definition. If being a team player is evaluated on the basis of co-operation with the tactical positions of the leader and caucus, he probably wasn't. Broadbent readily acknowledges that 90 per cent of the time, Robinson acted in solidarity. But in politics, that isn't good enough. "The main negative about Svend as a caucus member was his failure to co-operate with other caucus members according to the collective sense of priorities established by the caucus," states Broadbent. "He would, probably more often than any other member, go offside."

If the definition of a team player is broadened, the question becomes more complex. In the interpersonal sense, Robinson was a very good team player. The compassion that drove him as a politician made him a caring friend as well. Many of his former colleagues volunteer stories of his unexpected sensitivity and thoughtfulness during difficult times. "I never doubted his support and his friendship, his warmth, his willingness to help out, his kindness. Never doubted that at all," emphasizes Lorne Nystrom, a friend in caucus for many years. When Nystrom was accused of shoplifting after he forgot to pay for contact lens cleaning fluid, Robinson was the first person he told. Robinson contacted lawyer Clayton Ruby and accompanied Nystrom to the press conference in which he admitted his mistake. It was support Nystrom never forgot. "Very kind guy and very, very supportive, and someone that you really appreciated being on your side in a personal sense," he says. Blaikie recalls how often Robinson would go out of his way to acknowledge colleagues who were ill or who had experienced a death in the family. "Very caring — the first to send somebody a note, even across the aisle." Steven Langdon, an NDP MP who regularly disagreed with Robinson in caucus, noted the same thing. Langdon developed a disorder that caused shaking and a distortion in his voice. Some colleagues didn't know how to react, but Robinson knew how to be supportive. "Svend came up and talked to me about it. Then he went away and did research and came back with all kinds of medical articles. That is the kind of personal solidarity he has with people," Langdon told reporters years later, when Robinson was running for the leadership of the NDP, and Langdon was supporting one of his opponents.

If the team includes New Democrats from other levels of government, Robinson's commitment to teamwork must be evaluated a third time. Despite his rocky relationship with the B.C. NDP, when provincial New Democrats came calling, or when sympathetic municipal politicians needed support on some initiative or another, Robinson was always willing to help. "People often say that he wasn't a team player, and that was the furthest thing from the truth," says Jane Pepper, one of Robinson's longest-serving assistants. "Svend was always, always available, to anybody. Municipal, provincial, federal — whatever colleague needed him to do something, if he could do it, he'd be there."

If being a team player includes respecting the policies developed by card-carrying New Democrats, whose energies put caucus members into office in the first place, many New Democrats would point to issues like the decriminalization of solicitation and argue that Robinson's record improves yet again. But arguably most important were the assessments of the marginalized Canadians who learned to count on him as their spokesperson. If sex workers were part of the team the NDP was supposed to represent, or if members of the Haida Nation were part of the team, maybe Robinson was the best team player of all.

At least as important as the perception that Robinson wasn't a team player was the belief that Robinson was making his caucus colleagues look bad. Politicians are by nature protective of their reputations, which are their stock in trade. Many in the NDP caucus felt they were as strongly committed to environmental and aboriginal issues as Robinson was. But by showing up at the Haida blockade while they all stayed away, Robinson made them look like they were less committed than he was. "How does that make the environment critic look? How does that make the local MP look?" asks Blaikie. "Like he didn't care. Now the local MP may know, in his heart of hearts, that the leadership there asked him not to come, so he's not worried about them. But he's worried about the entire environmental constituency in B.C. that says, 'Why wasn't he there? Jim Fulton wasn't there. But good old Svend, he was there. He cares.'"

It wasn't the first or last time caucus members would feel that way. In 1981, the first time U.S. President Ronald Reagan addressed the House of Commons, the NDP caucus discussed wearing black armbands during his speech to protest American foreign policy in Central America. (Under Reagan, the U.S. supported the Contra rebels, accused of committing human rights abuses against Nicaraguan civilians in their rebellion against the socialist Sandinista government.) The NDP eventually decided that wearing armbands would be counterproductive, and that any ensuing media attention would probably focus on the armbands and the unparliamentary behaviour of the NDP instead of on Reagan's policies. Defying that decision, Robinson, Blaikie and several other NDP MPs wore the armbands anyway. In an experience Blaikie likens to being sent to the principal's office, the offending MPs were summoned to a meeting with Broadbent, where their leader chastised them, urging them to respect caucus solidarity. "It was from that point on that I was persuaded of the wisdom of that particular approach, although Svend never was," Blaikie says.

When Reagan visited the House a second time, in 1987, his entrance was marked by a thunderous standing ovation from the PCs, polite applause from the Liberals and stony silence from the NDP. As Reagan expounded on his vision for America and the world, his remarks occasionally punctuated by enthusiastic applause from supportive MPs, Robinson bided his time. For many Canadians, the Republican president's reputation as an international rogue and an ally of the wealthy and powerful had solidified in the years since his previous visit. Robinson had hoped to find an NDP MP willing to unfurl a banner with him, but had been unsuccessful. Still, he wasn't going to allow the only interruptions to Reagan's speech to be the repeated ovations from supportive MPs. When Reagan creatively called his Star Wars missile defence scheme, which critics feared would reignite the arms race with the Soviets, an impetus for arms reduction talks, Robinson saw his chance.

"No way!" he bellowed to a stunned House. "Stop Star Wars now!"

Momentarily startled, Reagan continued his speech. But when Reagan blamed the Soviets for destabilizing Central America through their support of the Sandinistas, Robinson heckled him again. "Nonsense. Absolute nonsense," he called out. "Stop fund-

ing the Contras, Reagan!" This time, NDP MPs Les Benjamin and
John Parry joined in.

"Is there an echo in here?" Reagan asked, to guffaws.

The unprecedented heckling of a foreign dignitary was a major
story, and it gave Robinson the opportunity to answer questions
about Reagan's controversial policies. "Reagan abused our hos-
pitality by lecturing us on subjects he knew many Canadians feel
strongly about," he told reporters. "Silence in such circumstances
implies consent." Some Canadians were appalled that he had been
disrespectful to the president, but many cheered, wishing they'd
had a chance to give Reagan a piece of their minds.

Telling the story today, Brian Mulroney insists that, behind the
scenes, Reagan found it funny. "Reagan dismissed him with some
kind of a quip, and that was the end of Svend that day. But look,
it's not every day that a backbench member of a third party in the
House of Commons gets an opportunity to be remembered for
yelling at the president of the United States. Svend knew that. That's
why he did it, to attract attention to whatever cause he happened
to be defending that day. He was very passionate about his causes,"
Mulroney says. "So I told Reagan after, when he said 'Who was that
guy anyway?' I said, 'That's just Svend. That's Svend being Svend,
Ron. You don't have to worry about that.' He just found it was
entertaining because, of course, as president of the United States,
not being part of a parliamentary body like ours, he wasn't used
to that kind of thing." However, politicians don't like public criticism. In 2004, when President George W. Bush visited Ottawa, he
chose not to address the House. Many Canadians despised Bush at
least as much as they had Reagan, and some media speculated that
Robinson's heckle was one reason why Prime Minister Paul Martin
ensconced Bush in the nearby Museum of Civilization, safe from
critical MPs and the dissent thundering in the streets outside.

Broadbent was not amused by Robinson's heckle. The NDP
leader was in Rome attending a conference, and he phoned Ottawa
as soon as he could. His bad back aggravated by the stress, he lay on
a sofa chastising Robinson, Benjamin and Parry by speakerphone.
Robinson refused to apologize, and in the end no discipline materi-

alized. Still, to some of his NDP colleagues, his heckling of Reagan seemed further proof that his willingness to act on his own initiative was making them look bad. "This kind of action made a hero out of the guy doing it, but it didn't do anything for the party. And it tended to make his colleagues look like maybe they weren't critical. So this is the crux of the matter," Blaikie contends. "He created the impression that somehow he was the only one who cared."

It is a fair point, but the fact that he appeared to gain political capital from his independent actions could suggest that the rest of the NDP caucus had taken the wrong positions in the first place. Perhaps they all should have heckled the president, or flown to Haida Gwaii, or publicly supported the decriminalization of solicitation. It wasn't his fault that they didn't. Alternatively, in the calculation of votes lost and gained, perhaps what Robinson gained from left-wing Canadians by being the sole MP willing to take certain stands was offset by what the NDP lost from mainstream Canadians in the ensuing controversies. Blaikie believes so, and also suggests that Robinson's uncompromising approach may have spurred the NDP's opponents to fight them more vociferously, when moderation might have blunted that willingness.

Perhaps more than teamwork, political capital was the crux of the issue. It's a matter of opinion what net effect his independent behaviour had on the NDP's poll numbers. But Robinson viewed the role of the NDP in a fundamentally different way than MPs like Broadbent and Blaikie. Broadbent was working to elect an NDP government. In his view, the party had to remain committed to its core principles, but it needed to communicate in a way that appealed to mainstream Canadians. That dictated a more cautious approach. If the NDP wasn't going to move to the centre of the political spectrum, its members needed to convince the centre to move to them by making careful, incremental changes to public discourse. What Robinson had done was leap decades ahead of the public, forcing the NDP to confront issues like the decriminalization of solicitation before the public was ready. "Ahead of his time? In some ways, if you're ahead of your time, you're not doing a good job," Broadbent submits. In part, Robinson was ahead of his time only because he failed to garner broad enough support for his position.

In contrast, although Robinson understood the power of popular support in creating change — and had used such support to his advantage — it was still a secondary consideration. More central to the way he did politics was the belief that principle had to come before power. This had been a consistent theme, both in his work as a young NDP activist pushing Dave Barrett's B.C. NDP government further left and in his work as an MP — and it would come up again. Robinson felt that if he wasn't speaking out on what he believed in, he wasn't doing his job, an approach that didn't require the sort of caution that Broadbent felt was necessary. Robinson understood what Broadbent was trying to achieve, but he couldn't make the compromises he saw some of his colleagues making. "I wouldn't question his sincerity," he says, in reference to one of his many disagreements with Broadbent. "His bottom line was just different from mine. He was genuinely committed. We just had very different perceptions of what was acceptable."

It was an attitude that earned Robinson a kind of second constituency of left-wing Canadians across the country. They were people who felt left behind by moderate messaging in the NDP and saw in him a political home they saw in no one else. One such person was a young theologian named Bill Siksay. "When I looked around and thought about who represented me in the House, I always said Svend Robinson was my MP, just because of the things I saw Svend working on," Siksay explains. "I had never lived in his riding at that time, but I always would tell people that that's who I saw as my MP."

Siksay became a chief political ally and was Robinson's assistant for 18 years, beginning in 1986. Robinson was beginning to inspire an extraordinary loyalty, not only in his office, but on the NDP's left flank, too. Some began to whisper his name in conversations about the next leader. But as that second constituency grew, so did the pressure. Many gay and lesbian activists, international human rights groups, environmentalists and aboriginal people began to wonder why they should bother writing to their own MPs and started writing to Robinson instead. His workload was already enormous, but, as always, he kept taking on more. To some of his colleagues and staff, it seemed as though there was no limit to his ability — or perhaps his compulsion — to keep adding cause after cause. But there was a limit, and by age 35, he was burned out. In the fall of 1987, he informed his constituency association in Burnaby that he'd decided to quit.

TEN

Leap Day

"If you think about Svend, and you think about the politics of being queer, and you think about him not being out, it just doesn't work, right?" reasons Bill Siksay. "It's not on, in terms of what we know about how Svend would deal with that kind of circumstance. It must have been a huge burden on him."

Robinson had always wanted to come out. The fire that had burned in him as a young married man who wanted to be open to the world about who he was now burned in him as a politician. A few times he nearly blurted it out. Once, speaking at a gay pride celebration in Vancouver, he referred to "our beautiful community." One reporter caught the surprising phrase and questioned him afterward. He wasn't ready to come out, but he had promised himself he would never lie, so he neither confirmed nor denied being gay and allowed his words to speak for themselves. The statement hadn't been direct enough to generate much attention, so as far as the general public was concerned, there was still no openly gay Canadian MP. Though he yearned to be open with the public, inevitably, he came to the same conclusion: the timing had to be just right. If he declared his homosexuality before his constituents were ready to accept it and was publicly crucified for doing so, who would ever try it again? If he miscalculated, he might set gay and lesbian acceptance back by a generation.

However, by the end of 1987, he had had enough of politics. The frantic pace, endless work, constant travel and fractious relationship with his colleagues had all taken their toll, and he wanted a normal life. He had options. He'd approached PC MP Perrin Beatty, and they'd discussed the possibility of Robinson coordinating the government's response to the AIDS crisis. The deadly disease was spreading rapidly, particularly among gay men, but it was poorly understood by the public at large, and the government had yet to organize a comprehensive strategy. Law beckoned, too. He could work on prisoners' rights or aboriginal law and maybe even have time for a relationship. He was an exhausted 35-year-old, and he still hadn't had a serious, long-term boyfriend. He had been in a relationship with a close friend, Chris Roehrs, for several years. The two had even lived together, but the relationship was on-again, off-again. "My personal life at that point was my work, and I realized that there had to be more than that," Robinson says.

He informed the disappointed members of his riding association that he wouldn't be running again and went to spend Christmas in Haida Gwaii with his adoptive family. As the exhaustion gradually abated, he reflected on his decision. It was the right choice, the healthy choice. The job, at least the way Robinson was doing it, was just too much. The decision made, he began to enjoy the holiday.

One night he and a young Haida friend drove to the spectacular beach at Rose Spit. There, as the cold Pacific pounded the shore, his friend broke down. He was so alone, he cried. There was no future in the world he knew. At first he wouldn't say why — he didn't think Robinson would understand.

"Because I'm gay!" the man finally burst out, crying again as though the act of saying those words had seared them into his flesh.

Robinson was stunned. He wasn't open with the public about his own sexuality, but he was sure that most of his good friends knew he was gay, and this was a good friend. When he replied that he was gay, too, the man's tears were halted by momentary confusion. "But you can't be gay . . . You're an MP," the man said, puzzled.

Those words hit Robinson hard. "It was one of those epiphany moments," he recalls. "It's so vivid: sitting in the front of that pickup truck, and him starting to cry, and my absolute astonishment when I found out that he didn't know I was gay." In that moment, more clearly than he ever had before, Robinson knew that he could make a difference. He had to show that being gay was not an impediment to success, even in the very public and image-driven realm of politics. He had to show that gay people were not predatory aliens but were trusted friends, neighbours and relatives who did not deserve discrimination and prejudice. Most of all, he had to show that being gay was nothing to hide or be ashamed of, but something that could be celebrated. "I didn't want anyone else to go through that pain, and that feeling of being all alone, and that sense that they had no future," he says. He couldn't throw away the privileged position he had as a member of Parliament with this injustice left to conquer. The normal life that had been just within his reach would have to wait.

But was Burnaby ready for an openly gay MP?

Siksay thought so. As a member of the United Church, and a leader in Affirm United, the church's lobby group for lesbian, gay, bisexual and transgender people, he closely followed the ongoing debate on the ordination of gay ministers. The respectful tone of that debate within the church suggested to Siksay that Canadians on the whole might be ready to engage the issue in an enlightened manner. Furthermore, two American congressmen and one British MP had recently declared their homosexuality and been accepted by the public. If it could happen in the U.S. and the U.K., it could happen in Canada, too. And if anyone could do it, it was Robinson. He was popular in the community and had earned the public's trust on a wide range of issues. Constituents had become used to controversy of one kind or another involving their MP, and they seemed to accept it as long as he kept delivering results for Burnaby. Siksay thought they would stick by Robinson through this controversy, too. "He was somebody who knew about taking risks politically, so if anybody had the experience of how to manage that kind of situation, he did," Siksay says. Furthermore, many people already knew he was gay. "It was out there. In the community, some people wondered why he hadn't come out already."

The members of Robinson's riding association were supportive. They consisted of youth, seniors, men, women, and constituents of diverse backgrounds and professions, and although they were all members of the NDP, they represented a reasonable cross-section of Burnaby. Their support was the most certain clue Robinson had that New Democrats, at least, were ready to back a gay candidate. Beyond that, no one knew what would happen. It wasn't easy to forget the homophobic remarks in the House or the hate mail. After all those years spent carefully cultivating his relationship with the riding, he was still going to have to trust his gut. "It was a leap into the unknown," he says.

In late February he informed the NDP caucus that he was taking that leap. The bitterness and tension that plagued his relationships with so many of his colleagues were put aside that day, and they reacted with a round of applause, hugs and promises of total support. He was planning his announcement carefully, he promised. He had arranged to appear on CBC's *The Journal* with Barbara Frum the next week, where he would tell Canadians that he was proud to be gay, that homosexuals were nothing to be afraid of and that it was time for discrimination against them to end.

Unfortunately, someone in the room blabbed to the wrong person, and the next day news of Robinson's imminent announcement was on the front page of the *Toronto Star*. Other reports followed. Outlandish rumours circulated: he had had an affair with former Liberal cabinet minister Ron Basford and was about to be named in a divorce proceeding; political opponents were about to out him; he was being blackmailed with pornographic pictures; he was dying of AIDS. The carefully orchestrated revelation he had prepared was pre-empted by uncontrolled gossip that threatened to undermine his positive message. The misinformation being spread was exactly the kind of nonsense he'd hoped to avoid with a dignified and — most importantly — voluntary affirmation that he was a politician who happened to be gay. With such bizarre rumours circulating, he couldn't answer the one simple question the media kept asking. If it looked as if he was being forced to respond to the rumours, it would appear he had been dragged out of the closet kicking and screaming. This was not the message he wanted to send, so for the time being he stayed quiet. The Frum interview was still four days away.

Two days after the reports first surfaced, Robinson arrived at his constituency office at 6340 Kingsway to find the windows smashed. As he surveyed the damage, every homophobic insult he'd ever heard flooded back to him. He recalled the schoolyard taunting, the wisecracks in the House and the T-shirt he'd recently seen a man wearing that proudly proclaimed "AIDS kills fags dead." He had been in that Kingsway office for eight years, and this was the first time there had been any vandalism. It hurt, but he knew it was another opportunity to illustrate his point. He called a press conference and showed the media this fresh evidence of the hatred that was faced by someone who was merely suspected of being a homosexual.

He still didn't answer questions about whether he was gay. Patiently, he waited for his appearance on CBC, when he would say what he needed to say, exactly the way he needed to say it. In Ottawa, the media kept buzzing. "Harvey Oberfeld of BCTV was literally camped in the hall with his sound guy and cameraman all day, peeking into the office every time the door opened," Siksay recalls. "Svend was in his office. So when he was leaving, we were going to make this mad dash and get him down to the taxi . . . We came out and ran down the hall, and Harvey chased him down the hall. The elevator was closing, and Svend was saying, 'I have no comment.' They waited all day for that!" Siksay says, laughing. As Robinson arrived at the airport to catch his flight back to Burnaby for his interview with Frum, he remembered one last, vital warning for his office staff. He'd been physically trapped in his office all day, and that had posed complications of a personal nature. He called his Ottawa staff and warned them emphatically not to drink the "apple juice" they found in his office fridge. No one did.

On February 29, 1988 — Leap Day — Robinson leapt. In his constituency office, with CBC cameras surrounding him, by making the following statement, he did what no other elected provincial or federal Canadian politician had ever done:

Yes, yes, I am gay ... I am proud to be a part of a community of very beautiful men and women ... What I'm telling Canadians is that I'm a member of Parliament who happens to be gay ... There are many other gays and lesbians in this country who are not able to live up to their full potential as human beings, who are subject to discrimination, who can lose their jobs, who can be thrown out of their homes, who can be the subject of violence. I guess it's a plea for understanding, for acceptance and for laws that say that we as a society don't tolerate this type of discrimination ... I'm hoping that perhaps by making a statement in a dignified way that this will make things just a little bit easier for gays and lesbians across this country to be open and honest about who they are as well ... If on a beautiful, sunny Sunday afternoon I'm walking through Stanley Park, I'd like to be able to walk perhaps hand in hand with the man that I care a lot about, and yet somehow that barrier is still there and very real.

Among friends, Robinson would come to call the announcement "The Big A." Today he laughs at the innocuousness of the statement that would cause such controversy in 1988. But he never forgot how it felt at the time. "It was just the most liberating moment you can imagine," he says. Friends and colleagues saw a change in him after that day. Jan Taylor, then one of his constituency assistants, recalls that Robinson seemed warmer and less guarded. He had always been confident, but his confidence seemed to flow mainly from a steadfast belief in his own capacity. After coming out, he had the confidence of a man who knew he was accepted by others. "Svend was like a different person," Taylor says. "He was like somebody who had blossomed. For me as a straight person, I don't think I had ever really understood the weight of being in the closet, how not being able to be who you are diminishes a person. What I saw when he came out was that he was just a nicer person, an easier person to be around."

Now that the full story was out, framed in Robinson's terms, media coverage was generally positive. "The precedent-setting pronouncement had been professional, dignified, and yet passionate. This wasn't amateur hour, and Robinson knew it. If the gay community had hand-picked someone to break the ice, they couldn't have done better," wrote Stan Persky in *Q Magazine*. "It had been a remarkably delicate task, calling for candour, but not cockiness, dignity without dogmatics. He had to get vastly diverse audiences to respond with a 'So What?' and simultaneously to see that it did indeed matter, not an easy trick."

Mainstreeting reporters found that his sexuality wasn't an issue for most people. A few editorials joked that Robinson coming out as gay was a bit like civil rights activist Jesse Jackson coming out as black. Far from turning him into a political pariah, his revelation was celebrated. At a crowded reception in West Block on Parliament Hill held by the gay and lesbian organization Egale a few days later, Laurier LaPierre, former host of the popular TV show *This Hour Has Seven Days*, announced that he was gay, too. LaPierre went on to be the guest speaker at Robinson's nomination meeting later that month in Burnaby.

Instead of Robinson, it was some of his homophobic colleagues in the House who suddenly found themselves the objects of scorn. "Until now, when the vicious barbs flew across the aisle of the Commons, the press gallery turned a deaf ear. To report the insults meant reporting Robinson's homosexuality," wrote journalist Susan Riley shortly after Robinson came out. "Sometimes it was difficult to stay silent. Robinson's critics are so coarse. Their pathetic little prejudices (and the deep fear they reveal) richly deserve to be exposed to public ridicule and contempt."

However, while some of his opponents might have skulked away in embarrassment, others couldn't denounce him fast enough. "I don't know whether we should really feel so good about people influencing young girls or young boys in this way," said Bill Vander Zalm, Social Credit premier of B.C., who went on to say that homosexuality was a sin. Similar comments were made by the PC premier of Saskatchewan, Grant Devine, who said that he felt the same compassion for homosexuals that he felt for bank robbers. Robinson was condemned from church pulpits across the country. One local Burnaby Catholic school told him he was no longer welcome to attend graduation ceremonies to present the scholarship he still sponsored with his own money (ironically, a few years later, the priest who spoke to him was charged with child abuse). Even reputable newspapers published intolerant editorials. "It is a scene to ponder, should the NDP come to power. There, in the sunshine of Stanley Park, smack in the heart of righteous [British Columbia], traipses Justice Minister Svend Robinson, hand in hand with his male lover. The totem poles would droop in embarrassment. Is Canada ready for this?" wrote Orland French in the *Globe and Mail*. "He is flaunting his sexuality in a crusade to promote gay rights, and that's the unsettling nature of his disclosure. If the NDP isn't cringing, it ought to be."

•　　　•　　　•

As anyone who has worked on Parliament Hill will confirm, even the meekest and most forgettable backbencher gets hate mail. Like many MPs, Robinson got hate mail for the policy positions of his party — and for the policy positions of other parties. He got hate mail for accepting his salary, or for sometimes giving parts of his speeches in French. More significantly, there had been a steady flow of gay-related hate mail since the Chicken Book allegations. He often responded to the letters personally, sometimes for catharsis and sometimes in the genuine hope of changing the correspondent's attitude. But while most of the public reaction after he came out as homosexual was positive, the volume and ferocity of the hate mail he received was like nothing he had seen before.

The National Archives in Ottawa today houses just a few of the massive files of hate mail that Robinson amassed over the years. It is a vulgar collection, filled with slurs, profanity, violent threats, bizarre descriptions of sexual acts, gleeful references to the AIDS crisis ravaging the gay community and prayers that Robinson himself would die of the disease, biblical condemnations and constant references to the fiery torments of a vengeful God. Intense loathing emanates from every page. One letter, signed by "the straight population of Canada," includes a bullet in the envelope and the suggestion that Robinson use it on himself. In the respectful silence of the Archives, opening a file to reveal a brass bullet taped to a sheet of paper is like hearing the sudden crack of the implied gunshot itself. In that environment of earnest, helpful librarians and impeccable filing systems, it is an experience as paralyzing and shocking today as it must have been when Robinson opened the envelope himself years ago. Following his retirement from politics, Robinson was invited to send a selection of his files to the Archives. He included some of the hate mail, believing that it could be of some value to future historians studying the social attitudes of our time. Undoubtedly it will be, but there is little point in exposing readers here to the hatred contained in such letters.

"I've gotten to know Romans and Leviticus pretty well," Robinson acknowledged shortly after coming out, referring to verses in the Bible condemning homosexuality.

Usually he downplayed the volume of the hate mail he received. Most of it was incoherent, barely literate ranting. Some of his correspondents were so ignorant that they addressed their letters to the B.C. Legislature instead of to Burnaby or Ottawa. It was hardly the sort of correspondence worth acknowledging. And yet, Robinson read it all. "I read everything. I wanted to know what people were saying. Some of it was very hurtful, too. Incredibly hurtful," he says.

Perhaps reading those letters helped fuel the relentlessness with which he continued to fight throughout his career for the acceptance of gays and lesbians. Robinson doesn't say much about the effects of exposing himself to that constant stream of hatred. It certainly must have contributed to the considerable strain he already felt. But by carefully reading every single one of them, he also came across letters like this one:

> I want to tell you that I admire you very much. I'm 19 years old, and I'm gay. I've just started coming out. I have no friends left, but I often think of how much you risked by coming out, and then I don't feel so bad. Thank you for being so honest about yourself . . . My life has been ruined by bigots, but I'm glad I have you to look up to. If you made it, I figure I can, too.

Young, gay Canadians from across the country wrote to Robinson, telling him that, because of him, they could envision a future without compromise. "I owe you my freedom," wrote one. These are the letters that had the greatest impact on him. He had become an important role model — a privilege but also a heavy responsibility. Being a role model meant that his behaviour was constantly being scrutinized, and that put increasing pressure on him. "I can stumble, but I can't fall. My life has to be squeaky clean in every conceivable way," he would later tell *Maclean's*. His positive public image had been instrumental in helping him bring homosexuality into the mainstream, but if that image was destroyed, either by political opponents or by a foolish decision of his own, that progress could be lost. "I won't allow that to happen. I will not allow that to happen," he told *Vancouver Magazine* a few years later. "That's not to say I'm infallible. I'm a human being, God knows. But to the extent that I can maintain a credible position politically and publicly, that means I can't in any way expose myself to vulnerability by doing dumb things personally." It was a rigid and narrow path that Robinson was able to walk for a long, long time.

•   •   •

The 1988 federal election is usually remembered by Canadians as the free-trade election, in which Brian Mulroney's PCs featured the Canada–United States Free Trade Agreement (FTA) as the central plank in their platform, while the Liberals and NDP, believing the FTA would turn Canada into a de facto economic colony of the U.S., dedicated their campaigns to opposing it. However, in Burnaby, free trade was not what the media wanted to discuss. Robinson still wanted to retire from politics, but after coming out, that was no longer an option. To prove that a homosexual could be accepted as a politician, he had to run again, and he had to win. Like it or not, in the new riding of Burnaby–Kingsway, the 1988 election had become a referendum on homosexuality.

Of course, homosexuality was not the only issue in his platform. "Certainly I am not a one-issue politician today any more than I was yesterday, or any more than I will be tomorrow," he said, trying to focus the campaign on substantive issues. But it was beyond his control. PC MP Chuck Cook, running in a nearby riding, suggested that Robinson's homosexuality made him a poor role model for children. Robinson's own PC opponent, John Bitonti, circulated campaign literature littered with references to "family values," and recounted stories he was told by constituents of the horror they felt when Robinson "ventured into the living rooms of the nation ... preaching his morality on sexual matters over the air to their kids." A group of fundamentalist Christians published a vicious pamphlet declaring "The end of Svend," describing his career with invented facts and referring to homosexuals as "tropical islands of exotic diseases."

Even Prime Minister Mulroney mused, "Wouldn't that be something, Svend as Minister of Defence? I'll tell you, that would make one fine ministerial meeting!" at a rally in B.C. during the campaign. Robinson's supporters interpreted Mulroney's comment as an implication that a gay man couldn't handle a job often perceived as masculine. "Look, in election campaigns, we all say things that we think are entertaining, and sometimes they turn out to be pretty stupid," Mulroney says, in reference to comments made by some of Robinson's opponents.

However, the attacks only bolstered Robinson's campaign. The campaign office started getting calls from former PC supporters, disgusted with the homophobia, who now pledged their support for Robinson. Mulroney's joke backfired, as NDP fundraisers made a fortune selling purple buttons saying "Svend Robinson for Defence Minister." (Robinson later met with Mulroney and thanked him for being one of his biggest campaign contributors, and the two had a good laugh.) In Saskatchewan, gay and lesbian activists, hurt by their premier's comments comparing homosexuals to bank robbers, held a "Bank Robbers' Ball" to raise money for Robinson's campaign. After the Frum interview, thousands of gay Canadians found a hero in Parliament, and that second constituency of Canadians from across the country who saw Robinson as their unofficial MP grew even larger. Donations poured in. The

Burnaby–Kingsway NDP raised over $100,000, more than any other NDP riding association in Canada during that election — a distinction Robinson's campaigns maintained in subsequent elections. "We had no problems money-wise. I just had to sit back and take the money in," recalls Lila Wing, the riding association treasurer. "I was the happiest official agent around."

Each homophobic insult seemed to give the campaign more momentum. Allies from previous political battles joined the fight. Robinson held a gala featuring speeches by his "little brother" David Suzuki and former B.C. Supreme Court justice Tom Berger, and performances by singers Shari Ulrich and Ferron. Legendary Haida artist Bill Reid designed campaign posters. New volunteers came out of the woodwork, and soon the Robinson team had a small army of over a thousand volunteers knocking on doors, putting up signs and making phone calls. By contrast, the PC and Liberal campaigns had one or two hundred volunteers each. There was a sense among the members of the Robinson team that they were part of something special.

On November 21, 1988, Robinson held his breath as he and about 400 supporters watched the election results at the Operating Engineers Hall in Burnaby. As usual in B.C., the national results were called before the final numbers had been counted in the west. The NDP made gains and the Liberals rebounded from their disastrous 1984 defeat, severely denting PC support, but Mulroney was re-elected with a majority government. (The results were a disappointment for Liberal Leader John Turner, who resigned before the next election; Jean Chrétien took over the leadership of the party.) As the results for Burnaby–Kingsway trickled in late that night, Robinson began to relax. His numbers were down, but they would be good enough. It turned out voters cared more about his hard work on behalf of the constituency than they did about his sexuality, just as he had always hoped they would. Robinson won with 43 per cent of the vote and became the first openly gay candidate in Canadian history to be elected in either a provincial or federal campaign.

"I believe this riding was very, very important. I believe Canada lost in this one," lamented Bitonti. But Robinson's vindication forged a bond with the community that would last throughout his career. People seemed to trust that if he was that honest with them about something so personal, he would be honest with them about anything. In an age of increasing cynicism about politics and politicians, that was credibility you couldn't buy. "I think Svend coming out made people more loyal to him," Siksay says. "They went through a special moment with him, a very public moment and a historic moment. People felt closer to him, felt like they had gone out on that limb and come out with him. When politicians have that kind of moment with their community, it's hard to break that bond."

The effect on Robinson's relationship with the homosexual community was even more profound. In the past, he had lived according to the creed of poet W.H. Auden: "Neither proclaim, nor pretend." That meant choosing his words carefully in order to avoid "outing" himself. But now that he was out, when he returned to the House to challenge the re-elected Mulroney government on gay and lesbian issues, he could bring a personal perspective to his speeches. When he proposed bills to do what Mulroney still had not done — follow through on John Crosbie's promise to add sexual orientation to the Human Rights Act — he spoke of "our" rights. When he proposed bills to include same-sex relationships in the Income Tax Act and the Canada Pension Plan, they were always "our" relationships. When he pushed the government to create an aggressive strategy to combat the devastation caused by the AIDS virus in the gay community, it was "our" community. This small change in syntax gave his words an authority they hadn't had before. "Frankly, as a gay man and as a member of Parliament, I am tired of hearing that somehow our relationships are not just as strong, and just as committed, and just as loving and caring as any other relationships in our society — that somehow we are incapable of being families," he told the House with renewed passion in his voice. "We should be entitled to full equality."

Speaking as a gay man didn't necessarily make progress happen any faster, however. Mulroney never did add sexual orientation to the Human Rights Act or recognize same-sex relationships for tax and pension benefits. Robinson considers the slow response to the AIDS crisis one of the most serious failures of the Mulroney government. But the fact that Robinson had publicly affirmed his sexuality did play an important role in one major victory for gay and lesbian acceptance during the Mulroney years.

For years, Robinson had opposed the policy preventing gays and lesbians from serving in the military. He had questioned successive defence ministers in the House and in committee. He had doggedly condemned the ban in the speeches on gay and lesbian issues he regularly made across the country. However, the Canadian Forces steadfastly maintained that allowing homosexual troops would negatively affect operational efficiency. Robinson knew such a groundless excuse wouldn't stand up in court, especially since the government had acknowledged, in Crosbie's historic response to the report of the 1985 subcommittee on equality rights, that sexual orientation was irrelevant to one's ability to perform a job. Without question, that included jobs in the Canadian Forces. In fact, the subcommittee report had explicitly recommended that the ban be rescinded. What Robinson needed was a soldier willing to go to court to challenge the ban. If he could find a gay or lesbian soldier with an impeccable service record who could prove that being a homosexual didn't have any operational consequences whatsoever, he was certain they would win.

After giving a speech at Ryerson University in 1989, Robinson thought he'd found that person. Captain Michelle Douglas was an officer with a perfect service record who loved being a soldier. However, she had recently become the subject of an investigation by military police who had discovered that she was a lesbian and had begun the process of discharging her from the army. When she introduced herself to Robinson after his speech, he was impressed by her eloquence. "My eyes lit up, and I thought, 'Yes, this is it!'" he remembers. But Douglas wasn't ready and didn't want to give him her contact information. She'd contact him instead, she promised, but she didn't. Later, in Chilliwack, B.C., Robinson gave another speech condemning the ban and mentioned the amazing woman he'd met at Ryerson. After the speech, a couple of lesbian soldiers from the nearby base discreetly met with him and told him they thought they knew who he meant. They were right. They put him in touch with Captain Douglas, and this time she agreed to launch a court challenge. Robinson introduced her to lawyer Clayton Ruby, who agreed to represent Douglas free of charge. Not one to watch from the sidelines, Robinson acted as Ruby's assistant, an arrangement both lawyers found useful. Together, they prepared a challenge that would be devastating to the government lawyers assigned the task of defending the discriminatory policy.

It never got that far. In October 1992, just as Douglas and Ruby were about to go through the doors of the Federal Court of Canada to argue their case, they received word that the military was abandoning the policy against homosexual members. The military knew what Robinson knew — that Crosbie's 1986 promise made it almost impossible for them to argue in favour of discrimination. It was a historic announcement — and one that came nearly 20 years before a similar about-face in the U.S.

The fact that Robinson came out first had been a persuasive element in Douglas's decision to sponsor the court challenge. The shy captain went on to become a respected, lifelong advocate for gay and lesbian acceptance. "You singularly gave me the guidance and support I needed to start this battle. Through your own personal example of strength, I realized that I too could stand up against the military," she later wrote to Robinson. "This experience has been incredibly empowering — I now feel the pride and dignity in being a lesbian, and I understand the inherent responsibility that gay men and lesbians carry ... Words do not seem enough to express my emotion in thanking you for your support, guidance and leadership."

It was another five years before a second MP, Réal Ménard of the Bloc Québécois, was willing to publicly affirm his homosexuality. Robinson used to joke that when he came out in 1988, he didn't exactly start a trend. But what mattered most was that people like

Captain Douglas knew, unequivocally, that there were people like her in Parliament, and that despite the discrimination gays and lesbians faced, it was still possible to take that brave step of coming out and be rewarded for it. Conversations like the one Robinson had with his friend in that pickup truck at Rose Spit in Haida Gwaii would never have to happen again. That was worth a little hate mail.

ELEVEN

The Front Lines

After nearly 15 years at the helm, in March 1989 Ed Broadbent stepped down as leader of the NDP. In the 1988 election he had led the NDP to what was to that time its best result — 43 seats — but he considered that a disappointment. The NDP had been riding high in the polls prior to the election, and some in the party had dared to dream about forming a government. "We set out in this campaign to do better than we did," he said after.

Many of Robinson's supporters urged him to run as a candidate to replace Broadbent, but he didn't think it was worth doing. "I wouldn't have had the support of that caucus in '89. That was out of the question. They would have gone ballistic if I had become leader," he explains. Instead, he pledged his support to Yukon MP Audrey McLaughlin and campaigned actively on her behalf. He saw McLaughlin as a committed social democrat and felt she would be more willing than past leadership had been to take unpopular but principled positions.

No woman had ever been chosen as the leader of a federal political party in Canada, but after what Robinson had just achieved as the first openly gay parliamentarian, that sort of barrier didn't faze him. The leadership contest against former B.C. NDP premier Dave Barrett and five other candidates was a bitter one, but McLaughlin forged an alliance with feminists and Ontario New Democrats and positioned herself alongside Barrett as one of the favourites. Robinson's support, and the overwhelming dedication that went with it, was also instrumental. "When Svend makes up his mind to be on somebody's side, he's really on your side," McLaughlin says, acknowledging the importance of his help. In the end, McLaughlin made history and prevailed in a fourth-ballot victory.

In caucus, McLaughlin and Robinson shared a mutual respect and worked well together. Their relationship wasn't plagued by the disagreements over caucus solidarity that had dominated Robinson's relationship with Broadbent. Robinson continued to earn the enmity of some of his colleagues — in 1991 he forced the B.C. NDP to return $85,000 in donations it had received in violation of party policy banning donations from corporations — but he maintained McLaughlin's support, and the two developed a personal friendship. "I don't think I've ever worked with anyone who was really as bright as Svend. He is a very clever person," McLaughlin says. "I am a great admirer."

When McLaughlin reassigned Robinson from justice to external affairs in September 1990, he accepted the change in critic responsibility eagerly. He had enjoyed his work as justice critic but had always maintained a strong interest in international issues as well. It was an important time to be on the file. Just one month earlier, under the leadership of dictator Saddam Hussein, Iraq had invaded Kuwait and gained access to one of the world's most lucrative oilfields. As the international community, most prominently the U.S., threatened to retaliate, Hussein took hostage the hundreds of foreign nationals living in Iraq, including 46 Canadians, perhaps hoping that the presence of hostages would stop Iraq's enemies from dropping bombs. The Canadian government demanded the hostages' release but couldn't be more forceful, lest they give the impression that the hostages were important enough to dissuade Canada from taking military action. The hostages' desperate families raised money and compiled a list of prominent Canadians they hoped to send to Iraq to negotiate their release. They successfully enlisted Robinson to lead the delegation. He was joined by Liberal

MP Lloyd Axworthy and PC MP Robert Corbett, and in November 1990 the small multi-party delegation left for Baghdad.

"It was one of the most frustrating times in my political life," Robinson recalls. "We went through a whole series of byzantine discussions with various people." The negotiations were delicate. If the Canadian MPs were too harsh in their criticisms of Hussein, they wouldn't get the hostages released. They might save more hostages if they were conciliatory, but then their statements could be used as pro-Hussein propaganda by a brutal regime. "It was a very, very tense time," says Robinson. "We weren't going to sacrifice any of our integrity in the process, but we were walking a fine line, because we wanted to save lives."

The three MPs ultimately returned home disappointed, having convinced Hussein to release only seven hostages. The poor results of the negotiations may have been due to Hussein's desire to maximize his leverage by releasing only a few hostages at a time. Similar delegations sent by other countries didn't fare much better than the Canadians. External Affairs Minister Joe Clark's tough-talking statements at home probably didn't help either. For example, Canada co-sponsored a UN Security Council resolution authorizing the use of force against Iraq.

Robinson's criticisms of the Hussein regime caused him problems of his own. The night before the delegation left, after a CTV national news interview Robinson conducted from Baghdad in which he decried Iraq's human rights record, he received a chilling telephone call in his room at the Al Rasheed Hotel. He took the heavily accented death threat seriously and quickly made up a will, which he gave to British MP Tony Benn, who was staying at the same hotel. It was clear that someone in Iraq hadn't liked his strong language, but Robinson safely left the country the next day.

He returned to the House in time to join a furious debate on whether Canada should join the U.S. in military action. He remained extremely critical of Hussein but was also firmly opposed to waging war. He saw the crisis as the first real opportunity since the end of the Cold War for the international community to use economic sanctions and negotiation in the UN to resolve a conflict without the brutality of war and the thousands of civilian deaths that always came with it. Many opponents of the war felt that the U.S. was primarily interested in gaining access to Middle Eastern oil, and that the Canadian hawks were intent on maintaining Canada's preferential status as a trading partner with the U.S. If the hawks were serious about wanting a humanitarian resolution to the crisis, as they insisted they were, and were not simply focused on narrower American or Canadian interests, they needed to give sanctions and negotiation more time. "Surely to God we in the latter part of the 20th century must have a better way of resolving conflicts between nations than resorting to war," Robinson told the House. "If there is to be a war in the world . . . let it not be a war with catastrophic consequences, not just for the Middle East but for the entire globe. Let it be a war on poverty, on homelessness, on environmental destruction, on AIDS, on racism and on sexism. Let it be a war on the obscenity of over a billion children on this planet living in poverty. Let that be the war that we collectively wage on behalf of the people of this planet."

In 1991 Canada joined the war on Iraq. That war drove Iraq from Kuwait, killed thousands of Iraqi civilians and protected American access to Middle Eastern oil reserves but left Hussein in power. Whether sanctions would have worked is a matter of debate. After the invasion of Kuwait, the UN did institute crippling sanctions on trade with Iraq, which were left in place until Hussein was ousted a decade later. Those sanctions are believed to have starved to death hundreds of thousands of Iraqis, but they never did succeed in forcing Iraq to rejoin the international community. On the other hand, perhaps there was nothing Hussein could have done that would have satisfied the West. Even after it was credibly demonstrated by international experts that Hussein had no weapons of mass destruction, the U.S. claimed that Hussein did have such weapons and used that as a pretext for an invasion in 2003 that killed over 100,000 Iraqi civilians. It may be that the war in 1991 was also inevitable — that the forces clamouring for war were too powerful, and that the messages of peace voiced by Robinson and others could never have prevented war no matter how eloquent they were. However, in leading the NDP opposition to the war, Robinson established that, as external affairs critic, he was a force to be reckoned with.

"One of my rules when I was Minister of External Affairs was, who do you have to be careful of on the other side?" Clark said years later. "There were two people I was extremely careful of." Clark went on to identify the two MPs who gave him so much trouble — one was fiery Liberal Sheila Copps, and the other was Robinson.

•   •   •

"Svend Robinson was engaging in direct action before anybody had even coined the term," NDP Leader Jack Layton told the audience at a celebration of Robinson's 25th year as an MP in 2004. It was an overstatement, but Robinson's willingness to go to the front lines to fight for his beliefs set him apart from his peers. While he excelled as a traditional parliamentary critic, haranguing cabinet ministers in the House and in committee, it was on the front lines that he truly defined himself as a politician. The lessons learned at Lyell Island in Haida Gwaii came to bear in his new role as external affairs critic. The media often characterizes any foreign travel a politician takes as a "junket," no matter what serious work is on the agenda. It's lazy, unfair journalism, but the cynicism is understandable — some parliamentarians do occasionally treat foreign travel as an excuse to go shopping, ride in limousines or eat at expensive restaurants on the public dime. Robinson wasn't one of them. As critic, he was invited to participate in fact-finding missions around the globe, and he always took full advantage of those learning opportunities. In January 1992 he packed his bags for such a mission. It was a journey that would lead him from his office in Burnaby to a police station in China and finally to a small hut deep in the Malaysian jungle. Along the way, he would terrify public servants, embarrass world leaders and directly challenge injustice in a way that Canadian politics has rarely seen before or since.

After the highly publicized massacre of hundreds of students who had called for basic democratic freedoms at a protest in Beijing's Tiananmen Square in 1989, Canada recalled its ambassador to China, suspended the sale of arms, cancelled development projects and announced that unless authoritarian China demonstrated an improved commitment to human rights, it could no longer count on business as usual with Canada. The Chinese government launched a public relations offensive, and relations with Canada eventually normalized. Trade between the two nations was worth about $3-billion a year, making Canada China's fifth-largest trading partner. Skeptical of China's statements lauding the government's commitment to human rights and political freedom, Chinese-Canadian groups sponsored a fact-finding delegation to travel to China to see if circumstances had really improved.

The delegation consisted of Robinson, Liberal MP Beryl Gaffney and PC MP Geoff Scott, along with Chinese-Canadian activist Richard Lee (later the B.C. Liberal MLA for Burnaby North), who assisted with translation and logistics. They arrived in Beijing on January 4, 1992, and began following the agenda the Chinese government had prepared for their visit. The delegation met with various government representatives and heard the official line, which was that Chinese authorities deeply respected human rights. Robinson, Gaffney and Scott got the sense that they were participating in scripted, rehearsed meetings, and that they weren't getting to the heart of the matter. However, they had also made other plans. During a break between meetings, they hailed a taxi — switching cars several times since they were afraid of being followed — and drove to a quiet restaurant in downtown Beijing, where they sat down to wait.

Robinson knew the dissidents they were hoping to meet were taking a huge risk in talking to them. "I was always torn about that, because I didn't want to put them at risk. But on the other hand, I thought it was sort of arrogant and presumptive of me to refuse to meet with them if they, fully aware of the risks, felt that the importance of meeting with me outweighed the risk to their personal safety," he explains. Despite that risk, 65-year-old Wu Yongfen entered the restaurant and sat down with the three MPs. Her son, who had since been imprisoned, had been a prominent organizer of the protests in Tiananmen Square. For the next hour, she shared stories of the treatment her son was facing in prison, and of the harassment the Chinese government still directed at the families of political dissidents.

At dinner that night with the president of the Chinese People's Institute of Foreign Affairs, the delegation learned that the Chinese government knew perfectly well what they'd been up to that day. They were told that no further departures from the approved itinerary would be tolerated. As guests of the Chinese government, the delegation had an obligation to behave. Robinson responded that not only did the delegation not want to visit the approved prison on the next day's agenda, but they had already made plans to visit a different prison and would be inviting journalists to join them. Furthermore, he said, the delegation also intended to lay a wreath at the grave of a dissident in commemoration of the victims of the massacre at Tiananmen Square. If the Chinese government was as committed to human rights as they claimed, surely they would have no objections. The officials were stunned at his audacity, and the president sat down, speechless.

The next day, the delegation sat through the morning meetings with the Chinese officials and then boarded the small bus their hosts had provided to return them to their hotel. They were planning on meeting the press there, and they already had a lot to say. However, instead of taking them to the hotel, the bus pulled into an austere concrete compound and stopped. A dozen armed policemen suddenly surrounded the vehicle. Dumbstruck, the Canadians stared out at the baffling show of force. Before they could process what had taken place, several officers boarded the bus. They took Gaffney by the arm and led her off, but the men were handled more roughly; Scott in particular was practically thrown from the bus. They were marched into the police station in the compound and told to wait. Two hours went by. Andrew Halper, the Canadian embassy official accompanying the delegation, insisted he be allowed to make a phone call to the embassy, but his demand was ignored. The MPs accused their captors of kidnapping them and breaking international law, but that protest was ignored, too. That was worrying. If diplomatic protocols meant nothing to the Chinese, how far might they go? Desperate to contact the ambassador, Scott even tried faking a heart attack so that Robinson could slip out in the ensuing confusion and try to get to a phone. As Scott clutched his heart, Robinson got up and moved towards the door. Just before grabbing the knob, he felt a firm grip on his shoulder. They were staying put.

It was an infuriating ordeal. "I have never, never seen anyone as unceremoniously manhandled and thrown around as I was and my companions were," Scott later said of the experience. The 61-year-old Gaffney, a grandmother, was shaken. "This was the most humiliating and degrading experience I have ever had in my entire life," she said.

Eventually, the officers informed the delegates that they were guilty of "activities incompatible with their status in China," and that they were to be taken immediately to the airport. They were finally granted their phone call to the embassy, and Ambassador Fred Bild raced to the airport, hoping to intervene. To buy time, Scott feigned another heart attack, but it was less convincing the second time around. The MPs' request to return to the hotel to retrieve their personal belongings was denied, and they were shoved back onto the bus. The MPs were furious at their treatment, but as the bus pulled out of the station, the tension they'd all felt when they didn't know just how far the Chinese would go began to abate. They saw that they had been given a glorious opportunity. They had been sent to learn the truth about Chinese human rights. As they counted a ludicrous total of 14 police cars escorting their bus to the airport, it was clear that the delegation had accomplished its mission.

"It was just gold. It was a massive miscalculation by the Chinese government, and it gave us an opportunity to speak about the human rights abuses in China," Robinson says. "I couldn't even imagine that they would overreact so foolishly."

The delegation arrived at the airport, where they were marched onto the tarmac and then onto the first flight to Hong Kong, which was British territory at the time. As they boarded the plane, they were handed their belongings, which had been taken from their hotel rooms and stuffed into garbage bags. They weren't allowed to see the ambassador, who had made it to the airport just on time.

When they arrived in Hong Kong, they held a massive press conference with media from around the globe. Robinson had held some huge press conferences in his career, but this was the biggest of them all. For the international media, foreign politicians scuffling with police and then being expelled from a nation bragging about its commitment to human rights was a major story. "It was the worst treatment of my life. We were roughed up, but the fact is there are thousands of people in China and Tibet who are getting much worse treatment. They're being harassed, tortured and even killed. We left. They have to stay," Robinson told the press conference. "It turned out to be a round trip into hell for a few hours for us. But for thousands and thousands of Chinese, they don't have round trip tickets."

The delegation also used the opportunity to call for a review of Chinese-Canadian relations, and for Canadian aid to be cut off until China's human rights record improved. Their story made headlines across the country and provoked serious concern at the highest levels about Canada's relationship with China. "I am particularly offended at this affront to the institution of Parliament and the treatment of democratically elected representatives of the Canadian people. We would all like to believe that the Chinese record on human rights is improving, but unfortunately the Chinese authorities continue to demonstrate no evidence of this," stated External Affairs Minister Barbara McDougall, who registered an official complaint with the Chinese ambassador.

"This mission was a success. It exposed the truth inside China," said Raymond Chan, a member of the Vancouver Society in Support of Democratic Movement and a future Liberal cabinet minister. Robinson, Gaffney and Scott, who had bonded through the experience and become good friends, were later invited to dinners organized by Chinese-Canadian groups to thank them for their work. Many Chinese Canadians believed that the actions of the three MPs had given hope to their friends and relatives struggling for democracy back in China. Robinson had condemned the Chinese human rights record before, in the House and in committee, but that hadn't given the issue anything like the kind of exposure that directly defying the Chinese authorities had. It seemed his provocative method had worked again.

Before the furor from this international incident died down, Robinson was already embroiled in another. As he flew directly from Hong Kong to Malaysia to conduct a second fact-finding mission, he considered how he might employ the same approach to draw attention to a very different humanitarian crisis. Sent by the Western Canada Wilderness Committee to investigate the deforestation of the Sarawak rainforests, Robinson left the five-star wining and dining of the typical diplomatic mission even further behind. The Malaysian state of Sarawak is roughly 13 per cent the size of B.C., but in the early 1990s it produced nearly 50 per cent of the world's tropical lumber. At the rate it was being logged, environmental scientists estimated it would be no more than 10 years before the rainforests were gone. Sarawak is home to the Penan, nomadic hunter-gatherers who have lived off the rainforests for as long as their history records. The Penan have a peaceful and egalitarian society, and it is said that in their language there is no word for "thank you," since helping one another is assumed. It is difficult to fathom what they must have felt when logging company representatives handed them little blue receipts and told them they were entitled to financial compensation — not for their land, but for the graves of their ancestors that had been dug up by loggers. They were then made to provide thumbprints as proof of receipt.

As their homeland was being destroyed, the Penan began to resist. In 1991 about 500 Penan erected a barricade on a logging road and drew the attention of the world to their plight. Their stand was symbolic of the international struggle between preservation of the natural environment and unchecked, ravenous human growth. "If we cannot save even a tiny remnant of the world's most ancient rainforests as a homeland for one of the world's only remaining hunter-gatherer tribes, there is not much hope for the rainforests elsewhere, or for any of us," said David Suzuki. "Whatever we let happen to Sarawak's forests will be symbolic of our values and actions for the next millennium."

In Sarawak, Robinson and Brendan McGivern, the Canadian High Commission official asked to accompany him, chartered a helicopter and arranged to fly over the rainforest. From above, they saw the glorious rainforest checkered with vast swathes of stumps and torn earth. Robinson had sent word to the Penan through a network of activists that he would be in Malaysia and wanted to learn more about their struggle. They invited him to visit them at their barricade in the middle of the rainforest, and he agreed to do so. But when the helicopter finally arrived at the barricade, the pilot refused to land. It wasn't safe, he claimed. Robinson was no pilot, but he couldn't see any reason why that would be true. It was an unexpected problem. Some of the Penan had walked for days to be at the barricade to meet him, and he was not going to let them down. If the pilot couldn't be convinced, he'd have to be threatened. Robinson put his hand on the door handle. "If you don't take me to see the Penan, I'm going to jump out of this aircraft, and if you think that's going to be good for you, or for Malaysia, you've got another thing coming," he told the pilot. "Now you take me there!"

Robinson's bluff was convincing, and the horrified pilot agreed to land.

McGivern couldn't believe what the MP had just done. "I was really appalled that Svend was second-guessing the pilot on these safety issues," McGivern remembers. "The pilot was in the best position to know if he could land and where, and it was simply foolhardy for Svend to try to substitute his judgment for that of the pilot." But meeting the Penan was Robinson's priority. What the pilot had to say about safety, which Robinson suspected had much more to do with Malaysian government interference than with actual safety concerns anyway, was simply secondary.

For hours, Robinson listened to the Penan tell stories of how the deforestation of Sarawak was destroying their way of life. That way of life was dramatically illustrated to Robinson and McGivern during their visit. "It was fantastic. We saw Penan in loincloth hunting with blowpipes," McGivern recalls. "All of the head men gathered to tell us how logging was ruining their way of life. This was a four-hour session, interrupted by a rainstorm. That night, we slept on the floor of a hut under mosquito nets." The next day, they were woken at sunrise by the prayers of the Penan. They were given gifts of blowpipes, baskets and bracelets made of bark. As Robinson and McGivern left, lines of Penan formed to say goodbye, and the women sang a prayer for a safe journey.

The barricade was a three-day trek from the nearest town, and the pilot, who hadn't wanted to land in the first place, wasn't coming back to pick them up. Penan guides led them through the rainforest, cutting a path with machetes. It was a beautiful but laborious and dangerous journey. "At one point, we had to walk across a large gorge on a slippery log, with Penan guides holding our arms. We really were in the middle of nowhere, and if we had fallen or were injured, there would have been absolutely no help available," McGivern says. After a few hours of hacking their way through the jungle, they reached a river and a small motorboat that had been left for them. The gas had been stolen, so they had to row. There were shallow rapids, and they got stuck several times. At sundown, they reached another Penan settlement and slept in a church. The next day followed the same pattern, and it was not until the day after that they reached a narrow, rugged, dirt road and took a jeep to Miri. While McGivern thought Robinson had been reckless in forcing the helicopter to land, he was pleasantly surprised by Robinson's willingness to get his hands dirty on the return trip. McGivern had travelled with parliamentarians before and had expected him to be yet another high-maintenance visitor. "There was a fair bit of physical labour involved in this trip, and Svend did more than his fair share of work," McGivern recalls. "He pitched right in and never expected others, either the Penan guides or me, to do his work for him."

By eschewing the traditional approach to international diplomacy and going straight to the front lines of the issue, Robinson gained first-hand knowledge that he wouldn't have been able to acquire any other way. Furthermore, his visit with the Penan provoked the Malaysian authorities into making the same mistake the

Chinese did. Following his visit, Robinson held a press conference denouncing the unsustainable logging taking place in Sarawak and the devastation it was wreaking on the Penan. He then called for the suspension of Canadian aid until such practices ended. The livid response from the Malaysian government brought far more exposure to the issue than Robinson ever could have by making a speech in Parliament or asking a question in committee. The Malaysians accused the unimpeachably professional McGivern of interfering in Malaysia's internal affairs and were on the verge of expelling him from the country until the Canadian High Commissioner interceded. One of the leading Penan activists who had met with Robinson, Anderson Mutang Urud, was arrested and later exiled to Canada. The Malaysian Minister of Primary Industries accused Robinson of inciting the Penan to use poisonous darts against loggers, a bizarre accusation McGivern confirms was entirely without foundation. Malaysian Prime Minister Mahathir bin Mohamad hotly condemned Canadian interference in Malaysian affairs, saying, "We are not interested in having lying, arm-twisting friends who feel that they are the only civilized people and know how to run this world." These hysterical responses and wild accusations made a great news story. Robinson and Suzuki, meanwhile, refuted the charge that environmentalists had no business interfering in Malaysia. Suzuki pointed out that nations and borders were irrelevant in the context of a global environment, and Robinson agreed. "An injury to the Penan is an injury to all of us as planetary citizens," he said.

The media exposure Robinson's tactics brought to injustices in China and Malaysia further vindicated the dramatic, direct-action approach he had been honing since he offered sanctuary to Galindo Madrid, the Chilean refugee, in 1979. Other successes using this approach were yet to come. But while Robinson has no regrets over the tactics he used, there is an important aspect of his engagement in foreign affairs in those early years that he has come to rethink. In 1991, Prime Minister Brian Mulroney pledged that Canadian aid would be provided only to countries that respected human rights. This would ensure that Canadian money couldn't be used to subsidize the repression of the people it was intended to help. It was a philosophy Robinson supported; after his missions to China and Malaysia, he recommended that aid to both countries be suspended. However, in the extensive international work he has done since his political career ended, he has developed a more nuanced view. "When you cut off aid entirely to countries in which there is massive suppression of traditional civil and political rights — freedom of speech, freedom of assembly, the right to organize, collective bargaining and so on — you have to be very careful that you don't end up denying basic humanitarian aid to their people. But it's a huge dilemma, because to the extent that you're subsidizing even food aid and so on, you're allowing brutal dictators to spend more money on weapons to suppress their people," he explains. "It's an incredibly complex and difficult issue, and just saying, 'We're going to cut off aid if China doesn't support freedom of speech' is far too simplistic." Robinson has since concluded that donor nations must listen more closely to the voices of dissent from within a country, and to whether they are recommending sanctions as a means of applying pressure. "Sometimes I was too quick to say, 'They abuse human rights? Cut 'em off!'" he says, snapping his fingers. "It was a far more complex issue than I was sometimes prepared to acknowledge."

It would have been nice to return to Burnaby after the stress of his missions to China and Malaysia, but Robinson still had work to do. Instead of going home, he joined Liberal MP Derek Lee and PC MP Barbara Greene in the Punjab and conducted an investigation into the conflict between Sikhs and the Indian government. Then he proceeded to Sri Lanka to look into the conflict between Tamils and the Sri Lankan government. After his visit to India, some Sikhs were upset that he had not spoken out more strongly against the repression of Sikhs. Asked today about the negative reaction to that trip, Robinson could argue. He could point out that he would have had difficulty meeting with detainees or visiting jails when he was accompanied by 12 armed guards. He could question whether anyone else would have stretched themselves as far as he had to fight for international human rights, on that trip to Asia or on the countless other trips he undertook as a parliamentarian. But he doesn't. Instead, he acknowledges their disappointment. "I don't fault people for saying, 'You could have done more,'" he says.

• • •

When Robinson finally returned to Burnaby after more than three weeks abroad, he began to sort through the mail that had piled up. When he got to the cream-coloured envelope with Chinese stamps, he frowned. Maybe he hadn't escaped official Chinese discipline as easily as he thought he had when the Chinese police stuffed his belongings into garbage bags and shoved them, and him, onto the first plane to Hong Kong. He opened the envelope. It read: "Dear Mr. S. J. Robinson, We were delighted to have you as our guest at Hotel Beijing and hope that your visit was as pleasant as it possibly could be. After your departure on January 7, 1992, our Information Clerk failed to locate the room key . . ."

• • •

Fifteen hundred years ago, as Victorius of Aquitaine was inventing the multiplication table, the Western red cedars that now tower over the forests of B.C.'s Clayoquot Sound were just tiny seedlings. Today, those seedlings have grown into the silent behemoths that are the dominant features of the west coast of Vancouver Island. While such forests may seem commonplace to British Columbians, they are actually an ecological rarity. "Some of the rarest kinds of terrestrial ecosystems worldwide are temperate rainforests. They occupy a tiny zone that only occurs on the western edges of large land masses in the temperate zone," Dr. Eliot Norse of the U.S. Centre for Marine Conservation explained to the *Ottawa Citizen*. "They only occur west of large mountain ranges that cause rainfall to occur in much larger quantities than would normally occur if the land were flat. They make up much less than 1 per cent of the terrestrial ecosystems on this planet."

Environmentalists, including the Friends of Clayoquot Sound, had always understood what a treasure they had in their backyard, and they had held periodic demonstrations for years, hoping to draw attention to the importance of preserving the forests of the sound. Successive B.C. governments had granted logging rights to the area, but environmentalists hoped the province's new NDP government, elected in 1991, would extinguish those rights and preserve the sound forever. When, in the spring of 1993, Premier Mike Harcourt announced that he was preserving one-third of the old-growth forest in Clayoquot Sound — leaving two-thirds of North America's largest remaining temperate rainforest to be logged — many environmentalists felt betrayed.

Robinson had hoped to use his status as an NDP insider to influence Harcourt's thinking on Clayoquot. Prior to Harcourt's decision, Robinson wrote to him warning against the destruction of old-growth forests. "It would be a terrible tragedy and a deep blow to the environmental credibility of our government," he wrote. When his attempts to lobby Harcourt and his ministers failed, he had no hesitation in attacking his own party. On April 16, 1993, he held a press conference denouncing Harcourt's decision as a betrayal of NDP principles. Robinson made it clear that the political stripes of the party in power made no difference to him; he would fight them the same way he fought his other opponents, on the front lines. "If my presence in a peaceful, non-violent demonstration of support would be helpful, I will be there," he said.

He wouldn't have to wait long. Friends of Clayoquot Sound, Greenpeace and other environmental groups were already mobilized, and the threat to Clayoquot drew international attention. Demonstrations took place in front of Canadian embassies in at least six countries. On Canada Day, over 100 protesters set up camp near the site of a clear-cut in Clayoquot known as "the Black Hole." But organizers soon decided they needed to take a more direct approach, and on July 5 they set up a blockade. That day, wearing a T-shirt proclaiming "My Canada includes trees," Robinson joined a dozen other protesters as they lined up across the Kennedy River Bridge, linked arms and refused to let the MacMillan Bloedel logging trucks pass.

"I agonized over this decision," he recalls. The memories of the battles in court and in caucus following his participation in the Haida blockade were still vivid. As he had done when he joined the blockade in Haida Gwaii, he met with the local aboriginal leaders prior to helping stop traffic on the Kennedy River Bridge. They, too, opposed the government's policy. Still, the decision to participate was a difficult one. There was already a court injunction in place to prevent the demonstration before it had even begun. "I thought, 'What if I lose my seat as a result of this? Then I have no platform whatsoever, no opportunity to speak out on this or on so many other issues.' But then I thought, once you destroy an ecosystem that's been here for centuries, there's no way of reversing that decision. It's final. It's irrevocable. And it's a massive betrayal of future generations. I could not be anywhere other than on that line that morning." Addressing the media, Robinson didn't mince words when asked to comment on Harcourt's position. "This decision is profoundly wrong and an abdication of leadership and vision," he said.

Clayoquot Sound became the story of the summer in B.C. More than 12,000 people attended the Clayoquot Sound Peace Camp over the next three months, including environmentalist Robert Kennedy Jr., painter Robert Bateman, and musicians Sarah McLachlan, Midnight Oil and Raffi, all of whom performed at the blockade. The protests drew an incredible diversity of supporters. Whole families showed up to join the camp. Every day at 4 a.m. an accordion player made his way through the temporary village, waking up the volunteers who then carpooled back to the Kennedy River Bridge and set up the blockade all over again. The blockade resulted in the largest mass arrest in B.C. history. On August 9 alone, 356 protesters were arrested, and by the time the blockade ended, 856 protesters had been arrested. "The camp and blockade experience changed lives and generated a new cohort of environmental activists," wrote Valerie Langer of Friends of Clayoquot Sound in *Common Ground* magazine. "The controversy, the uniqueness of the actions, the grandmothers and doctors and hippies together, made Clayoquot famous." While Robinson had only joined the blockade for an hour and a half on the first day, his presence helped generate the media attention that turned a small group of dedicated environmentalists into a massive movement and a game-changer for the logging industry in B.C.

It was attention the provincial government couldn't ignore. The following spring, Harcourt announced that an accord had been signed with all stakeholders, including the Nuu-chah-nulth First Nation, which had not consented to the original decision. More of the forest would be preserved, and the area still to be logged was subject to stricter regulation to prevent clear-cutting. The new agreement was seen as a victory for the environmental movement, and within 10 years the amount of logging in Clayoquot Sound had been reduced to 20 per cent of what it was in 1993. For the thousands of activists who had stood up for Clayoquot that summer, the victory was a powerful confirmation of one of Robinson's favourite quotes, from the American cultural anthropologist Margaret Mead, who said, "Never doubt that a small group of thoughtful, committed citizens can change the world. Indeed, it is the only thing that ever has."

Predictably, Robinson's criticism of the B.C. NDP government infuriated some of his NDP colleagues. "Svend represents no one other than himself in the federal caucus. He's a loose cannon whose position on Clayoquot does not reflect the views of his federal colleagues," stated NDP MP Lyle MacWilliam. He was exaggerating — some of his caucus colleagues did agree with Robinson's stand — but Audrey McLaughlin had to resist demands that she remove Robinson's critic responsibility as a punishment. Logging unions were also enraged. "Our ties are with the NDP, not with Svend Robinson. He's proved over the years that he's no great friend of working people. His intent when he was up there was to put people out of work," said Dave Haggard, president of the Port Alberni local of the Industrial Wood and Allied Workers of Canada.

Some of the B.C. NDP felt that Robinson didn't understand the responsibilities of being in government. "Oh my God, nobody can understand it unless you've actually lived that life and that culture. I think he would have felt he understood it, but he hadn't been in that position where he had to make the compromises, weigh a whole bunch of uncomfortable options and find a way to tiptoe through decisions that, philosophically as New Democrats, we may have abhorred, but as a government for all of the people, we had to make anyway," says Joan Sawicki, Speaker of the B.C. Legislature at that time. Sawicki was a dedicated environmentalist who had been a member of Robinson's riding association and a close friend for many years. Like other members of the B.C. NDP government, she was deeply torn on the issue but wished that Robinson hadn't jumped into the fray and made a tough issue even more difficult. Their friendship survived the conflict, but it wasn't easy. "We didn't talk about that substantively for quite a few months," Sawicki says. "It was one of those things that we just agreed to be on opposite sides on, and we managed to get through it, but it was definitely the low point in our relationship."

Further tension with New Democrats was not the only price Robinson had to pay. Some of the Clayoquot protesters received prison sentences of up to 45 days for their participation in the blockade, but Robinson had not been charged. He had only been present on the first day of the blockade, and the arrests began on the second day. Furthermore, the RCMP officer in charge of the investigation, Bernie Johnstone, had personally recommended against charging protesters for the first day's blockade when filing his report to the Crown. "From my perspective, the efforts to prosecute the blockade of July 5 would only escalate the problem, giving police, Crown and government further bad press, just what the environmentalists are looking for," Johnstone wrote. It was standard RCMP policy for an investigating officer to present the case against a suspect in a written report, but also to include a personal recommendation about whether to lay charges. Johnstone's report made it clear that Robinson could reasonably be charged, but he also stated that, in his professional opinion, it wasn't advisable. Furthermore, it would be unusual for the Crown to ignore a recommendation from a senior RCMP officer. Nevertheless, on February 4, 1994, *The Province* chose to run a more provocative front-page headline: "RCMP Urge Attorney-General: CHARGE SVEND." The B.C. tabloid, owned by Southam Inc., later printed a two-inch retraction on page 4, but the damage had been done. The Attorney-General had to charge Robinson or risk the appearance that an NDP MP had received preferential treatment from an NDP government. The Attorney-General's office appointed a Special Prosecutor and on May 10, 1994, announced that Robinson was being charged with criminal contempt for defying a Supreme Court order prohibiting the obstruction of logging in Clayoquot Sound.

"I have come prepared today to fully accept the punishment that this Court deems fit and just in the circumstances," Robinson told the B.C. Supreme Court as he pled guilty. "I don't want any public perception I was treated any differently from the others."

"It's not going to be an easy case to decide," acknowledged Justice Wally Oppal. During Robinson's sentencing, Oppal stated that he found it refreshing that Robinson had taken responsibility for his actions as unequivocally as he had. "I must also take into consideration Mr. Robinson's lengthy record for public service and his otherwise unimpeachable character," he said. In his ruling, he affirmed the value of civil disobedience, referring to the examples of Mahatma Gandhi and Martin Luther King, and readily agreed that the practice had been "instrumental for many great human purposes." Nevertheless, Robinson had a duty to uphold the law, not only as a citizen, but also as an MP and a lawyer. Furthermore, he had a prior record for a similar offence, committed eight years previously in Haida Gwaii. On July 26, 1994, Oppal sentenced him to 14 days in prison. Corrections officials offered him the opportunity to serve his sentence at home with an electronic monitoring bracelet. Robinson declined the bracelet, noting that the option had not been offered to all of the other activists who had been convicted. In his view, in a matter of civil disobedience, one had to accept the full consequences of the law. From the courtroom, he was taken directly to Ford Mountain Correctional Centre to begin his sentence.

On Parliament Hill, members of Parliament are treated like aristocrats. If a member offhandedly voices a preference for chocolate milk instead of regular milk, chocolate milk is waiting at the next committee meeting, along with a plate of cookies. Special green buses run throughout the day so that MPs can be ferried from one parliamentary building to another 200 metres away. On Parliament Hill, nobody ever tells a member to wash out flower pots for the greenhouse, collapse and stack cardboard boxes, or bag pop cans, but that's what Robinson did at Ford Mountain. He lived in a unit with 54 other inmates and was treated like any other prisoner. He earned $3 a day performing the same menial tasks assigned to the other inmates, including painting an outhouse and clearing brush (but, as he would later joke, not old-growth rainforest). Like everyone else, he ate in the cafeteria and had to wait in line to use the phone. Although he had visited prisons many times in his career, the sense of restriction he felt as an inmate was still startling. "It was very real," he says. "Your liberty is a very important part of your ability to live a full life. Even to be able to make just one phone call a day, and not to be able to move outside the confines of the prison walls, is enormously serious."

Joan Sawicki came to see him on visitation day, and they sat in the prison yard at a picnic table with two little plastic cups of watered-down juice. "He was subdued, somewhat shaken. The term 'bowed but not broken' came to mind. The most significant thing, I guess, was that he was not in control of his surroundings. For one of the first times, he wasn't able to control everything around him, and I think more than anything else that was the most difficult thing for Svend to accept," Sawicki recalls of the experience. "He needed that sense of freedom in every regard."

Bill Blaikie was also able to visit. Although the two caucus colleagues were frequently at loggerheads, they got along well. "I always had this vision of having you contained in some way, and I just had to come and enjoy it," Blaikie recalls joking to Robinson.

Despite his discomfort, Robinson tried to glean something positive from the experience. He found that guards and prisoners alike were willing to speak candidly with him about the challenges faced by the correctional system. With his background in criminal justice, both as a lawyer and as the former NDP justice critic, he was able to make genuine connections with the people he met. When

Bill Siksay arrived to pick him up upon his release, he couldn't believe how much luggage Robinson had somehow acquired. "He'd been buying stuff they make in the shop, and there were things people had given him. We're loading the truck up. He had all this stuff. It was hilarious. You're not supposed to come away from jail with souvenirs!" Siksay says, laughing.

Released for good behaviour after having served two-thirds of his sentence, Robinson was mobbed by the media outside the prison gates. "What are you guys doing here?" he joked. Sporting the shadow of a beard for the first time in his career, he used the opportunity to share his reflections on the prison system. "The prison system is an abject failure. Society will look back not many years from now in shame and bewilderment at our response to crime in this country," he said. "I think if anyone belongs in prison in this country, it's corporate executives who are destroying our environment."

Robinson had relinquished his salary as a member of Parliament for the duration of his imprisonment and had donated the $27 of prisoner's salary he'd earned to the Inmate Welfare Fund, but opponents still called for a federal ethics investigation. The controversy over a sitting member of Parliament serving time in prison sparked a national discussion on the merits of civil disobedience. Some argued that in a free and democratic society, in which laws were properly constituted and in which avenues of redress were available, citizens could not simply break laws just because they disagreed with them. Others argued that laws of conscience carried greater authority than laws of government. Some challenged Robinson's notion that a parliamentarian could engage in direct action. If he believed that protest on the front lines was more valuable than parliamentary debate, they argued, he should resign his seat. Others were impressed at how he managed to use both approaches so effectively. "His critics say he goes too far, and down the wrong path. His supporters say the means he employs are justified by a higher law," Guido Marziali wrote in the *Burnaby News*. "But Robinson is sure of one thing. No one says he doesn't go far enough."

Five years after the famous protests, the small town of Tofino,

B.C., hosted what may have been the largest gathering of convicts in Canadian history. The reunion was called "Clayoquatraz," and it brought many of the environmentalists who had been involved in the blockade back to the site of their victory. Robert Kennedy Jr. and Robinson gave speeches, and the arrestees proudly wore white armbands symbolizing the sacrifices they'd made to protect the sound. In spite of those efforts, the ancient rainforests of the Pacific Northwest are still threatened by logging. However, the dedication of the activists that summer in Clayoquot Sound proved that the muscular interests fuelling the destruction of the environment didn't hold all the power, and that drums, face paint, signs, songs and, most importantly, peaceful, direct-action civil disobedience really could make a difference.

TWELVE

The Last Word

"It was numbing. I was going to funerals all the time. A gay friend would get sick or develop a cough, and we'd all be terrified," Robinson recalls of the AIDS epidemic devastating the gay community. Friends were dying at an incredible rate, and Christian fundamentalists seized upon the disease as proof that God had sent a pestilence to strike down the wicked. Many of those afflicted died alone, more afraid of coming out than they were of the disease.

If Mitch Jacobson had known what dying of AIDS was going to be like, he would have killed himself while he still had the strength to do it. Blind, nearly deaf, unable to taste — pain was about the only thing he could still feel. Thanks to Robinson's assistance, Jacobson became the first AIDS patient admitted for palliative care at Ottawa's Elisabeth Bruyère Health Centre. Robinson came to see him regularly. On one of these visits, Jacobson begged Robinson to help him do what he had become too weak to do on his own: end his life. "If I had known, I would have jumped," he said, pointing out the window at a nearby bridge. It was heartbreaking to watch a friend beg for help and be unable to give it. Jacobson died in 1986, but Robinson never forgot that helpless, impotent feeling. In 1991, PC MP Bob Wenman introduced a private member's bill that would have allowed doctors, in certain circumstances, to stop treatments and allow patients to die. When Robinson rose to speak, he remembered Jacobson's painful end. "Surely to God, we must allow a man or a woman to avoid that kind of death, to allow them to make the decision for themselves to end that terrible, agonizing pain. As Mitch said, 'Let me go.' I could not let him go," he said.

The bill didn't pass, but after his speech, Robinson was contacted by John Hofsess of the Right to Die Society, and Hofsess introduced him to an exceptional woman. Sue Rodriguez was athletic and free-spirited, a loving mother coping with her recent separation from her husband. At age 41, Rodriguez noticed a strange, recurring twitch in her hands. She travelled from her home in Victoria to see a specialist in Vancouver who told her that she had amyotrophic lateral sclerosis, commonly known as ALS or "Lou Gehrig's disease." The motor neurons in her spinal cord would slowly destroy themselves, and while her mind would remain as sharp as ever, she would lose her ability to walk, then to talk and eventually to breathe. She'd be paralyzed, hooked up to a machine pumping fluid from her lungs to keep her from suffocating. She wouldn't be able to speak with her son or even hold him. She would constantly feel like she was drowning. Within five years, the doctor told her, she would be dead.

On the ferry back to Victoria, Rodriguez was in shock. She couldn't keep her eyes off the elderly people riding the ferry with her. "All of a sudden, I felt envy for people that were in their seventies, knowing that I wasn't going to reach that age," she said of the experience. An active woman who loved to run and cross-country ski, Rodriguez determined that if she had to die young, then at least she would die with dignity. However, she knew that by the time the pain became too much to endure, she would no longer have the physical ability to end her life herself. She would need help from a friend, but assisting a suicide carried a penalty of up to 14 years in prison. Nevertheless, she contacted the Right to Die Society, and Hofsess agreed to help. He was haunted by the memory of a friend with early-onset Alzheimer's disease who had asked him to help end his life. Hofsess refused, and later the man jumped from a bridge, terrified and alone. Determined not to let that happen again, Hofsess signed a contract with Rodriguez in which he promised to help her end her life, at the time and in the manner of her choosing. They were prepared to do it no matter what, but they hoped that when the time came, they would be able to do it without breaking the law.

Laws could be changed in one of two ways: through the courts or through Parliament. The courts seemed more promising. With the help of Victoria lawyer Chris Considine, Rodriguez challenged the constitutionality of the prohibition on assisted suicide. First in the B.C. Supreme Court and then in the B.C. Court of Appeal, Considine argued that the right to "security of the person," guaranteed by Section 7 of the Charter of Rights and Freedoms, gave Rodriguez the right to make decisions about her own body, and that included the decision to end her life. That right was being infringed if Rodriguez, by virtue of her disease and the necessity of obtaining assistance, was prevented from ending her life by Criminal Code sanctions against assisted suicide. Section 7 had been successfully used to argue that women had the right to make decisions about their own bodies in terminating a pregnancy. The Supreme Court had struck down laws against abortion in 1988, and Considine hoped the courts would also strike down laws against assisted suicide.

Meanwhile, Robinson was Rodriguez's chief ally in Parliament. In addition to arguing passionately in favour of legalizing physician-assisted suicide, he helped her to appear before the justice committee. In a pre-recorded video played for the members of the committee, Rodriguez put a human face on what was, for many, an abstract concept. "Whose body is this? Who owns my life?" she asked the MPs.

As media interest in the issue intensified, her eloquence and spirit captivated Canadians. She gradually realized that she had become a powerful spokesperson for a right she felt all Canadians should have, and she embraced that role willingly. She would allow cameras to film her as she good-naturedly struggled to put on makeup or get dressed. "I feel like I'm in a slow motion movie. It takes forever!" she laughed. When she spoke, in a rhythm that was becoming ever slower and more laborious as her speech deteriorated, her large eyes expressed only earnestness and honesty. While Robinson and Hofsess occasionally adopted a combative tone when addressing opponents to physician-assisted suicide, Rodriguez didn't. It seemed as if she didn't want to fight, but only to reach out to people. When she answered reporters' questions, every answer ended with the broad, open-hearted smile that seemed to burst from her whenever she had nothing left to say, as though that warmth was the default feeling she had to express.

Canadians admired Rodriguez and followed her case with compassion. "People were moved by her bravery. Sue was an articulate person who did not seem to be out to gain anything for herself. She didn't do books, sell rights to television or anything of that nature. She would explain the plight that she found herself in," Considine says. He recalls leaving the Bedford Hotel in Victoria after a press conference with Rodriguez and Robinson, and stepping out onto Government Street. "As we came out, it seemed as if the street stopped," he says. Strangers began to applaud. "They applauded for Sue. They recognized her and applauded her bravery and courage . . . It was very moving."

While polls showed that a majority of Canadians supported the legalization of physician-assisted suicide, the concept had — and has — many committed opponents. For some Christians, it is a religious matter: condoning any form of suicide is contrary to their interpretation of the Bible. Many other Canadians feel passionately that allowing voluntary, physician-assisted suicide would devalue human life, and could lead to the legal killing of people with disabilities. Complicating the debate, in 1993, Saskatchewan farmer Robert Latimer killed his severely disabled daughter to spare her further pain. While Robinson called for compassion for Latimer and opposed the harsh sentence he received for his act, he also emphasized that the crucial difference between what Latimer had done and what Rodriguez was proposing was the element of personal choice. That distinction wasn't always heard. As Rodriguez continued her battle, some opponents believed that she was becoming a victim herself. They did not believe that she was making her own decisions; instead, they suspected she was being manipulated by Robinson and Hofsess for political gains. "The kind of legislation that she — or those acting on her behalf — say that she wants will not be passed so long as I am a legislator, because it is wrong," declared Liberal MP Don Boudria after Rodriguez's video was shown to the justice committee.

Rodriguez lost at the B.C. Supreme Court and at the B.C. Court of Appeal, but the Chief Justice dissented, and Rodriguez and her supporters thought they had a good chance to win at the Supreme Court of Canada. On September 30, 1993, the Supreme Court rendered its decision. The Court found that the Criminal Code did violate the security of the person provision of Section 7 of the Charter, just as Considine had argued it did, but that that violation was in accordance with the overriding principles of "fundamental justice" also guaranteed by Section 7. "Given the concerns about abuse that have been expressed and the great difficulty in creating appropriate safeguards to prevent these, it can not be said that the blanket prohibition on assisted suicide is arbitrary or unfair, or that it is not reflective of fundamental values at play in our society," wrote Justice John Sopinka. By the narrowest majority, 5–4, the Supreme Court ruled that the prohibition on assisted suicide was constitutional. (Among the dissenters was Beverley McLachlin, who became Chief Justice in 2000.)

Robinson was disappointed, and felt strongly that the court had come to the wrong legal conclusion. Notably, as a member of the committee studying the draft Charter in 1981, Robinson had argued against including the undefined phrase "fundamental justice," precisely because he felt it left too much discretion to the courts. Of the many ways in which his arguments to the committee had been vindicated over the years, this offered the least comfort. As he fumed about the court's decision, Rodriguez calmed him. "Svend, the Court may have spoken, but remember, I have the last word," she said. Both she and Robinson were also comforted by the eloquent words of dissenting Justice Peter Cory, who wrote: "The life of an individual must include dying. Dying is the final act in the drama of life. If, as I believe, dying is an integral part of living ... It follows that the right to die with dignity should be as well protected as is any other aspect of the right to life. State prohibitions that would force a dreadful, painful death on a rational but incapacitated terminally-ill patient are an affront to human dignity."

As they worked together, Robinson and Rodriguez became friends. When Rodriguez needed to be in Vancouver, she would stay at the historic Sylvia Hotel on English Bay, and she and Robinson would go for walks together on the seawall, Robinson pushing her in her wheelchair. Away from the prying eyes of the media, he would visit her at her home on the weekends, and she would offer him advice on his love life. "We just clicked from the first time we met," he recalls. "We had, I guess, a similar sense of humour. I don't know. There was just a real link there, a real personal link there, that became a very close friendship." Rodriguez's estranged husband had moved back to help out during that difficult time, but Rodriguez also valued having someone from outside the family that she could trust. "I think that Svend had a lot of empathy for Sue," Considine says. "Sue found him to be a tremendous comfort to her."

At Christmas, Rodriguez decided it was time. As the doctors had predicted, she no longer had control over her body and was in constant agony. Her relationship with Hofsess had deteriorated due to remarks he had made to the media on her behalf, and Rodriguez had decided to dissociate herself from the Right to Die Society. That meant she needed someone else to help her end her life when the time came, so she asked Robinson. He felt privileged to be asked, and despite the serious legal risk, he agreed to help. However, when Rodriguez chose February 12, 1994, as the date for her passing, it seemed incredibly close. "I foolishly argued with her and said that she should hang on longer, that things might improve, that it might just be a temporary depression driving her feelings at that time. But Sue angrily rejected that," Robinson says. "As the date approached, I became more and more tormented by her decision, and anguished by the knowledge that this remarkable woman, whom I had come not only to respect but also to love, would die. Yet, as we met to plan the details of that day, I was in awe of her sense of calm and control. She never, ever wavered in her determination," he says.

When Rodriguez gave what would be her last media interview, her speech had become so slow and unclear that the media needed to subtitle her when broadcasting it. She couldn't share the exact details of her plan, partly because it was illegal and partly because she feared religious extremists would try to stop her. (Two Christian fundamentalists had recently found her home, entered without permission and begun praying at her bedside while she watched helplessly.) But her spirit still shone. "I know it's right for me, and I feel I've done all I can to contribute to life, and it's time for me to move on," Rodriguez said, still ending with that glorious, wide smile.

Advocating for the right to die dominated Robinson's political life at that time. He received over 2,000 letters, many describing moving personal stories. "That was one of the most difficult times working in the office. People were phoning from all across the country, telling you these stories about their own preparations for death, or some relative's," Bill Siksay recalls. "I spent hours on the phone with people in horrible situations. I'd be in tears the whole time. There would just be gut-wrenching, gut-wrenching stories." Robinson was impressed by the dedication and sensitivity of his staff in handling those difficult situations. But in the matter of assisting Rodriguez herself, he had to work alone. He discreetly sought the assistance of a physician, but those he approached were understandably reluctant to help because of the legal implications. Eventually he enlisted the help of a foreign doctor. "Initially Svend would tell me what was going on, and I eventually said, 'Svend, we have to stop having these conversations. I don't want the cops coming here and asking me what I know. I don't want to know anything. I'm not that good at not telling people what I know,'" Siksay says.

On February 11, 1994, Rodriguez had one last family dinner with her husband and son. The next morning, Robinson took the ferry to Victoria and drove to Rodriguez's home. He parked on a nearby street and walked the rest of the way. Robinson describes what happened:

> I entered through the back yard and through the sliding glass door, which had been left open for me. Sue was alone in her bed downstairs. She was very calm and clear. I again asked her if she was certain that she wanted to go ahead that day, and told her there was absolutely no problem in putting it off. She was very firm and told me that she knew that this was the time. She said that her husband had taken her son away to a movie and lunch, but would call in the afternoon to make sure that everything was okay. She had decided upon the music that she wanted played at the time of her death, [German recording artist] Deuter, and I put the tape in the player and turned up the volume after she said it was too quiet. She laughed at one point and said that I was more nervous than she was, and she calmed me. I was in tears and felt so helpless, but also so inspired by her great courage. After she received a lethal dose of secobarbital, she asked me to hold her as she listened to the music. I got into bed beside her and held her in my arms. At one point the doorbell rang, and I panicked and looked out the window, only to see two earnest Jehovah's Witnesses at the door. Eventually they left, much to our relief.
>
> Sue slipped into unconsciousness, but it took a very long time for her heart to stop beating. I lay with her until that time. It was so painful, but I was also very glad that I was able to be with her at the end, as I had promised her. When I was certain that she was dead, I covered her head with a sheet and went upstairs to call her family doctor to ask him to come and pronounce her dead. As well, I called the local RCMP detachment and told them that Sue had died with the assistance of a physician, and that they should come to her home . . . I made a very brief statement and told them that I would be retaining legal counsel, and then called my friend and lawyer Clayton Ruby. They then let me leave the house, and I drove to the nearby town of Sidney where I spent the night at the Sidney Hotel. I did not sleep much that night.

The next day, Robinson flew to Ottawa, where he carefully prepared his statement for the press. With Ruby's help, he redrafted his statement several times. Even though he had read it many times over, he was still overcome with emotion as he spoke to the press from the podium in the Charles Lynch Room in Centre Block. He had to stop several times, apologizing for his tears. It was a side of Robinson few had seen before. "That was him at his most open — no political mask. I think that was true Svend at that press conference. Going down to the press conference and going back with him was probably the closest I ever felt to him," says former assistant Jane Pepper. When Hugh Winsor of the *Globe and Mail* asked Robinson about his duty as a member of Parliament to uphold the law, Robinson's response was simple, vulnerable and human. Those present that day saw it was how he truly felt. "The highest duty of a member of Parliament is love," he said, fighting back tears.

•   •   •

Section 241 of the Criminal Code states: "Anyone who (a) counsels a person to commit suicide or (b) aids or abets a person to commit suicide, whether suicide ensues or not, is guilty of an indictable offence and liable to imprisonment for a term not exceeding 14 years." On January 10, 1995, the Attorney-General of B.C. appointed a Special Prosecutor to determine whether Robinson should face charges. Special Prosecutor Robert Johnston's investigation concluded that, although it was clear that Rodriguez could not have administered the drugs that killed her, it could not be proven who had.

Robinson had stated that he was present and had alluded to the involvement of a doctor, but had not gone into any further detail about what happened. "The presence of Mr. Robinson proves only that he had an opportunity to commit an offence by assisting in the suicide," Johnston wrote in his report. "Proof of opportunity is at best circumstantial evidence, and the law imposes a more rigorous burden on the prosecution where the evidence is circumstantial." With only circumstantial evidence, the case against Robinson would have been far too weak. He couldn't be charged with obstructing justice by refusing to identify the doctor involved, either. "Mr. Robinson, like every other person, has a constitutionally-protected right to remain silent. He is under no legal obligation to provide information to the police," wrote Johnston. Charges based on counselling suicide were rejected as well. "During the period during which her application for the right to an assisted suicide was before the courts, there were many public expressions of support for her position and sympathy for her plight, as well as considerable public debate on the moral and ethical issues raised by her application," Johnston noted. "There is no evidence that any of this had any influence on Sue Rodriguez sufficient to warrant a criminal charge."

After Johnston released his report, Robinson expressed his relief. "I will work hard to ensure that, hopefully soon, no other caring and compassionate doctor, no other loving friend, will have to fear criminal prosecution for honouring the request to end the suffering, pain and indignity of the terminal or incurable illness of a competent adult, at the time they choose," he said. True to his word, he continued to argue in the House for changes to the law. Convinced that the public was on his side, he encouraged MPs to meet with their constituents to solicit their views. Shortly after Rodriguez's death, Justice Minister Allan Rock promised that the newly elected Liberal government would bring the issue before the House for a free vote. Robinson introduced a bill the next day. However, like most private members' bills in those days, it was officially designated "non-votable" by the Liberal-dominated committee in charge of regulating private members' business, a committee that included opponents to physician-assisted suicide like Don Boudria, but did not have an NDP representative. Therefore, after being debated, the bill was dropped from the Order Paper (the list of business that can be debated by the House). The same fate befell his next bill to legalize physician-assisted suicide. Years later, the government still hadn't brought forward a proposal of its own. In 1997 Robinson proposed a motion to create a special committee to develop legislation legalizing physician-assisted suicide. Finally he got his free vote. However, an overwhelming majority of both the Liberal and Reform MPs opposed his motion, and it was defeated 169–65.

Robinson never identified the doctor involved in Rodriguez's suicide and still won't go into any greater detail about what happened the day she died. He chose his words carefully in 1994 and is determined to leave it at that. He remains a passionate advocate for the right to die with dignity and continues to follow the issue closely from his home in Switzerland, where physician-assisted suicide is legal. He was disappointed to see Bloc Québécois MP Francine Lalonde's bill to legalize physician-assisted suicide defeated in 2010. What was even more disappointing was seeing that, this time, even a majority of the NDP MPs joined with the bill's opponents to crush it. Nearly two decades after Rodriguez's death, her dream is still unrealized. Robinson is comforted by the knowledge that her pain is over, and that she ended her life in the manner of her choosing. "You lose a close friend, of course you feel a sense of loss. But time marches on," he says. "She was an amazing woman, and I treasure the memories of the time we spent together." Even today, her legacy endures. Robinson says Canadians still approach him to tell him how impressed they were with the courage and determination Rodriguez showed.

In June 2012 the B.C. Supreme Court ruled in a case remarkably similar to that of Rodriguez, involving Gloria Taylor, a grandmother who was terminally ill with ALS. Taylor was represented by prominent human rights lawyer Joe Arvay, who consulted with Robinson while preparing his case. His arguments before the court were successful; the court ruled that the laws prohibiting physician-assisted suicide are indeed unconstitutional but suspended the effects of the ruling for one year in order to allow Parliament to make necessary changes in the law. Taylor, meanwhile, was granted an exemption from the current law and allowed the freedom to die with dignity at the moment of her choosing. "I'm so grateful to know that if I choose to do so I will be allowed to seek a doctor's help to a peaceful and dignified death. This brings me great solace and comfort," Taylor said. On the day of the ruling, opponents of physician-assisted suicide pledged to appeal. Within a month, so did Stephen Harper's Conservative government, announcing it would appeal not only the ruling, but Taylor's exemption as well. The B.C. Court of Appeal rejected the government's request to overturn Taylor's exemption, but in the fall of 2012, before her terminal illness had made her life too painful to continue, Taylor died suddenly of an infection caused by a perforated colon.

While physician-assisted suicide remains illegal in Canada, it is permitted in several European countries and even in several U.S. states. Quebec is reportedly seriously considering legalization. Of all Robinson's political battles, this was the one he says resonated with Canadians the most. As reluctant as ever to give up the fight, he would say that this struggle, like so many others, isn't over yet.

THIRTEEN

The Silence of our Friends

Even before Jack Layton moved into Stornoway, the official residence of the Leader of the Opposition, the NDP had a long history of wielding power from the opposition benches. It is sometimes said that the height of their influence was when they held the balance of power during the minority parliaments of the 1960s and 1970s, when they helped pass such legislation as Medicare and public pensions, but the NDP had a significant impact in the 1980s, too. "One of the great parliamentarians, and most influential people in modern times, was Ed Broadbent on the floor of the House of Commons," says Brian Mulroney. "Third parties can have an impact." That extended to Robinson, too. "While Svend was not a leader of a party, he was a prominent member and spokesperson of it, and because he was driven very strongly in the area of human rights, I think he made a difference — a positive difference — in the lives of many Canadians," Mulroney says. It was occasionally suggested that Robinson's forceful style may have put political opponents on the defensive, causing them to adopt a combative stance rather than a receptive one, but he and Mulroney had a productive working relationship. "I enjoyed his comments. I enjoyed his speeches in the House. I could have done without some of his questions, but he was always polite and respectful with me and my family, so I listened carefully to his causes when he spoke about them, and his positions on AIDS and human rights and so on, and I would invite him over from time to time in the House of Commons to chat with me," Mulroney says.

But that was before the 1993 election. When Mulroney retired, he left office as one of the most unpopular politicians in Canadian history. Patronage, the introduction of the Goods and Services Tax, and controversial deficit spending ($4.8-billion on new helicopters for the military just as the Cold War was ending, for example) had tarnished his legacy. As the 1993 election campaign progressed, it became clear that Mulroney's successor, Kim Campbell, couldn't undo the damage to the PC brand, and Jean Chrétien's Liberals soared in the national polls. Voters were eager to punish the PCs, and that didn't leave a lot of room for the NDP.

In Burnaby, Robinson ran on his personal record rather than the party's. His campaign materials were green, instead of NDP orange, and they included scant mention of the national party. The allies he had collected in his various political battles lined up in support of his campaign. Haida artist Bill Reid again designed a poster — a drawing of a snarling wolf, with the confident slogan "Who's afraid?" — and David Suzuki and Raffi were featured at campaign events. Again Robinson was well-funded and able to count on an army of loyal volunteers, but on the doorsteps, he got the sense that it would be a close race and that the Liberal candidate, Kwangyul Peck, was a real threat.

Then someone on Peck's team blew it. Midway through the campaign, a constituent Robinson had helped with an immigration issue sent him a flyer she'd received in the mail. It was a bilingual flyer, in English and Chinese, featuring Peck's smiling face. However, the Chinese side featured an additional paragraph that wasn't written on the English side: "The present member of Parliament of the New Democratic Party, who was even openly proud of his homosexual lifestyle, and therefore was expelled by the Malaysian as well as the Chinese Government, has a bad influence on our children, hence he should not be a parliamentary representative."

In a single flyer, Peck's supporters had offended homosexuals, made the inappropriate assumption that Chinese-speaking Burnaby residents would be more likely than their English-speaking neighbours to object to homosexuality, and lied about what had happened to Robinson in Asia. Peck immediately apologized and said he hadn't seen or approved the version with the offending paragraph, but it was to no avail. Throughout the riding, Liberal signs were replaced by NDP signs, and on election day Robinson was re-elected with just under 34 per cent of the vote.

Few other NDP candidates were as successful in the 1993 election. In B.C., the NDP went from 19 seats to just two, with only Robinson and Nelson Riis hanging on. The Reform Party supplanted the PCs as the most powerful conservative force in the country, and they dominated the western provinces. Led by the populist Preston Manning, they sent 52 MPs to the House of Commons, while the PCs were reduced to a caucus of two. Meanwhile, the separatist Bloc Québécois dominated Quebec, and the Liberals won everywhere else, storming to victory with a majority government. The NDP won only nine seats in total, three short of the 12 required for official party status. Without that status for the first time in their history, the party was not entitled to public funding or membership on parliamentary committees, and received almost no time in Question Period.

With no strong opposing voice on the left, the Liberals veered right in their approach to the deficit. In opposition and during the campaign, they had railed against Mulroney's cuts to health and education, but once in government, Chrétien and his Finance Minister, Paul Martin, cut them even further. They cut unemployment insurance, old age benefits and the CBC. Foreign aid, already much less than half of 1 per cent of the gross national product, was slashed by 20 per cent over three years. They cancelled the Canada Assistance Plan, which had helped the provinces provide welfare since the days of Lester B. Pearson's government. They instituted a harsh cap on funding increases for First Nations' programs and services, including education and child welfare, regardless of inflation or demographic changes. As the aboriginal population boomed, the cap stayed the same, and aboriginal students and children in care received dramatically less per capita funding than non-aboriginal children. Not all of the Liberals' economic policies came from the right; along with cutting services, they also raised corporate taxes, reduced military spending and cut certain business subsidies (for example, subsidies to an asbestos lobby group, which had been receiving taxpayer dollars to promote the use of asbestos in some of the world's poorest countries since 1984, were suspended in 1993 before being resumed in 1997). Nevertheless, it seemed to some that the burden of lifting Canada out of a difficult economic quagmire had fallen disproportionately on social services, and on poor and underprivileged Canadians.

The new PC leader, Jean Charest, who had replaced the defeated Kim Campbell, suggested that the shift in Liberal policy was a vindication of Mulroney's government. "What the Liberals fought for nine years, they have now adopted. Free trade, NAFTA [North American Free Trade Agreement], tax reform, the Conservative government's energy policies, deregulation, privatization, deficit reduction. What's next? Buying new helicopters?" Charest joked in an article in the *Globe and Mail* in 1995. The Liberals were so conservative that they even earned begrudging praise from Reform MP Stephen Harper, the future Conservative prime minister. "The current Liberal government is more conservative on most issues than the previous Progressive Conservative government," Harper noted in an article he wrote with prominent conservative Tom Flanagan in *Next City* magazine, after Chrétien's first few years in power.

At least as important as the demise of the NDP was the rising influence of the socially and fiscally conservative Reform Party on the national discourse. "Conservative voters are getting better results as outsiders influencing a Liberal government than they did as an inside influence within a Progressive Conservative government," continued Harper and Flanagan. Robinson, for his part, attacked Reform with harsher language than he'd used for previous political opponents and warned against their growing influence. "I think the Reform Party represents a very dangerous political movement. They pander to the worst in people by attacking immigrants, by attacking gays and lesbians, by attacking equality for women. They're a mean, nasty group of intolerant politicians. But, because they're a populist group, they play to people's fears. Their strength can't be discounted," he said.

It was a dismal time to be left-wing in Canada. "I certainly wouldn't claim to have had any particularly significant impact, looking at those barren years from '93 to '97. I was one of nine members of the New Democrat caucus, jumping up and down in the farthest corner of the House of Commons trying to get the attention of the Speaker for one or two questions a week, and not a formal member of any parliamentary committee. Those were bleak and challenging years," Robinson says. To him, the first Chrétien years were a time of betrayal. "I think back on those cuts, and they were so savage, and the long-term implications of them were so serious. That axe could have been wielded with a vengeance so easily by Mulroney." There is a certain bitterness in his voice as he reflects on the image the Liberals crafted of being a centre-left alternative to the PCs. "I had such contempt for them in so many different ways. They were frauds, parading as being in the centre of the political spectrum, but they were frauds, political frauds. They were fundamentally conservative," he says. "At least with conservatives, true conservatives, you know what to expect. You know where they stand. You can have a vigorous debate with them, and at the end of the day, vote against them, disagree profoundly, but at least have some sense of respect that they have some intellectual honesty."

There was progress on gay and lesbian issues during Chrétien's first term. Justice Minister Allan Rock added sexual orientation to hate crime legislation and to the prohibited grounds of discrimination in the Human Rights Act. According to former Liberal MP Bill Graham, a strong supporter of gay and lesbian rights, Robinson's constant advocacy helped play a role in influencing the government. "Where Svend was great was, he was consistent through the whole piece. Everybody knew where he was coming from," says Graham. Although Robinson felt there was still much more to accomplish, it was a relief to see John Crosbie's 1986 promise to add sexual orientation to the Human Rights Act finally come to fruition. "I thank the Minister of Justice for moving ahead with this legislation. It is an important step forward. For 16 long years I have been battling for this," he said. "This is an important day."

However, even this progress was accompanied by homophobia. During the hate crime debate, Liberal MP Roseanne Skoke went on several rants, declaring that homosexuality was "defiling humanity, destroying families and annihilating mankind." While there were other MPs who shared her views, few in 1994 still spoke with such venom. "She was a really, seriously bad piece of work. Not all the opponents were like her," Graham says of his former colleague. Robinson called for her ouster from the Liberal caucus, hoping her punishment would demonstrate just how out of line her comments were. When it became apparent that Chrétien had no intention of disciplining her, Robinson's response in *Briarpatch* magazine was scathing: "Martin Luther King said that when history records the struggle for equality of black people in America, what will be most shameful is not 'the hatred of our enemies, but the silence of our friends.' And our friends have been deafening in their silence." Many Liberals, such as Graham, Sheila Copps and Hedy Fry, were passionate supporters of gay rights, but they faced a culture war in their own caucus that made progress painfully slow. When Rock's bill to amend the Human Rights Act was adopted by the House, 44 Reformers and 31 Liberals voted against it. If Canadians hoped that the election of the Liberals would soon result in further progress (such as the recognition of same-sex relationships for pensions and benefits, protection from hate propaganda, or the legalization of same-sex marriage), the negative reaction Rock got from the Reform Party and the social conservatives in the Liberal caucus suggested they would have a lot longer to wait.

The NDP also disappointed Robinson in those years. When the Liberals proposed Bill C-68, which would require all gun owners to be licensed and all firearms to be registered, he strongly supported the initiative. He worked closely with the Coalition for Gun Control, headed by Wendy Cukier in Toronto, but found himself working against his NDP colleagues. The NDP was in a difficult position. Philosophically, many New Democrats were in favour of gun control. However, five of the nine MPs elected in 1993 were from Saskatchewan, while leader Audrey McLaughlin was from the Yukon — both areas where the bill was highly unpopular. Some New Democrats worried that a misstep on this issue might cost the party its few remaining seats. McLaughlin allowed a free vote, and Robinson was furious when his colleagues voted against the bill. "I have no doubt that the caucus is out of step, not only with the party, but also with public opinion," he said. He was the only New Democrat to vote in favour.

Relegated to the backbenches in a House dominated by more conservative forces, Robinson focused most of his attention outside Ottawa during Chrétien's first term. He was part of a small group of Canadian parliamentarians sent by the Department of Foreign Affairs to monitor the historic 1994 South African election, the first election in which black South Africans were entitled to vote. Prior to the election, there was concern that there might be violence, that there might not be enough polling stations, and that the polling stations would be distributed unequally between white and black neighbourhoods. In that context, international observers would have an important role. "Your attendance is, given the situation in South Africa, highly desirable. We can not emphasize too much how important it is that you attend," stated a memo Robinson received from the department.

The multi-party delegation was accompanied by a former RCMP officer for security, and each of the MPs was given a radio and a code name; Robinson was "Oscar 2." In South Africa, the delegation witnessed both the ugliness of racism and the dignity of hope. "Would you let your dog vote?" sneered a white South African within the Canadians' earshot. But Robinson also recalls getting up early to observe the voting with Liberal MP Jean Augustine, the first black woman elected to the Canadian Parliament. By 5 a.m., there was already a long line-up at the voting station. Robinson and Augustine spoke with an elderly woman and her son, who were lucky enough to be at the front. The woman had been brought there in a wheelbarrow. "We asked them how they had managed to be the first in line, and they proudly replied that they had left their home the night before so they could come and vote for this man," Robinson says, recalling how the woman pulled out a folded-up picture of Nelson Mandela. "We asked how far they had come. Her son pointed to the nearby hills and said, 'About 25 kilometres.'"

Robinson also travelled to Turkey to meet with members of the oppressed Kurdish minority. Upon his return, Robinson condemned the sale of Canadian weaponry to Turkey and became an outspoken advocate of the Kurdish cause. In a 1999 incident that demonstrated not only the high esteem with which he was held in the Kurdish community, but also his commitment to peaceful protest, he was praised by the RCMP for his actions at a protest that had threatened to turn violent outside the Turkish Embassy in Ottawa. "Your prompt intervention with the Kurdish demonstrators and words denouncing senseless acts of violence had a calming effect on what was otherwise a very violent crowd. I praise you for your courage," wrote the officer in charge in a thank-you letter to Robinson.

Of course, Robinson continued to focus extraordinary attention on Burnaby. For years, Canadian firefighters had been lobbying the federal government for funding to create a computerized database of hazardous materials. At first the government argued that the new system would be too expensive and that the current system was satisfactory. In 1996, after lobbying bureaucrats and MPs, Robinson convinced the government to establish a test site for the database. Unsurprisingly, Burnaby was chosen as the location for that test site.

When the Liberals proposed a ban on imported unpasteurized cheeses that same year, Burnaby's sizeable Italian-Canadian community was upset. They went to Robinson, and he went to the Liberals. He convinced the government that the ban was unpopular with Italian-Canadian voters in Burnaby, and the decision was reversed. In his view, Liberal hopes of winning the riding in the next election gave him a leverage he could use on Burnaby's behalf. "To the extent that they were gunning for me, they had to be very aware of the impact of their decisions on the ground in key communities in Burnaby, and I milked that relentlessly," he says. It kept working, and in 1996 Robinson was voted the best local politician in a poll commissioned by the *Georgia Straight*.

His effectiveness was hard for opponents to dispute. However, it became commonplace in the 1990s for the media — the same media that had helped Robinson galvanize public opinion on so many issues in the past — to deride him as a shameless attention-seeker, a theatrical stuntman in love with seeing his name in print. "Accused by critics of being willing to attend 'opening of an envelope' so long as TV cameras are there. Would likely assail opener of envelope for infringing on envelope's inviolable right to remain sealed," wrote Scott Feschuk in the *Globe and Mail*, in an article entitled "Canada's Hungriest Publicity Hounds." Most attacks didn't have Feschuk's wit, but the message was the same: Robinson's stands against injustice could be dismissed because he was only motivated by publicity.

Those who knew him best suspected that he did enjoy the lime-light. Maybe all politicians do. Maybe Robinson did more than most — even in his later years in Parliament he still carefully saved newspaper clippings documenting his accomplishments. But whether he enjoyed having microphones thrust in his face under the glare of TV lights was fundamentally irrelevant; his use of the media was a calculated tactic and a major reason he was so effective. It was how the Galindo Madrid formula worked — injustice, dramatic action, media attention, result. "For an opposition MP to have influence requires publicity," University of Toronto political scientist David Rayside told the *Georgia Straight*. "To use the pub-licity-seeking angle as a criticism in and of itself misdiagnoses the political role." According to Ed Broadbent, MPs are not doing their jobs if they are not interested in media attention. "I would have liked many of my other MPs to have been as successful, frankly, as Svend was with the media. I don't fault him at all for that. Quite the contrary," Broadbent says. Furthermore, Robinson didn't have a gun to the head of journalists, forcing them to cover him. He sim-ply ensured that, in his efforts to draw attention to causes, he did things that were newsworthy. "Nowhere else that I worked did five reporters stand outside the office door waiting," recalls Sonja van Dieen, one of his assistants in his later years in Parliament. "When you're working with other people, you're begging them to cover you, whereas with Svend, they all just came." Robinson himself was unapologetic. "Of course I use the media!" he told *Vancouver Magazine*. "I mean, I can stand and speak for hours in Metrotown in Burnaby, but if I'm not speaking beyond the immediate crowd, then I'm not effective, right?"

There may have been a political purpose behind the ridicule. In the latter half of the 1990s, B.C.'s most influential papers had come to have a decidedly conservative bent. Both *The Province* and the *Vancouver Sun* were owned by Southam Inc. The majority owner of Southam Inc. was Hollinger Inc., the holding company that owned the *National Post*, which was also widely read in B.C. The majority shareholder of Hollinger was multi-millionaire and staunch conservative Conrad Black. These papers couldn't afford to ignore a major newsmaker like Robinson, but they often didn't like what he had to say. They had the power, however, to define his image as a self-interested publicity hound, whose opinions were amusing but should ultimately be discounted. Predictably, the Hollinger papers were among the cruellest in ridiculing him. "The right-wing press resents that I am getting my message out, which in many cases they diametrically disagree with. But I'm using their pages or their newscasts to do it, right? So the way they compensate for that is by snarkiness and publishing nasty commentaries," he said. Friends suggest it hurt more than he let on. "While Svend didn't show it, I suspect that in his own way he suffered from the criticism," McLaughlin says. "I think that he has a fragility that he doesn't show."

•   •   •

With the responsibility of being one of the last voices on the left in Parliament, and under the weight of persistent media criticism, Robinson continued to feel immense pressure. But every time he thought he was at the end of his rope, he'd receive either a desperate request for help or heartfelt encouragement to keep fighting. Those messages of support made a huge difference. "I was in constant turmoil, battles with my caucus colleagues. But if I had that external support and solidarity and respect, that helped to keep me going," he says. "Eventually it broke me. It took a while, but eventually it broke me."

That was yet to come. In the meantime, he forged ahead, often alone. He still didn't have the solace of a partner, who could give him strength or, perhaps, encourage him to slow down. He had had a few boyfriends, but he avoided long-term romances. One relationship was with journalist Laurier LaPierre. It was intense, passionate, turbulent — and short. "We had many happy times together. But, in the end, we both realized that our strong personalities and roving eyes meant that the relationship could not last," he says. He had many friends, but few intimate friendships. It is a trait commonly seen in people with an alcoholic parent. "They have no frame of reference for a healthy, intimate relationship because they have never seen one," wrote Janet Woititz in *Adult Children of Alcoholics*. "Not knowing what it is like to have a consistent, day-to-day, healthy, intimate relationship with another person makes building one very painful and complicated."

"I don't think he was depressed. I didn't get that sense. I think he might have been lonely," suggests Bill Siksay. "I don't think he saw clearly as an out gay man how relationships could work. I can see that if you're already in a very public job, like a member of Parliament, it would be even harder to figure that out."

Robinson couldn't imagine another person sharing his hectic existence, accompanying him to political events and putting up with the constant turbulence in his life. In his early 40s, he had given up on love. "But I ask myself, 'Is the price too high?'" he told *Maclean's* candidly in 1994. "Will I wake up 10 years from now and say, 'You fool. What about your humanity? What about love?'"

But it wasn't in his nature to slow down. If he did, it would leave an even larger void on the political left. Instead, he ran for the leadership of the NDP.

FOURTEEN

The Rainbow Coalition

The NDP was in a state of crisis. With the party hovering between 4 and 9 per cent in the polls, in April 1994 Audrey McLaughlin decided to step down as leader. "Without a dramatic reversal of fortune, the future of the New Democrats lies west of irrelevance and east of oblivion," proclaimed an editorial in the *Globe and Mail*, which went on to compare the leadership race sparked by McLaughlin's resignation to "blind men fighting over a pair of glasses." The *Ottawa Sun* said it had "all the excitement of a two-car funeral." Political cartoons depicted, for example, a dead horse and a whip, runners sprinting towards a cliff, and Robinson sitting in the crow's nest of a sinking ship.

Although the media seemed to delight in informing everyone just how much no one cared about the NDP, the party itself took the 1995 leadership race extremely seriously. It was a matter of survival. Choose incorrectly, and the party could lose its few remaining seats and become nothing more than a glorified debating society. "I mean, it's touch and go. The party may be over," former NDP MP Ian Waddell told the *Georgia Straight*.

However, nothing energizes the NDP grassroots like a lost cause. Thousands of volunteers across the country, who had toiled for years on impossible-to-win campaigns, rewarded only with the mocking tone of the mainstream media as it dismissed the causes they were most passionate about, were never going to let their party die. The central question they faced was not one of commitment, but tactics. To survive, the NDP had to choose between moving to the centre to attract disaffected Liberals, or moving to the left to attract the progressive activists outside the mainstream who had not yet found a political home. "That split, which has been part of the NDP landscape since its beginnings in the Co-operative Commonwealth Federation, is now practically the party's defining feature, its central doctrinal schism," wrote Mark Kingwell in *Saturday Night*.

For those who wanted to push the NDP to the left, the dream candidate was obvious. In a caucus of 43, Robinson had been imposing. In a caucus of nine, he was a giant. "Robinson would bring to the contest a proven track record as a winner, a wealth of parliamentary experience, a coherent set of principles, and a media profile that no NDP dollars could buy in the best of times," wrote Daniel Gawthrop in the *Georgia Straight*. Robinson gave all the right non-answers when reporters asked if he would run; no politicians ever want to look like they covet the leadership too much. But the vision he outlined next made it clear that he wanted the job.

"I think if the party moves to the mushy middle, we're doomed, and we deserve to be doomed," he told *Canadian Forum*. "Anyone who suggests we abandon that commitment to fundamental and profound socialist change by moving to the political centre is not only betraying the vision of the founders of this party, but is condemning this party to oblivion." He went on to describe what he called a "rainbow coalition" of minorities, gays, lesbians, students, seniors and the disabled, and activists from environmental, peace, women's rights and anti-poverty movements that could unite under the NDP. The party had become too obsessed with parliamentary debates and Question Period, Robinson said, and had lost touch with the social movements it purported to represent. "We have an opportunity to not just bathe in our own bath water," he added, as he explained how the NDP would connect with the grassroots year-round instead of just at election time. He also saw a greater role for Quebec in the future of the NDP. "We have some extraordinary opportunities in Quebec. Some people say I'm dreaming, but there's a very strong social democratic movement in Quebec, and there are many solid social democrats with the Bloc Québécois," he said. A second referendum on secession was planned for the fall, and the federalists were expected to win. Robinson hoped that if the separatists failed, the social democrats among them would turn their attention to issues championed by the NDP. "If the referendum is defeated, these people will be looking for a political home."

On April 27, 1995, Robinson launched his campaign. "The time has come for new politics: one that puts people before profits, principles before power, has respect for the environment, and promotes human rights in Canada and the world," he announced to over 100 cheering supporters in Burnaby. Backed by banners emblazoned with his slogan, "New politics," and the campaign hotline number, 1-800-95-SVEND, Robinson spoke with the authority of a seasoned parliamentarian and the fresh energy of a student radical. Long gone was the lanky, bespectacled nerd who was so mercilessly bullied as a child. In his place was a photogenic, athletic firebrand who looked equally comfortable debating in the House in a suit and tie, or in a plaid shirt with rolled-up sleeves, talking with supporters at a union meeting. His platform, "Economics for People and a Planet," told the sort of truths politicians are normally convinced Canadians cannot handle. The economy needed to function within the limits of the environment, and, contrary to our national myths, Canada was not doing its part to fight international poverty and starvation. "Our demand for constant and unequally-distributed growth is not only unfair, it is suicidal for us all," he wrote.

The campaign, managed by Bill Siksay, drew several high-profile endorsements, including Buzz Hargrove, president of the Canadian Auto Workers (CAW), one of Canada's largest unions; Judy Rebick, former head of the National Action Committee on the Status of Women; and David Suzuki. "Marginalized segments of society desperately need models to look up to for hope and inspiration.

Svend Robinson is one such person," stated Suzuki. "He stands up on issues as a matter of principle." Toronto city councillors Jack Layton and Olivia Chow were impressed by Robinson, too, and the couple joined the campaign team. Layton was put in charge of fundraising, and the Ontario campaign was launched in the living room of the home he and Chow shared.

Despite the enthusiastic support Robinson received from the left flank of the NDP, it was clear that the party establishment would prefer to be led by almost anyone else. They still saw him as a maverick who refused to play ball on tactical questions. "That was a serious deficiency," says Broadbent, who remained influential in the party, even though he was no longer an MP. "It wasn't a matter of intelligence, or capacity to work. It was his sense of solidarity that I think a leader has to intuitively feel and demonstrate before he or she runs for the leadership."

The affable Lorne Nystrom didn't have that deficiency. He had decades of experience in the House of Commons and projected a calm, prime ministerial image. If elected leader, he promised to focus on economic issues. "We have to deal with the deficit and debt. We have ceded that issue to the right. We can't do that and be credible," he said. "I don't see us reconnecting unless we come up with a substantive program focusing on two or three pocket-book issues of concern to ordinary people." Popular in the prairies, where support for the NDP was the strongest, the Saskatchewan-born Nystrom was a formidable candidate. As the leadership campaign progressed, he obtained more endorsements from NDP MPs and MLAs than the other candidates combined.

The other candidates — Vancouver writer Herschel Hardin and Nova Scotia NDP Leader Alexa McDonough — were not expected to be serious contenders. Hardin was an intellectual without any experience as an elected official. McDonough was supported by several heavy-hitters, including Ontario NDP Leader Bob Rae, former Ontario leader Stephen Lewis, and the United Steelworkers of America, but her campaign was being run with a single phone and a fax machine in a Winnipeg basement. Furthermore, the Nova Scotia NDP had never won more than three seats under her leadership. "No one seriously believes Alexa McDonough, a silver-spooned socialist from Nova Scotia, has a hope of victory. McDonough has simply failed to catch fire with rank and file social democrats who hold the future of the party in their hands," wrote Robert Fife of the *Ottawa Sun*.

Hoping to generate media interest and engage party membership, the NDP adopted a unique system for choosing the leader. In what was the first step by a federal political party towards a "one member, one vote" leadership race, the candidates first faced off in U.S.-style regional primaries, in which every card-carrying member of the NDP had a chance to vote. Then, any candidate who either won an individual primary or received 15 per cent of the total vote from all the primaries was put on the ballot for the traditional leadership convention. To be successful in the race, a candidate had to attract support from both rank-and-file New Democrats across the country, and the convention delegates elected by local riding associations.

To connect with voters, Robinson crossed the country by rail, dropping in on communities and picket lines along the way. He easily deflected concerns that his sexuality would work against him, pointing out the federal NDP's history in electing the first Jewish leader (David Lewis) and the first female leader (Audrey McLaughlin) in Canadian history. "New Democrats have never elected leaders based on the fears or prejudices of others," he said. His opponents repeated the old complaints about how he wasn't enough of a team player, and Industrial Wood and Allied Workers of Canada president Jack Munro said it would be "insanity" to elect the man who had stood against the logging unions in the Clayoquot Sound protests. Nevertheless, Robinson struck a chord with the rainbow coalition, and new members, particularly youth, flocked to his campaign. As the primaries approached, he felt good about his chances.

The first primary was Quebec, which Robinson won handily. He had the best French of all four candidates, and the highest profile in that province, where the NDP was still an afterthought at best. The next was a special primary for the labour movement, which would count for 25 per cent of the final total. Nystrom was expected to dominate, which he did, but Robinson came in second with a surprisingly high 32 per cent, thanks to support from the CAW. McDonough won the Atlantic, and Robinson placed second again. After he won the next two primaries, Ontario and B.C., he had a lead of nearly 20 per cent. Because Robinson, Nystrom and McDonough had each won an individual primary, they would all be on the convention ballot, regardless of who finished first over-all. However, convention delegates would be paying close atten-tion to the wishes of the grassroots and might feel duty-bound to vote for the winner of the primaries, especially if the winner had taken over 50 per cent of the primary vote.

As the candidates took part in the final primary — the prairies — the reality of the deep gulf in the NDP became inescapably clear. Robinson's mostly urban rainbow coalition, with its emphasis on social justice and international human rights, just didn't see eye-to-eye with the traditional, rural, prairie New Democrats, who were focused on farming and bread-and-butter economic issues. For Robinson, the drive through rural Saskatchewan in a doomed attempt to muster support for his vision was one of the loneliest car trips he had ever made. "I tried. I really tried. I looked really hard for common ground. I studied up on the family farm, and I knew more about Saskatchewan agriculture than most members of cau-cus, then or since, probably. So I looked really hard, but for many of them, the reality was that my brand of politics wasn't something that resonated," he recalls. "Overall, they were glad to see the back of me when I left." Because the prairies held almost as many NDP members as the other regions put together, Nystrom's massive win catapulted him into first place. After labour's 25 per cent was fac-tored in, Nystrom was declared the winner of the primaries with just under 45 per cent of the vote, followed by Robinson with 32 and McDonough with 18. Hardin, with less than 5 per cent and no victory in any of the regions, was eliminated.

Heading into the convention in Ottawa, Robinson's strategy was clear. If the delegates voted the way the rank-and-file party mem-bers did during the primaries, Nystrom and Robinson would finish

first and second on the first ballot. With McDonough then eliminated, her delegates would play a crucial role on the second ballot:
whoever they supported would end up becoming the next leader
of the NDP. According to polls, up to 80 per cent of McDonough's
delegates, many of them young and female, would support Robinson over Nystrom. The leadership was his to lose. During the
final speeches before the first ballot, Robinson maintained the cool
confidence of the frontrunner. He didn't attack his fellow candidates, instead describing his vision of environmental sustainabil-
ity, participatory democracy and fair taxes. He acknowledged that
a leader needed a greater commitment to caucus solidarity than an
individual MP and pledged to be a better team player. In closing,
he quoted Tennyson: "Come, my friends, 'tis not too late to seek a
newer world. For our purpose holds, to strive, to seek, to find, and
not to yield!" As his speech ended, the Ottawa Congress Centre
erupted with chants of "Svend-DP! Svend-DP!"

• • •

As McDonough's campaign manager, Judy Wasylycia-Leis, later
explained, the McDonough team came into the convention in a
much stronger position than people realized. Instead of focusing
on securing votes from rank-and-file members in the primaries,
they had focused on delegate selection and convention strategy.
Even in Robinson's next-door riding of New Westminster–Burnaby, for example, a majority of the delegates elected for the convention by the riding association were committed to McDonough.
Meanwhile, a number of Nystrom and McDonough supporters
had come to the same conclusion as Robinson's team: regardless of
who finished ahead on the first ballot, if McDonough came in last
and was eliminated, most of her delegates would support Robinson, and the dreaded maverick would win. While Nystrom circulated throughout the room, encouraging delegates to vote for him,
Bob Rae and other key McDonough supporters were spreading a
different message: a vote for Nystrom was a vote for Robinson.

Olivia Chow still won't say exactly how she found out that dozens of Nystrom delegates had followed Rae's logic and left the convention floor without voting. "I'm pretty good at hearing rumours," she says, smiling. But the ramifications were clear. Without those votes, Nystrom might finish third. If Nystrom was eliminated instead of McDonough, his centrist, prairie supporters were sure to support McDonough on the second ballot, and Robinson would be sunk. In order to keep McDonough in third, Chow suggested, Robinson would have to intentionally get some of his own delegates to vote for Nystrom to rebalance the equation. Robinson considered Chow one of his shrewdest political advisors and had learned to listen when she spoke. However, if this was how badly the establishment didn't want him as leader, he'd never truly be able to lead them. On that basis, he declined. The only thing to do was hope that McDonough's team hadn't swayed enough delegates to make it work. He returned to the bright lights of the convention floor, carefully returning the smile to his face.

Of course. I should have known they'd never let me get any farther than this.

Years later, he said that it felt like getting kicked in the gut. When the results of the first ballot were announced, a giant cheer went up from the McDonough camp. Robinson led with 655 votes, followed by McDonough with 566. Nystrom had garnered only 514, and he would be eliminated. Stunned, the veteran prairie politician waved to the crowd and began to move towards McDonough. When he announced his support for her, it was all but over.

Seeing only that their candidate was in the lead, Robinson's supporters were as ecstatic as McDonough's. Robinson cheered, too, raising his fist in the air like a warrior leading his charges into battle, but he knew that by the end of the night he would not be the leader of the NDP. Robinson, Siksay, Layton, Chow, advisor David Pepper and a handful of other key members of the team stepped out into the hallway. "I know I'm going to regret this for the rest of my life, but I'll leave you alone," said the CBC reporter who happened to be there. When the reporter was gone, Siksay reminded the team of a conversation they'd had prior to the convention. A lesson the team had learned from previous NDP leadership races was that the candidate from the left usually reached somewhere around 40 per cent support and then lost to a compromise candidate from the centre. "We talked about how supporters of those left candidates tended to get marginalized afterwards, and how the left had to build its way back up in the party again. We were talking about how to avoid that," Siksay recalls. "Somebody said, 'Why not stop that from happening by making a pitch for party unity? If it's clear that we aren't going to win, why not have Svend withdraw?'" The acrimonious 1989 leadership race between McLaughlin and Dave Barrett had left deep divisions within the party, and some members of the Robinson team saw withdrawing as a way to prevent that from happening again. It would be unprecedented in Canadian politics for a first-place candidate to withdraw and support the second-place candidate, but the idea had some merit. The winner would inherit a party that had suddenly become united, and the loser would appear magnanimous and, above all, a consummate team player.

In a decision that proved to be one of the few major political errors of his career, Robinson agreed. With his volunteers still valiantly pursuing Nystrom delegates, he made his way slowly across the convention floor. When he reached McDonough's table, she didn't seem to know how to react. She started to suggest that they wait to speak until after the second ballot, but Robinson cut her off. "Alexa, I'm telling you we don't have to wait for a final ballot," he said, amid a crush of reporters. "I'm here to support you. I want to pull this party together, and you've done a superb job. You'll be a great leader, and I'll be proud to work with you." With that, Robinson moved that the election of Alexa McDonough be made unanimous. Nystrom seconded the motion, and the former social worker from Nova Scotia, who had been written off from the start of the campaign, became the new leader of the NDP.

The prospect of McDonough as leader had always appealed to Robinson. In fact, Siksay suggests, had McDonough announced her candidacy first, Robinson might well have decided to campaign on her behalf instead of running himself. As a legislator in Nova Scotia, she had been a strong supporter of the gay and lesbian community. She had fought for same-sex spousal benefits, the inclusion of sexual orientation in the provincial human rights code and more funding for the fight against AIDS. Those accomplishments had earned her Robinson's respect. When McDonough decided to run, she called Robinson to inform him before launching her campaign. Their conversation was friendly, and Robinson told her he'd be happy to see either of them as leader. "He was always a fan of Alexa's," Siksay says.

After a long leadership race, Robinson saw withdrawing as a public olive branch, a sign that he supported McDonough and was sincerely eager to serve under her leadership. McDonough takes that rationale at face value. "I believe to this day that it was genuinely meant to be a unity gesture. I really do," she says. "I think Svend was being Svend, with all that was wonderful and sometimes outrageous about him." Nevertheless, what he planned as a noble gesture was woefully misinterpreted by some of the NDP establishment. So deep was their mistrust of Robinson that they saw his decision to withdraw from the race as an attempt to steal McDonough's thunder. It was a "manipulative ploy to snatch front page from the jaws of defeat," as the *Vancouver Sun*'s Peter O'Neil put it, describing the reaction of many New Democrats behind the scenes. Robinson had seen the writing on the wall, they guessed, and had only supported McDonough in an attempt to rebrand himself as a team player for a future leadership run. Dropping out left McDonough defending the legitimacy of her win — not what she expected she'd have to do on her first day as leader. "It denied Alexa a clean victory," explains former party advisor Jamey Heath. "That accomplishment should have been hers." Siksay and several other New Democrats with prominent roles on both sides maintain that McDonough misunderstood Robinson's intentions. "Alexa always saw that as Svend trying to screw up her moment, or steal her moment, when the reality was it was really an attempt to make a statement about party unity," he says. "So I think they got off on a bad foot from the beginning — from literally the first moment — of her leadership."

The verdict from Robinson's supporters was just as bad. "I know many of you feel a sense of anguish and betrayal," he told them in a speech following McDonough's victory. "I share that. But I plead with you, we must all come together in solidarity and unity," he said. However, many of his supporters still felt cheated. They had come to believe that Robinson would not compromise his vision by succumbing to brokerage-style politics, and they admired him for that. It was part of what made him different. Over the course of the campaign, they had worked long hours to get him elected because they were truly inspired by the clarity of his purpose and the force of his charisma. In a leadership race, it's easy to forget that everyone is fighting under the same banner. Many of Robinson's delegates had begun to feel less like New Democrats and more like a new political breed: Robinson New Democrats. On convention day itself, fuelled by adrenaline and emotion (and rarely food), they'd cheered and chanted until their voices were hoarse and their ears were ringing. They were willing to lose but wanted their immense investment of energy to be rewarded with the opportunity to keep voting for him until the bitter end. When he withdrew, they were bewildered and hurt.

During his concession speech, some of his former supporters threw down their "Svend!" pins in disgust. A few even booed. There was a fear that the young members he had recruited to the NDP during his leadership run would leave the party. "I was furious at him, like many people. We were livid that he'd dropped out," recalls Libby Davies, then working for the Hospital Employees' Union and volunteering on the campaign. Later they became close friends and frequent political allies, but at the time she wrote to Robinson to tell him how disillusioned she was. Many of his high-profile endorsers wondered why they hadn't been consulted before he made his decision. "Svend will, of course, have to defend this decision, and especially how it was made," Buzz Hargrove wrote in a letter to CAW members. Judy Rebick agreed. "The importance of process has always been Svend's weakness. He blew it in the end," she says. "I thought I'd never come to another NDP convention after that debacle." There was a genuine crisis of faith for many in the party. McDonough's two sons, both in their 20s, had been by their mother's side during the leadership campaign.

After her victory, instead of celebrating, they spent the evening trying to build bridges with Robinson's devastated supporters.

Robinson revealed how it felt to deliver that message of solidarity to his supporters in David Rayside's *On the Fringe: Gays and Lesbians in Politics*. "It was like an out-of-body experience, because I couldn't speak from the heart to those people," he said. "I had to do this thing about 'Let's rally around Alexa' and you know, that was important to do, important to say. But fundamentally I wasn't speaking from my heart to them. I was speaking to the media . . . The message that had to come out publicly was this message of solidarity and unity."

In the hours of interviews conducted with Robinson to prepare this biography, he is nearly always completely at ease. He munches a sandwich, combs his dogs or putters about, tidying his shed. As he describes the betrayal his supporters felt following his decision to drop out, he stops what he is doing and leans forward. His eyes widen. The relaxed, confident — sometimes almost distracted — air he has displayed through much of the interview process disappears, and he seems on the verge of confiding something deeply personal. Like many people, he is good at pointing out his faults in the abstract and joking about them, but he finds it more difficult to admit to an individual mistake. Nearly two decades after the fact, he is now willing to publicly admit that he made an error in judgment in 1995. "It was a mistake. It was absolutely the wrong decision not to go to a second ballot. I didn't honour and respect enough my own supporters at that convention. Even though the outcome was a foregone conclusion, they should have had the right to cast that ballot. And in my desire to build bridges and hopefully bring the party together, I didn't give that enough weight, and I deeply regret that," he says. "They saw in my actions that I was just doing politics the old way, and they really felt betrayed. It was devastating. It was. I felt terrible. And I absolutely wasn't expecting that."

It was the first time that Robinson had ever lost an election, but it wasn't losing that bothered him. "I wasn't devastated or crushed, because I ran on a very radical platform," he says. "The forces against me had to move heaven and earth to manipulate the convention in the most crass possible way in order to ultimately triumph." He was proud of the campaign he'd run, and proud that he'd brought new members to the party. What was most painful was seeing those new members drift away, feeling disillusioned and abandoned by the man who'd brought them in. "But losing? No. In fact, I knew that if I had won, I would have taken over a caucus that was actively opposed to me," he explains. "For the establishment in the party, I was the devil incarnate."

•   •   •

His friendship with Nystrom withstood the pressures of the leadership race, but rumours of McDonough's mistrust of Robinson's motives for supporting her never dissipated. "I think an echo of that permeated the whole caucus relationship between Svend and Alexa," says Davies, who joined them in caucus as the MP for Vancouver East in 1997. Robinson feels he never got the opportunity to become the better team player that he wanted to be after that leadership race. "Alexa didn't in any way reach out to me. Instead of taking advantage of that opportunity to build bridges, she just consolidated her position with her own circle and never reached out to me," he says. It wasn't up to him to reach out to her, he reasoned. In his view, he had already done so by withdrawing and supporting her. "But she just didn't take it. There was no change. So I remained the bad boy of caucus."

"The NDP will find itself where it was before they decided to replace Audrey McLaughlin: near the bottom of the public opinion polls and stuck with a leader who has neither the charisma nor the credibility to lead it out of the political wilderness," wrote the *Winnipeg Free Press*. "Ms. McDonough has a reputation in party circles for being brainy, but during the leadership campaign she did little more than mouth the usual platitudes about sharing and caring. At a time when New Democrats had to elect a leader who could help redefine what it means to be a New Democrat in the 1990s, they decided to elect someone who defines what it was to be a New Democrat in the 1970s or 80s." An editorial in Montreal's

La Presse had the headline "Alexa qui?" Others joked that at least McDonough could reuse Audrey McLaughlin's "AM for PM" campaign materials.

The party establishment rejected the candidate who had the most media savvy, who had the highest profile in Quebec (the province that would play a major role in giving the NDP Official Opposition status in 2011), and who had brought the most youth to the party. Robinson, in turn, alienated his own supporters with a fatal political miscalculation at the climax of the convention. The left flank of the NDP had to rebuild once again. But during the race, one particular member of Robinson's campaign team earned a respect that wouldn't quickly be forgotten. "Svend has the courage, the audacity and the creativity, and Jack had the ability to work with people, build relationships and be supportive, and you need both those things to be a good leader," Judy Rebick says. "If you could make Svend and Jack one person, that would be the perfect leader."

• • •

The moment of anger and remorse Robinson feels as he describes what happened in 1995 passes, and he resumes grooming his yelping dogs. Although the leadership race took place at a crucial juncture in the history of the NDP, when the very survival of the left seemed at stake, he reminds himself that it was all nearly 20 years ago, and he begins to laugh. "And that's politics!" he says, grinning. "With a vengeance!"

FIFTEEN

Falling

Svend and his partner, Max, are an exercise in contrast. Born in Las Tunas, Cuba, in 1972, Maximo Lazaro Riveron Dominguez enjoyed a childhood that bore little resemblance to the upbringing of the man he would one day love. He grew up in the suburb of Havana where, in Revolution Square, Fidel Castro made his speeches to the nation. The only child of two officers in the Cuban military, Max was enrolled in literary clubs and youth associations by his devoted parents. Despite being born only 13 years after the revolution, he had the stable childhood that Svend never had. "I had a good life," Max says. "I was spoiled rotten by my parents and the whole family." He spent his free time biking, target-shooting and fishing. "Going fishing — that was a thing I would do every weekend if I could," he says. "I would go to a dam close to where we lived, go into the water and spend the whole day there."

On August 19, 1994, his life changed forever. Almost 22 years old and a gifted student of language and literature at the University of Havana, Max was hired to interpret at a dinner being organized for a visiting Canadian–Cuban solidarity association. He prepared for his task the way he would for an exam: by studying the topics that were likely to be under discussion. He studied the guest list, too, and it was intimidating. The most prominent name was that of Svend

Robinson, a 15-year veteran of the Canadian House of Commons. After researching the Canadian MP's long and illustrious career, Max expected to meet a grizzled old man. When he met the trim 42-year-old politician, it was, in his own words, "love at first sight."

Svend felt that way, too. There were important officials from the Communist Party in attendance, but the guest of honour seemed to see no one but the interpreter. "He was very charming and very gracious and very beautiful," Robinson recalls, "so I invited him back to my hotel, and he said no!" They exchanged addresses and telephone numbers and parted. Over the next months they remained in contact, and when Svend returned to Havana for a World Solidarity Meeting that November, they met again. "That time I was more successful in persuading him to come and visit the hotel," he says. For the next year and a half they continued to communicate, and Svend took every possible opportunity to return to Havana. The loneliness he had felt during most of his adult life vanished, and he knew he'd met the love of his life. "I knew right away," he says. "I knew this was special. I knew this was the person I wanted to spend my life with."

They looked for a way to get Max to Canada and found one: he was accepted to an educational exchange program between the University of Havana and SFU, and on Canada Day, 1996, he left Cuba for the first time in his life. In his first week in Canada, Max was invited to accompany Svend to a local festival, and he was shocked to find himself sitting at the same table as B.C. Premier Glen Clark. "I was just this guy who had just arrived from Cuba, already sitting across from the premier!" he recalls, laughing at how quickly he had to adjust to the life of dating a political celebrity. "I was like, 'Oh my God. Am I allowed in here?'"

He fit right in. Voluble, cheerful and friendly, Max made friends easily. He was an immediate hit with the other parliamentary spouses in Ottawa. The seniors in Svend's neighbourhood in Burnaby loved him — Svend joked that they'd formed a fan club. As Max's exchange program drew to a close, he was asked to make a life-changing decision. "After I finished my program, I was going to go back to Cuba," Max says. "And then I remember Svend took me to a Greek restaurant on Broadway, and that's when we talked. He said he didn't want me to go back to Cuba. I never thought I would stay in Canada. He was my lover, but I never thought I was coming here forever." Part of what made the decision so difficult was that Max was frustrated by Svend's hectic schedule. "He was almost never there. He'd be coming for the weekend, and then leaving again. And then I'd go to I don't know how many political events with him on the weekend," he recalls. However, this was the first time Svend had shown how serious his feelings were, and Max agreed to stay. Canada accepted him as a landed immigrant under the provisions allowing the reunification of same-sex couples, which Svend himself had pushed the Mulroney government to institute. Max was expected to return to Cuba after his exchange; when he didn't, it meant he had left the country illegally. At the time, the Cuban government imposed harsh restrictions on which Cubans could leave the country, and for what length of time. But Svend harassed the Cuban bureaucracy with every diplomatic trick he knew, and Max was finally granted a rare multi-entry permit allowing him to come and go as he pleased. Comfortable in his new home, Max did graduate work in second-language education at SFU, and in 2000 he became a Canadian citizen.

The romance continued to flourish, and in each other, Svend and Max found a lover, a partner and a best friend. However, Max had to adjust to more differences in Canada than just busier shopping malls, newer computers and dinners with the premier. He also had to adjust to life with an out gay man. In Cuba, while there was no longer any legal restriction on homosexuality, there was still strong societal pressure to conform to a heterosexual lifestyle. Max had never told his parents that he was gay, but Svend had already lived that life of hiding who he really was, and he wasn't willing to return to it. If they were going to last as a couple and have the kind of relationship they hoped to have with Max's parents, Svend felt that Mami and Papi needed to know the truth. During their next visit to Havana, Svend told Max's mom about their relationship. She was shaken, but her love for her son overcame her unfamiliarity with homosexuality, and she accepted it. However, both she and Max insisted that Svend say nothing to Max's father. Of course, Svend was no better at following instructions in his personal life than he was in his political life, and as soon as they were alone together, Svend told Papi anyway. "But my Spanish wasn't very good, certainly not good enough to be able to communicate something so sensitive. I tried my best to explain it all to him, and he just nodded and smiled," Robinson recalls. "I knew he didn't really get it. Meanwhile, in the next room, Max and his mom were hyperventilating with outrage."

Max felt betrayed, but he knew it could have been much worse. He hoped that Svend would feel that he had been honest — without having caused any real damage — and would now leave the issue alone. But that night at dinner in a restaurant, Svend persisted. He kept pointing to people's wedding rings and then to himself and Max, trying to explain that marriage was similar to the relationship they had. "I had to hit him over the head with it," Robinson recalls. Eventually, Papi nodded, got up and left the table. He was gone for a long time. When he returned, he had tears in his eyes. He didn't say anything until the next morning, when he found Svend alone. "I've been thinking a lot about what you told me," Papi said in Spanish. "I understand that you love Papito. I don't really understand all of this, but I know that you love him, and for me that's very important. And I love you, too, and now I have two sons." They hugged, and Papi remained supportive of their relationship until he died. Max forgave Svend, and in the end was glad his parents knew he'd found love. But if his parents hadn't reacted with such acceptance, Max concedes that he would have been beyond furious with Svend. "He wouldn't be alive today!" he says, laughing.

An even more difficult adjustment for Max was learning to live with the hate mail that Svend received. Worse still were the death threats that sometimes accompanied the letters. "We would get messages under our door, and he would just ignore them," Max says. "The only times he would pay attention were when they were sent to his office, and his staff would force him to." Staff felt understandably threatened, and Svend was willing to placate them by calling the police. At home, he didn't care. "But I did care. That's why I always had cameras and alarms and everything else. And I always had an escape plan," Max says. "I always had one at home, of how to get out of there, how long it would take me and what to do. I had to think about those things. He wouldn't." Max agrees that Svend had a cavalier attitude towards his own safety. "All his life, he never cared about it," he says. "Some people value their life a lot, and others don't care. He just never cared about dying. He was never afraid. That's for sure. He's never been afraid of anything."

It is their differences that make Svend and Max such an extraordinary couple. While Svend has trouble turning on a television or using an Interac machine, Max is a computer expert who entertains himself for hours hooking up electronics. Like the skilled mechanics of his homeland, who keep 50-year-old classic cars running with boat engines, Max finds inventive ways to hook up antennas and get the best signals for their devices. Svend loves to kayak, hike and camp. To the extent that he ever takes time off to recharge, he prefers physical activity in the serenity of nature. Max, however, has no interest in roughing it; the camping trip he went on at age 13 in the Sierra Maestra mountains with a Cuban youth organization was his first and last. Svend is firmly atheist, while Max believes in a higher power and has been known to have premonitions. As already noted, Svend isn't safety-conscious but Max is, prompting a steady flow of jokes about speed limits, helmets and lifejackets. They tease each other constantly — what sometimes happens when two strong-willed, intelligent people meet and fall in love.

One might have expected that if Svend were to fall for a Cuban, he would be a revolutionary cut from the same cloth as Fidel Castro or Che Guevara. That's not Max. Surprisingly, he's on the centre-right of the political spectrum, a Red Tory in favour of liberal social policies but conservative economics. As such, he delights in making mild political jokes at Svend's expense. Sometimes Svend takes the bait; other times he doesn't. "I tolerate his conservatism, and he tolerates my radical leftism," Robinson says. "I've got no choice. That's the way it is. I'm not going to change him, and he's not going to change me. We live with it." Max's version is slightly different. "I love it!" he says. "I helped him move a bit towards me . . . he would have done crazier things!" When it's suggested that it wouldn't be possible for Svend to be any further to the left, Max laughs. "Oh, you have no idea!"

•   •   •

With Max in his life, Svend became part of a new family, and after a few years, he and Max became godparents to the daughter of one of Robinson's assistants. Coro Strandberg saw Svend and Max as the perfect role models for her daughter. But as Svend's new family grew, his family of origin continued to fall apart.

His oldest sister, Gretchen, had married, but her husband turned out to be an abusive alcoholic, and eventually they divorced. Unlike rabble-rousing Svend, Gretchen took a long time to feel comfortable sticking up for herself. Today, remarried, she is a friendly free spirit, an animal lover who rescues cats from shelters, a woman of faith. Far more overtly emotional than Svend, she feels that their differences have resulted in tension at certain points in their adult relationship. "He can be very businesslike, and sometimes I feel like he looks at me cross-eyed because our personalities are different," Gretchen says. "I still love him, though. I don't always agree with everything he's said and done, but he's still my brother." She moved to Seattle and now works as a retail demonstrator for Safeway. Her relationship with her brother is not intimate, but it is warm. For Svend, it is the sibling relationship that has been the least turbulent over the years.

Ingrid, the sister to whom Svend felt closest as a child, left home at 15 and turned to drugs and prostitution. "It was a hellish, hellish existence," Robinson recalls. Eventually, Ingrid came to her brother for help. Staff recall Svend devoting considerable time to her. Some felt she was taking advantage of him. He gave her a place to live and supported her financially until it became clear that all he was doing was funding her habit. Her son, Jason, wasn't receiving proper care. Concerned for his nephew's well-being, Svend called Child and Family Services, and Jason was sent to live with his father. Despite an increasingly difficult relationship with Ingrid, Svend played an active role in his nephew's life. "Truthfully, I always had a better relationship with Svend than I had with my own mother," Jason says. "Svend really cared about me. I can't remember a birthday that he didn't call or write." Jason recalls one birthday when Svend arrived at his house with a gift bag. "He said, 'Okay, Jason, I want you to be really careful. I want you to open this bag, because there's something inside.' And I can't remember if he shook it a little bit, but he made it look like there was something that was alive in there. And I opened it up, and it was a stuffed animal — I think it was a porcupine or something — and I thought it was alive!" Jason recalls. "We all had a good laugh. So there was a funny side about him, too."

When Jason was young, Svend used to take him on ski trips to Whistler. After one such trip, Svend learned that Ingrid was upset. Suddenly she had a problem with Jason's father allowing their son to be alone with Svend. The accusation implicit in Ingrid's anxiety — that Svend's homosexuality made him some sort of a threat to his nephew — was deeply hurtful. "My mom was known to be manipulative. She was known to lie. She was probably right in the middle of falling off the wagon as well," Jason explains. "Was she jealous of the relationship that we had, maybe? I don't know." Whatever the reason for the baseless and cruel innuendo, it prompted a bitter estrangement between her and Svend. Despite the extraordinary energy he had devoted to helping her fight her demons, Ingrid seemed determined to sabotage their relationship. She remarried and moved to Kelowna, where she continued to be overwhelmed by addiction. "She just lost it at that point," Jason says. "I lost contact with her. I kept writing her letters. I never received anything in return."

Svend's father, Wayne, had returned to Burnaby after several more years of wandering. Despite the hostility they still felt for each other, Svend took Wayne to The Pantry restaurant every weekend. He even bought him a summer home in Denmark, on the island of Bornholm where Wayne and Edith had met, when Wayne believed he was dying. "I just wanted to look after him. He was my father, right?" Robinson says. "There was not a lot of love or anything like that, but I thought that he deserved to be treated with dignity and respect." The uneasy equilibrium in their relationship was shattered when Svend introduced him to Max. Wayne might have been able to ignore his son's homosexuality when he was single, but he could not accept seeing Svend and Max together. Wayne informed Svend that he wouldn't allow Max in his home, and Svend responded that if the man he loved wasn't welcome, he didn't feel welcome either. Faced with that ultimatum, Wayne chose to sever his relationship with his son.

Svend lost contact with his youngest sister, too. Born 10 years later than Svend, Kim had missed the worst of Wayne's alcoholism and had a much better relationship with him than Svend and his other sisters had. "He was like a mentor, a best friend to her. Kim's role was very different from my role with Father, or Svend's," Gretchen says. In later years, Kim became Wayne's primary caregiver. Perhaps because of their close relationship, after Wayne cut Svend from his life, so did Kim. "She subscribed to the Svend-is-the-devil theory, so she didn't have any contact with me either," Robinson says. "Sadly, nothing has changed on that front." Svend periodically tried to re-establish contact with his father and sister, but when he did, they threatened to call the police.

It seemed that Svend's family had indeed fallen apart. His relationship with Gretchen was distant. Ingrid was a mess. Wayne and Kim seemed to loathe him. That might have been the last of Svend's contact with his family. However, Ingrid had strength that no one expected. It takes a superhuman effort to escape drug and alcohol addiction, but she did it. Jason understandably found it difficult to have his mother back in his life, fearing that she had come back only to abandon him again, but her recovery allowed her to mend her relationship with Svend. When she was diagnosed with multiple sclerosis (MS) in 2002, she had her brother for support. "He was certainly able to put a lot of things behind him with my mom," Jason says. "I know Svend fought for her. He fought for her to have a place in a home. He had her best interests in mind, and he had to forgive her for a lot of things."

She was still difficult to handle. Like Svend, she could be extremely demanding, causing constant headaches for the staff in her care home, whom Svend would then have to pacify. But he and Max visited regularly, and Ingrid and Max became friends. "She was so happy. I can still see her smiling that bad girl smile that she'd give me whenever she'd do something wrong," Max remembers. Ingrid died from MS in 2007. "She was a really special person. She did a lot of good in her life," Robinson says, referring to a period in which she worked at the first needle exchange in Vancouver's heroin-plagued Downtown Eastside. There she showed an activist streak and was an effective resource for addicts. After so much strife, Svend and Ingrid's relationship was excellent in the last few years of her life, just as it had been when they were children.

When Wayne died in 2008, Kim did not even inform her brother.

•　　　•　　　•

Svend's body hit the ground. The air rushed out of his chest as he slammed onto the stones at the bottom of the cliff. After that sickening, guttural grunt, the only sounds were the few loose stones that followed his body over the precipice and clattered down the rock face. Then, silence.

Two hours later, he began to moan. The sound cut the stillness of the cold, misty forest. At the bottom of the 18-metre cliff, he lifted his head and tried to think. It was too early to think. He tried to breathe instead. That worked better. The pain was excruciating, and it seemed to come from everywhere, but at least his head began to clear. He tried to get up, but the first movement of his right leg brought even more agony. With effort, he turned to look at his leg. It was covered in blood, but it didn't look as bad as it felt, and that was good. He hadn't seen the bone protruding from his torn ankle yet.

He turned to face forward again and saw the blood dripping from his face onto the rocks below. Too much blood. He seemed to have some pebbles or dirt in his mouth, so he tried to spit. He screamed in pain. They were bones inside his mouth — his jaw was shattered, and he would later learn he was missing eight teeth. By now totally lucid, Svend took stock of his situation. He wasn't suffering from amnesia, at least. He knew the date: December 31, 1997. He and Max had spent Christmas in Haida Gwaii and the last four days in the Gulf Islands. He had been hiking alone on Mount Sutil on Galiano Island, where he and Max had a cabin. That's where Max was, packing for their return to the mainland, and Svend was at the bottom of a cliff. He looked up and saw how far he'd fallen. He should be dead, but he wasn't. His arms, back and left leg were okay. He tried to move his right leg again and knew that would be the last time he'd try. He saw the bone sticking out of his ankle and slumped back down.

Next, he tried to call for help. Nothing. He wiped the blood from his watch and tried to angle it in order to catch the reflection of the sun. If anyone was looking for him, at least they'd have an idea of where to start. But he was cold, and losing blood fast. "I knew I had to get out of there to survive," Robinson recalls. He knew the area well and determined that his best chance for survival would be to make his way towards the beach, through the forest sloping away from the cliff. If he was where he thought he was, there would be a row of cabins about a half-kilometre of dense coastal rainforest away. If he wasn't, at least he'd be on the beach, where he'd be more visible to anyone looking for him.

Using a heavy stick to help prop himself up, he dragged himself through bushes, across jagged rocks and over the twisted roots of the arbutus trees and evergreens that seemed to stretch endlessly in all directions. He crawled through cold, winter mud until his hands were numb. He had to stop frequently to rest. He reached a giant tree stump with a mass of twisted roots, and his heart sank. It was too difficult to go over and too wide to go around. He thought he had just enough strength left to get to the beach, but not enough for this. The voice of doubt telling him he wasn't going to make it grew louder.

He tried not to listen. Using his good leg to brace himself, he heaved himself onto the roots of the stump. With another huge heave, he dragged his chest a little farther across. That was too far. The roots buckled, and his good leg fell through the rotted wood.

His leg was wedged in a hole, and no matter how hard he pulled, he couldn't get it out. He was now almost totally immobile.

I'm not going to survive this.

He had never feared death, so he faced it with acceptance. He had travelled the world and made a difference. He had suffered, and he had loved. If this was the end, he was ready. Exhausted, cold and weak from the loss of blood, he drifted in and out of consciousness. The forest was silent again.

Max!

The feeling was so powerful that it shot through his body like an electric current.

Never again. No more us, ever. Left totally alone.

The thought tore his heart from his chest.

"It did save my life. That's how strong it was," Robinson says. The image of his partner fuelled one last, immense heave, and he pulled himself out of the fallen log and continued to drag himself through the forest. Finally, he saw a cabin. It was the last house in the row on the waterfront.

· · ·

"The hospital was just flooded with flowers," Robinson remembers. "People were just amazing." He'd been airlifted to Vancouver General Hospital, and during his treatment he received hundreds of cards and bouquets from well-wishers across the country. There were far too many flowers for his room, so he had them distributed to other patients in the hospital. Visitors included Glen Clark, David Suzuki and new caucus colleague Libby Davies. Although he didn't hear a word from his father, he got a phone call from Brian Mulroney. With his jaw wired shut, he communicated with his guests using pen and paper. He wrote a standard note he could use to greet them: "The doctors have warned me I've been slowing recovery and increasing the risk of complications by talking way too much! (Are you surprised?)" Here Svend drew a happy face. "So — please understand. Talk to me as much as you like. I'll respond with nods etc. Feel truly blessed!"

"There he was, lying on the bed, totally wired up, broken — he looked just awful," says Jane Pepper, one of Svend's assistants. "I can remember going up and saying, 'Oh my God,' and shaking his hand, and him looking at me and asking, 'Are you okay?'" Pepper laughs as she recalls her battered boss inquiring after her well-being.

At night, Svend felt as if knives were sticking into his ankle from all sides. He had nightmares. The first jaw surgery was unsuccessful, and the jawbone had to be re-broken. The nurses put wire cutters beside his bed, because with his jaw wired shut there was a risk he might vomit and drown. He was heavily medicated. According to his official patient file, doctors were surprised that he had relatively normal sensation after what he'd been through. Svend recalls overhearing one doctor confirming what he'd already suspected: that he was lucky to be alive. Nevertheless, there was some cynical speculation in the media that he'd exaggerated his injuries and was remaining in hospital unnecessarily. Such accusations prompted a statement from hospital CEO Murray T. Martin. "This is an inaccurate and unfair perception about Mr. Robinson's condition and about the standards of practice at Vancouver Hospital," Martin stated. "None of the 37,000 in-patients annually cared for in our hospital stays a day longer than their condition justifies."

In fact, hospital staff were probably looking forward to the day he was healthy enough to leave. "Svend before the accident was difficult to work for. Svend after the accident was probably one of the most horrific times of our lives with him," says Pepper. Frustrated with the immobility and pain, he was more demanding than ever. His hospital bed became his office. His political judgment suddenly confused Bill Siksay. "Svend is a really hyperactive, really creative kind of guy. But Svend on drugs is really scary. And because Svend was always in charge of his political career, always in charge of what happened, and always the decision-maker, it was hard to know how to function in that period," Siksay says. "Initially we just tried to function normally, and it became clear that probably wasn't such a great idea, at least while he was in the hospital. He was prone to some flights of fancy." He recalls Svend having grandiose ideas for negotiating aboriginal land claims and engaging in advocacy on behalf of other patients in the hospital. It took a while for him to recover his sense of what could and couldn't be accomplished. "It was very difficult. It was hard on all of us. It was hard on the nursing staff. It was hard on the public relations people in the hospital," Siksay says. "It wasn't a pleasant time."

After two weeks, Svend was released from the hospital. He was given a wheelchair, which he would use for the next three months. Max, who had never learned to drive and had never cooked a meal in his life, was thrust into the role of caregiver. He helped Svend shower, dress and eat. Svend wasn't an easy patient at home, either. "He was terrible. Just terrible. He's a pain to take care of," Max says. "It was always his way, the way he wanted. He doesn't like to take directions. And he didn't want to feel weak, or that idea of having any disability. That was out of the question." It was understandably difficult for Svend to adjust to a life of dependence. So much of what was central to his identity had been taken away. He was a politician who could barely speak because of the wires still in his jaw. He was a hiker who couldn't move. The square-jawed, scarred face in the mirror didn't look like his. For the first time, people said he looked older than his age.

Svend's doctor encouraged him to seek counselling for post-traumatic stress and referred him to a psychiatrist. He visited once and never returned. "I just didn't have the sense that it would be particularly helpful to see him again," Robinson says. Instead of focusing on his recovery, Svend returned to the House for the first day of the winter session. When the Speaker acknowledged his presence, Svend was welcomed with the first and only standing ovation he would ever receive from his fellow parliamentarians. Speaking from his wheelchair, his speech distorted because of the wires in his jaw, he thanked Max and his doctors, and joked that an all-party delegation, led by Prime Minister Jean Chrétien and NDP Leader Alexa McDonough, had urged his surgeon to wire his jaw permanently shut. (In response, on Svend's birthday, Chrétien sent him a handwritten note in French saying that it wasn't true, and that without Svend "Parliament would be even more dull.")

Svend's sense of humour disguised an unwavering determination to show he remained a titan. "He was sending a message: I'm still alive. I'm getting stronger, and every day I feel better," Max says. He couldn't maintain his pace from before the fall, but he still worked between 60 and 70 hours a week. He added advocacy for the disabled to his list of causes and took CBC reporters on a tour of Parliament Hill, pointing out areas that were inaccessible to a person in a wheelchair. He flew back and forth between Ottawa and Burnaby every chance he got. Libby Davies, a constant source of support and friendship during this time, recalls Svend asking her to drive him to a meeting in Richmond, B.C. "I mean, he just about drove me mad. I drove him around in my little Honda, and he was demanding to go to the fisheries committee," she says. "He couldn't speak, because he was all wired up. He couldn't basically move. And he insisted — and I stupidly agreed — to drive him to the fisheries committee. I don't even think he was on the damn fisheries committee! And even on the way there, out to Richmond . . . he was convinced that I wasn't taking the right route, and that I needed to take a faster route. So here he is, in the front of my car, all wired up, trying to give me instructions about how I'm taking the wrong road in Richmond. I basically told him to fuck off."

Years later, some of his former assistants express regret that they didn't force him to focus on his health. Svend, too, acknowledges that he returned to work far too early. Now in his early 60s, he walks with a noticeable limp and still takes medication for the pain in his foot. As doctors had warned might happen, he developed osteoarthritis in his foot. (Not one to accept limitations, he still hikes and skis. He even returned to Mount Sutil. "I wanted to see if any of my teeth were still there!" he says, laughing.) The effect the trauma may have had on his mental health is difficult to gauge. He jokes about the fall and regularly brings it up in conversation, calling it "The Big F." When the subject is discussed in depth, though, he clearly finds it uncomfortable. If he was suffering from post-traumatic stress in the months after the fall, professional help might have been beneficial. The day he would be forced to take his mental and emotional health seriously was still years away.

Despite the trauma of his injuries, Svend managed to use the attention to achieve something positive. Max had never been paraded before the media the way some politicians put their families on display. *Xtra! West*, a popular gay and lesbian newspaper, had once approached Svend and Max in the hopes of doing an in-depth profile on their relationship, but they had refused. After the fall, Svend felt differently. "In this particular story — above all, of survival, of love, of hope — Max is at the absolute heart of it," he wrote in the journal he sometimes kept. He hoped that he could use the story of his fall to demonstrate that the love between homosexual partners was as real and as powerful as the love between heterosexual partners. When he greeted the media upon his release from the hospital and described his ordeal in the forest, Max was at his side. "I thought of people I am close to, people I loved, and I came to terms with that. I was ready to go," Robinson said. Then he gestured to Max. "And then, somehow, I thought of this guy here . . ." (Svend hadn't informed Max ahead of time that they would be doing a press conference together. Because he was pushing Svend's wheelchair, Max simply found himself present. But he took it in stride. "By that time, I was already used to anything coming from Svend," Max says.)

Svend didn't deny that he was using their relationship for political ends. "But I see that as politics in the best sense of politics. Over the years I've learned that some of the most powerful political statements are personal statements, and if you can put a human dimension on something that's otherwise abstract, you help to transform people's perceptions, and you educate people," Robinson told *Xtra! West*, which was finally allowed to publish a profile on him and Max. "If you look back over my life as a politician, you can point to some of those moments when I've tried to do that. This is one of those moments, unquestionably."

Just as introducing the lesbian mothers to members of the sub-committee on equality rights in Burnaby in 1985 had helped shape the MPs' views, Svend feels that sharing his love for Max with the public also had a positive impact. He gives the example of a man who had been leaving hateful messages on his constituency office voice mail for years. He remembers listening to his messages one morning and hearing the man's voice:

> Hey, Robinson. You know who this is. I've left a lot of messages for you over the past few years. I just want you to know — I can't change anything I've said — but from the bottom of my heart, I want to apologize to you. I feel so terrible about what I've done and what I've said. It wasn't until I saw you in that hospital with your friend beside you, and I heard you speaking, that I finally understood what an idiot I was. And I just want to apologize and let you know that I'll never, ever be calling your office again with that kind of message.

"I thought, if I had gotten through to him, how many other people in the country may have been moved by that?" Robinson says. He didn't pretend that he and Max had a white picket fence, a golden retriever and 2.5 kids. But by choosing to use his near-fatal fall to illustrate his love for his companion, he told a story that resonated in the heterosexual world. Love is love, after all.

SIXTEEN

The Exclusion of all Others

Partway through the 1997 election campaign, the Liberals claimed Robinson was running third in the new riding of Burnaby–Douglas. Their candidate, Mobina Jaffer, was a heavyweight behind the scenes in the party, and Jean Chrétien himself paid a visit to the riding during the campaign. But after nearly 20 years of delivering results for Burnaby, Robinson couldn't be dislodged by bravado and a glad-handing prime minister. On election day the veteran New Democrat prevailed with 43 per cent of the vote, and it was Jaffer who finished third. Meanwhile, led by Alexa McDonough, the NDP achieved a modest breakthrough in Atlantic Canada and regained official party status with 21 seats. The Reform Party made gains and solidified its status as the Liberals' chief threat, the PCs returned to respectability with 20 seats, and the Bloc Québécois remained the major power in Quebec. The divided opposition, and Chrétien's reputation as a generally competent public administrator, allowed the Liberals to hold on to a majority government. There were 10 openly gay candidates running in that election. "In every newspaper story, I was 'openly gay candidate' like it was my new first name," recalls Jamey Heath, who ran for the NDP in Ottawa Centre. He remembers Robinson calling him and offering moral support. But in Burnaby, for the first time since the Chicken

Book allegations, Robinson's sexuality played almost no role in the campaign.

Progress was slower in Parliament than in Burnaby. There may be no better example than the fight to legalize same-sex marriage. Robinson had been arguing in favour since the Mulroney years. He had prepared a bill, but it languished on the Order Paper, awaiting its turn for debate. Most MPs didn't want to touch the issue. Still, there was some public support for same-sex marriage, and that worried MPs in the socially conservative Reform Party. On June 8, 1999, Reform MP Eric Lowther proposed a motion stating that "marriage is and should remain the union of one man and one woman to the exclusion of all others," and insisting that Parliament "take all necessary steps to preserve that definition." The debate that followed featured arguments that supporters of same-sex marriage found difficult to take seriously. "Marriage provides a healthy biological design for procreation. Other types of relationships are technically incomplete," stated Lowther. Reform MP Monte Solberg went even further. "Homosexual couples, by the very definition of what that means, discriminate against heterosexuals," Solberg declared. Another Reform MP, Gurmant Grewal, told the House that the prohibition on same-sex marriage was an important consideration for immigrants who chose to come to Canada. "That was one of the reasons I came to Canada," Grewal said. In speech after speech, MPs recounted touching anecdotes of their own loving marriages, while at the same time denying that homosexuals should be entitled to marry. They seemed to fear that their most cherished institutions would come crashing down if they had to be shared with people who were different.

"The fact is that gay and lesbian people also enter into committed, loving, lifelong relationships. I have to ask the honourable member a question. How is it any threat to a heterosexual marriage to recognize and affirm our relationships as well?" Robinson asked Lowther. But the mathematical reality was that it didn't matter what Lowther or the other Reform MPs thought. Parliament was dominated by a Liberal majority, and they alone would decide the fate of the Reform motion endorsing the ban on same-sex marriage. "Let me clearly state that the Government of Canada will be supporting the motion in the House today. The fact that we will be supporting the motion should come as a surprise to no one," stated Justice Minister Anne McLellan, to Robinson's disappointment. "Let me state again, for the record, that the government has no intention of changing the definition of marriage or of legislating same-sex marriage."

In 2000, after the Ontario Court of Appeal and the Supreme Court ruled that same-sex relationships should be treated in the same manner as opposite-sex relationships in survivor pension and spousal support cases, the Liberals proposed legislation extending benefits such as the Canada Pension Plan to same-sex couples. To placate the religious right, they included a clause stating that the changes would not affect the definition of marriage. "For someone like Anne [McLellan], I don't think she had a problem with the gay marriage thing, but she had to deal with the members of caucus to get their support," explains former Liberal MP Bill Graham, a long-time supporter of same-sex marriage. When Robinson proposed an amendment to the benefits bill that would have legalized same-sex marriage, Graham was one of only seven Liberals to vote for it. "It was a funny thing, to be voting in favour of Svend's amendment against the government, I'll tell you," he says. "I did get a fair bit of shit from the whip, but it was worth it in the long run, because it was certainly the right side to be on."

Behind the scenes, Liberals like Graham and Hedy Fry lobbied their caucus colleagues in an attempt to change their party's stance. "It was a long, complicated and interesting period, and one where the legislation evolved, parliamentarians evolved, and Prime Minister Chrétien himself personally evolved, from not really being in favour of it," Graham says. "We had a huge caucus meeting and a big fight about it, in Sudbury, I think. He came out of caucus, and when he was asked by the press about the issue, he said, 'Well, it's a human right under the Charter. A Charter right is a Charter right.' But I don't think he would have said that 10 years earlier. So, we all evolved." In Graham's view, there were two types of opponents to same-sex marriage. Some MPs were opposed on religious grounds, while others feared a political backlash. "I would divide it into the ideologues and the pragmatists. Ultimately the pragmatists were brought around, and there was nothing you could do about the ideologues."

As the internal debate in the Liberal Party continued, Robinson proposed more bills legalizing same-sex marriage. During debate on one of his bills in 2001, Libby Davies became the first female MP in Canadian history to publicly affirm that she was in a same-sex relationship. "At the end of the day, it comes down to this: we either have equality in the country, or we do not. We cannot have half equality," Davies stated.

The Reform Party — rebranded as the Canadian Alliance and led by former Reform MP Stephen Harper — continued its opposition. In 2003 the Ontario Court of Appeal ruled that the ban on same-sex marriage was unconstitutional. In September of that year, in a final attempt to preserve the ban, Harper moved that "it is necessary, in light of public debate around recent court decisions, to reaffirm that marriage is and should remain the union of one man and one woman to the exclusion of all others." Harper's motion was supported by his own party and by most of the PCs. The Bloc Québécois and NDP were nearly unanimous in their opposition, but they were outnumbered by nearly 2 to 1. Once again, the Liberal majority would decide the fate of same-sex marriage. MPs like Robinson, Graham and Fry had made remarkable progress promoting their views, but a third of the Liberal caucus still supported Harper's motion. With over 50 Liberal MPs on Harper's side, the vote would be very close. When the Speaker announced the result, the House divided into victorious cheers and sighs of disgust. The motion had failed by five votes, and, for the first time, the House had affirmed its support for same-sex marriage.

After the law was officially changed in 2005, Robinson was asked to officiate at a wedding. Gurmant Grewal had warned that immigrants would shy away from a country where homosexuals could marry. The two men who stood before Robinson, hand in hand and deeply in love, were Hawaiians who could not marry under

American law. They were just one of many loving couples who would come to Canada in the next years, because here they could express their commitment to each other by marrying. For supporters of same-sex marriage, that is a source of abiding national pride.

•   •   •

Restored to official party status after the 1997 election, the NDP could once again make an impact. Back on the foreign affairs committee, Robinson resumed his role as one of the most effective critics of Canadian foreign policy. "His lawyer's background and his own intellectual clarity allowed him to ... ask questions in a way that he could get what he wanted to get very effectively," says Bill Graham, who chaired the committee and later became Minister of Foreign Affairs. "Svend was a flamboyant character in many ways, but it was flamboyance with a hard purpose behind it, and he was very tough. So, as a critic, he was a tough critic, but he was a fair critic."

Opponents often accused Robinson of being an incorrigible ideologue, but as foreign affairs critic he reacted to changing circumstances with flexibility, not rigid ideology. Typically, political pundits might have expected the NDP to oppose any use of military intervention without UN sanction. However, after reports that Serbs were massacring thousands of ethnic Albanians in the Yugoslavian province of Kosovo, Robinson supported the 1999 North Atlantic Treaty Organization (NATO) campaign against the Serbs. The UN had failed to prevent the massacre of Tutsis in Rwanda and had taken three years to intervene when the Serbs attacked Bosnia. With the body count rising in Kosovo, Robinson felt that the international community could not rely upon the UN for a swift response. "There are times when the global community must respond to serious human rights violations not just with words but with actions. I profoundly regret to say that we have now reached that point of humanitarian tragedy," he said. "We in the New Democratic Party accept that the use of military force as a last resort is sometimes necessary in grave humanitarian crises, when all efforts at diplomatic settlement have failed, and we believe this meets that test."

With the support of the NDP, Canada participated in the NATO bombing campaign against the Serbs. Robinson had set aside his intense aversion to the U.S.-dominated military alliance because, in this case, he believed its intervention was the only way to resolve the crisis. Nevertheless, he watched the situation carefully. It soon became clear that NATO bombs were only exacerbating the conflict, as Serbs accelerated their attacks on Albanians in retaliation. The NATO campaign had utterly failed to achieve its political purpose of intimidating the Serbs into submission. As a military operation, the campaign was horribly bungled as well. NATO failed to avoid civilian targets, bombing residential areas, the Chinese embassy, a television station and a passenger train. Hundreds of civilians were killed. According to a leaked document from the British Ministry of Defence, 60 per cent of the Royal Air Force's cluster bombs and 98 per cent of its unguided bombs missed their intended targets. A week after the bombing began, Robinson urged a return to negotiation. "There is no shame in ending a strategy that is not working," he said.

In May, as the bombs continued to fall, Robinson went to Kosovo. He was the only foreign politician to visit the war zone at the time. "I wanted to atone for the initial support for this campaign, that quite clearly was costing many innocent lives," he explains. Despite warnings from the Canadian Department of Foreign Affairs that it could not guarantee his safety, he accompanied journalists and Yugoslavian officials on a tour of the devastation. As he met with the Yugoslavian Foreign Minister in Belgrade, two NATO bombs exploded outside. In Pristina he stayed at the Grand Hotel, where, waiting in the lobby, he saw Russian mercenaries who told him they were there to kill Muslims. He visited refugee camps in Macedonia and heard horrific accounts of the ongoing attacks against Albanians. On the highway out of Belgrade, veering on and off the road to avoid the damage caused by the bombs, he passed a dozen destroyed villages and did not see a single person. "It really drove home to me the importance of strengthening the United Nations and never again allowing NATO to become the world police. What happened in Kosovo was terrible, but NATO's bombings did not make the situation any better," he said upon his return.

As a critic, Robinson was willing to admit a mistake and absorb the political cost of changing his position. More commonly he was a model of consistency, taking a principled position and trying to generate support for it. The Indonesian annexation of East Timor is one such example. Robinson became the founding Canadian member of Parliamentarians for East Timor in 1988 and steadfastly opposed the violence perpetrated on East Timorese civilians by Indonesian militants. Prior to the 1999 referendum on East Timor's independence, he travelled to the region and learned that East Timorese leaders feared a bloodbath would follow the vote. Hoping Canada could help prevent that violence, upon his return he called for the intervention of UN peacekeepers and an end to the sale of Canadian weapons to Indonesia.

As the East Timorese leaders had predicted, violence escalated after the vote. Canada's response, however, was to produce a press release congratulating the Indonesian government on the referendum. After a massacre in Dili, Foreign Affairs Minister Lloyd Axworthy was prodded into saying he was "deeply concerned." That cautious understatement provoked a scathing rebuke from East Timorese leader José Ramos-Horta. "Then he has the audacity to call on all parties to declare an immediate cease-fire. Cease-fire between whom? Between the children and women who are slaughtered in a churchyard and the Indonesian army?" Ramos-Horta said. Canada had over $6-billion in direct investment in Indonesia, and activists suspected that Canadian reluctance to criticize the Indonesian human rights record had something to do with that. Canada eventually played a leading role in getting the UN to authorize a peacekeeping mission to end the post-referendum violence, but Robinson felt that Axworthy had waited far too long. Robinson's early support, however, was not forgotten by the

East Timorese. In May 2012 he was presented with the country's highest honour — the Order of Timor-Leste — by Ramos-Horta, who had since become president of an independent East Timor.

In Robinson's view, Liberal foreign policy was driven by Canadian economic interests, while the human cost of our prosperity was often disregarded. Many Canadians saw the Summit of the Americas, held in Quebec City in April 2001, as an opportunity to challenge that approach. The Summit was one of the first significant free-trade conferences since the famed "Battle in Seattle." That clash between activists and police, which author Naomi Klein called the "coming-out party of a movement," shut down the World Trade Organization conference in Seattle in 1999. In anticipation of mass protests, Summit organizers in Quebec erected a four-kilometre-long, three-metre-high steel fence to separate the delegates from the protesters. Along with thousands of environmentalists and human rights activists who didn't trust that the assembled world leaders would put social needs ahead of private profits, Robinson and the entire NDP caucus gathered outside the fence as the Summit began.

• • •

"This is what democracy looks like!" sang the 20-something woman in the baggy wool sweater as she danced to the rhythm of her own chant. The crowd around her repeated the refrain. Amid the bongos and the carnival atmosphere, there was an unmistakable sense of purpose in the crowd. It wasn't rage that brought thousands to Quebec City, although a lot about what international power brokers had done in recent years was outrageous. Instead, it was optimism that fuelled the energy in the streets. Here were thousands of people who felt that the world could afford to be less violent and more generous. With Quebec City's narrow, winding streets so crammed with people that the neighbourhoods seemed like one living, breathing being, protesters felt empowered. If so many people wanted it, they had to be able to make a change. Clad in a black leather jacket with an orange NDP bandana around his neck, Robinson admired the crowd. It looked so much like the rainbow coalition he had envisioned during his leadership run in 1995.

A moment later came a harsh voice on a bullhorn, followed by the sting of tear gas.

• • •

While the rest of the NDP caucus stayed with the main body of protesters during the Summit, Robinson unsurprisingly gravitated towards the front lines, joining several hundred others who had gathered near a hole in the fence. A line of riot police quickly formed and ordered them to disperse. Since the protesters intended to be peaceful, they saw no reason to comply. Without further warning the police advanced, releasing tear gas and wielding batons. That left the protesters little choice. They could leave, or they could stay and be bludgeoned by police batons. Most chose to run, blindly and with tears streaming if they were among the unfortunates who'd been gassed. Hoping to get away before the plastic bullets were fired, Robinson turned to leave. As he did, he heard what sounded like a gun and felt a sharp pain in the back of his leg. He looked down and saw that his pants were torn and his leg was bleeding.

Some of the protesters at the Quebec Summit were indeed violent and destructive. Robinson felt that their tactics played into the hands of the corporate elite, allowing the media to focus on the kids-versus-cops blame game rather than on the substance of the protesters' concerns. When he saw so-called black bloc protesters throwing stones at police, he told them their tactics were counter-productive, but his warnings went unheeded. Robinson had no sympathy for such acts of destruction, which led to an uneasy relationship with some segments of the protest movement. However, it was clear that the police were making little distinction between the violent minority and the majority of the protesters who were peacefully exercising their democratic rights.

In the end, the brutal actions of the police officers assigned to the event are remembered more than the speeches of the demonstrators or the vague "Plan of Action" agreed to by the member states. Police fired over 900 plastic bullets and emptied over 5,000 canisters of tear gas, conducted indiscriminate mass arrests, and attacked peaceful protesters with batons. The Human Rights League of Quebec documented further cases of police brutality, and Amnesty International called for a public inquiry. One protester who was shot in the throat with a plastic bullet ended up with a crushed larynx. After that injury he could barely talk and had to breathe through a small hole in the steel pipe inserted in his throat.

Disgusted with the heavy-handed tactics of the police, Robinson later filed a grievance with the Commission for Public Complaints Against the RCMP. The report that followed the commission's investigation was damning. It concluded that the protesters gathered near the hole in the fence had posed no threat, and that the tear gas had been released unnecessarily and without adequate warning. The report also documented several other cases of police abuse. In one incident, a man lying on the ground as an act of peaceful protest was tasered. The commission saw video evidence of officers laughing as they used the laser sights on their guns to aim at a man's crotch. Other officers were caught on tape mocking protesters' English skills. According to the report, these incidents showed that certain members of the O Division tactical troop "abused their power and authority without justification" and that "the circumstances of each encounter could not have remotely called for such disgraceful conduct." In conclusion, the commission recommended disciplinary measures against several of the officers involved, and an apology to Robinson as a representative of the protesters. The RCMP refused to apologize, and Robinson filed a lawsuit. In 2004 they reached a settlement, and he received $10,000 (most of which went towards covering his legal costs) and an apology.

The police had clearly behaved inappropriately, but readers of the National Post were treated to a different version of events. In his press conference with Alexa McDonough following the Summit, Robinson explained why he was taking action against the RCMP, carefully pointing out that he was more concerned with the broader implications of the police crackdown on dissent than he was with his own personal well-being. "I don't want to exaggerate what happened to me, however. I was very fortunate that it wasn't more serious. I lost a pair of pants and I have a wound on my leg. But for that young [man] who was hit with a plastic bullet in the throat, the consequences were devastating," he said. Despite Robinson's comments, when the April 24, 2001, edition of the *National Post* appeared, the front-page article focused primarily on the damage to Robinson's pants. "Plastic bullet ruined my pants at Quebec Summit, NDP MP says," read the title. In a mocking tone, the story implied that Robinson was pursuing a petty crusade against the RCMP simply because his clothing had been torn. The article entreated readers to make contributions to the "New Pants for Svend" fund and provided the address of the *National Post*. Later editions featured updates on the pants campaign and irate, pants-related letters to the editor.

The New Pants for Svend campaign made Robinson an easy target for barbs from political opponents, even those who usually treated him with respect. When, during Question Period the day after the first pants article appeared, he asked Foreign Affairs Minister John Manley a question about the Armenian genocide, Manley's response didn't include a single word about Armenia. "Mr. Speaker, first I am very pleased to know that there is a fund being accumulated for the honourable member's trousers. I hope to contribute to it," Manley said. It was later reported that Manley sent $10 to the fund. Not to be outdone, Canadian Alliance MP Monte Solberg tried to amend the budget to include an extra $18 for pants repair. "I'm just looking for Mr. Robinson's pants in here. I can't find them," replied Bill Graham. "They may be nuclear, Mr. Chairman," offered Joe Clark. "Well, they're certainly radioactive," Graham replied. With his reputation in danger of being seriously damaged, Robinson sued the *National Post* for libel.

In an examination for discovery (a pre-trial process in which testimony is gathered), journalist Michael Higgins testified that he'd been instructed to rewrite Justine Hunter's story to focus on the pants, and to remove a reference Hunter had included to Robinson's leg being cut. Both Higgins and Hunter also acknowledged that the *National Post* fully realized that Robinson had only mentioned the pants as evidence of widespread police brutality. More than two years later, Robinson and the paper settled out of court, and the *National Post* finally issued what was something like an apology. "The need to replace Mr. Robinson's pants was raised only by the *National Post*," explained the short paragraph. "The *National Post* regrets any misunderstanding." As part of the settlement, the *National Post* also donated $15,000 to charity, including a donation to the Burnaby Hospital.

Robinson had faced unfair criticism in the media before, but the *National Post* seemed to have an ideological vendetta against him that bordered on fanatical. Prior to his trip to Kosovo, the *National Post* ran an article that portrayed his fact-finding mission as the ill-prepared, foolhardy jaunt of either a lunatic or an idiot. Taking pains to point out that Robinson didn't speak Serbian or own a cell phone, Christopher Michael wrote that he was "planning on purchasing a map," that "someone will probably interview him" and that he "plans to visit some buildings, apparently." This unprofessional journalism was repeated when Robinson visited Iraq in 2000. His mission was to investigate the effects of the ongoing bombings and economic sanctions, which had reportedly killed hundreds of thousands of Iraqi children since the end of the Gulf War. Upon his return, he condemned the bombings and sanctions, as well as the human rights atrocities still being committed by Iraqi dictator Saddam Hussein. In another mocking article, the *National Post*'s Alexander Rose wrote, "According to Svend, once upon a time pre-sanctions Iraq was a fairy kingdom . . . an NDP wonderland — just like Cuba! . . . strife beset this Paradise when America (always the Bad Guy in Svend's World, especially since it persists in interfering with his favourite dictatorships) forced the UN to impose sanctions."

Eventually Robinson, the supposed media hound, refused interview requests from the *National Post*. His office staff stopped using the *Post*'s articles for research. In their view, the *Post* had demonstrated that it simply wasn't a legitimate news source.

•　　•　　•

Despite such ridicule, Robinson continued to present his positions with a boldness and precision that almost no one else would. After the al-Qaeda terrorist attacks on the U.S. on September 11, 2001, the Western world responded with one voice. For the next several months, nearly every speech in the House of Commons seemed to include a variation of the phrase "standing shoulder to shoulder with our American friends and allies." It was clear that the attacks on the world's strongest and richest nation had provoked a systematic restructuring of how world powers interacted, with each other and with their populations at home. The U.S. attacked Afghanistan, and President George W. Bush tried to divide the world into allies and terrorists. It was a dichotomy that troubled many Canadian politicians, but in the emotionally charged atmosphere, criticism was muted at first. Despite the initial timidity of other politicians, Robinson immediately and boldly rejected the new doctrine. "President Bush said tonight to the people of America and the people of the world, 'Either you are with us, or you are with the terrorists.' I say no to the President of the United States. We are not with him as he embarks upon this path of unilateral, massive military assaults. We are certainly not with the terrorists. There is a third way which calls for respect for international law as we bring these perpetrators to justice," he said, a little over a week after September 11. "By what perverted logic can it be suggested that killing thousands of Afghanis who are fleeing from the terror of the Taliban will save any lives anywhere else in the world?"

The Liberals enacted anti-terrorism legislation and committed Canada to the invasion of Afghanistan. Robinson saw the Liberal reaction as a knee-jerk response designed to send a message of solidarity to the U.S., not as a principled approach to a complex international issue. In his view, the new legal definition of terrorism in the anti-terrorism bill went too far and would have prevented Canadians from assisting the African National Congress (ANC) in its struggle against apartheid in South Africa, for example, if the definition had existed at that time. The question of whether to oppose the bill at second reading, when the House votes on the principle of a bill before sending it to committee for detailed study and amendment, sparked a fierce debate in caucus. Some MPs thought that the party could support the bill in principle and seek amendments at a later stage, while Robinson felt the bill was bad enough that it should be rejected outright. Robinson recalls a heated exchange with Bill Blaikie, in which Blaikie dramatically threw down his pen, sending it skidding across the table. Nevertheless, the NDP was the only party to vote against the bill on principle at second reading, before being joined by the Bloc Québécois at third reading.

Canada's response to President Bush in the months after September 11 troubled human rights activists, who feared that under the new world order, basic civil liberties would be eroded in the guise of rooting out terrorists. Robinson was the first parliamentarian to raise the issue of Omar Khadr, a child soldier and Canadian citizen being held without trial in the U.S. military prison in Guantanamo Bay after allegedly killing a U.S. soldier in a battle in Afghanistan. Robinson called it a "blatant violation of international law," but Canada stood by and let Khadr languish in Guantanamo Bay for a decade, until he was the last Western citizen in the military prison who had not been brought home by his government.

Speaking in the House, Robinson passionately condemned the Liberal policies. He also tried to return attention to the issues which, after September 11, seemed to have no further relevance to his fellow legislators. "September 11 was a day of unbelievable tragedy and anguish, as we saw over 6,000 people die in the crimes against humanity involved in the terrorist attacks on New York, on Washington and in Pennsylvania," Robinson said. "As well, September 11 was a day on which 30,000 children around this planet died of preventable disease and hunger. UNICEF has reminded us that each and every day on this planet 30,000 children die of preventable disease and hunger — on September 11, on September 12, on September 13 and on every single day since then. There is no CNN, no publicity, but there is death, despair, famine and hopelessness."

Returning that perspective to the debate earned Robinson admiration from Canadians who felt that the response to the attacks of September 11 had been both dangerous and disproportionate. When he applied that same fearless use of language to the conflict between Israelis and Palestinians, he provoked another of the great controversies of his career. In the spring of 2002, the Israeli army entered the Jenin refugee camp in the West Bank. Later accounts of the conflict put the number of dead at 52 Palestinians and 23 Israelis, but at the time it was reported that hundreds of Palestinian civilians might have been killed. "It looks as if an earthquake has hit the heart of the refugee camp here. There's a stench of decaying corpses all over the place," reported UN Special Envoy Terje Roed-Larsen, who called for an investigation into Israeli actions. Other UN officials made similar comments. "The world is watching, and Israel needs to end this pitiless assault on civilian refugees," stated Peter Hansen, Commissioner-General of the UN Relief and Works Agency for Palestine Refugees.

As foreign affairs critic, Robinson supported a two-state solution to the decades-old conflict, an end to suicide bombings targeting Israeli civilians, and Israel's withdrawal from lands seized from Palestinians in the 1967 Arab-Israeli War. After the incident in Jenin, he conducted a fact-finding mission, spending most of his time in Tel Aviv, where he met with Israeli peace activists. He also tried to meet with members of the Israeli government, although his requests were denied. Another important element of his mission (and the only part reported by the media) was an attempt to visit Palestinian Authority President Yasser Arafat, who was under siege by the Israeli army in his compound in Ramallah. Robinson knew he had little chance of meeting Arafat, but he hoped that by trying he could draw attention to the Israeli occupation of Palestinian lands. "Of course, this was all symbolic. I knew I'd either be stopped or shot, and wasn't sure which," he says. Wearing a blue bullet-proof vest, he approached the checkpoint on the road to Ramallah. Israeli soldiers told him to turn around. He replied that they were guarding land over which they had no authority, and he continued down the road. After a shoving match, he was dragged back, shaken but unharmed.

Robinson held a press conference in Jerusalem. In his description of the Israeli occupation of Palestinian territories, he stated that the Israeli military was guilty of torture and murder. When most Canadian politicians address the conflict, they usually devote equal time to condemning the occupation of Palestinian lands and the suicide bombings carried out by Palestinian terrorists. Robinson was already on record condemning such acts of terrorism. But when he didn't mention suicide bombings in his press conference, media asked if he had taken sides in the conflict. "I plead guilty, yes. I am taking sides. I am taking the side of peace over war, I am taking the side of the oppressed over the oppressor, I am taking the side of life over death, and I am taking the side of justice over tyranny," he replied.

Robinson's comments were similar to remarks from other political commentators at the time. NDP Leader Alexa McDonough condemned the actions of the Israeli military, referring to "state terrorism." Several prominent Jewish observers used similar language. "The Palestinians have been under a military occupation for 35 years. It has been harsh and brutal and violent throughout — racist, humiliating, destructive," said Noam Chomsky. "There's been Palestinian terrorism all the way through. I have always opposed it. I oppose it now. But it's very small compared to the U.S.-backed Israeli terrorism." British Labour MP Gerald Kaufman called Israeli Prime Minister Ariel Sharon a "war criminal" and suggested that his actions were "staining the Star of David with blood."

Nevertheless, reaction to Robinson's comments was furious. Many supporters of Israel felt that his choice of words, and the fact that he had tried to visit Arafat, had demonstrated an imbalance. Both the Canadian Jewish Congress and the Canada-Israel Committee called for him to be fired as foreign affairs critic. "Accusations of mass murder, genocide and all of those blood-libelous statements simply weren't true, and for a member of Parliament to participate in any way, shape or form — by giving credence to that kind of a lie — was very unnerving for us," says Frank Dimant, executive vice-president of B'nai Brith Canada. Angry calls flooded Robinson's office as well as McDonough's. "I got screamed at for weeks," says Sonja van Dieen, then working for McDonough. "I could have had a nervous breakdown over the Palestine trip. It was just vicious and relentless. My voicemail inbox would fill up while I was listening to the messages." Bob Rae, former premier of Ontario, publicly announced he was permanently dissociating himself from the NDP, in part because of Robinson's actions. "If Svend Robinson's foray had been a solitary event, it might have been possible to brush it off as yet another escapade from a histrionic crank. But he is the foreign affairs critic of the New Democratic Party," Rae wrote.

In an effort to contain the damage, McDonough released a statement. "My caucus has condemned terror wherever it has occurred, and we will continue to do so. For us, there is no justification that allows suicide bombers to target innocent civilians, nor do we support the Israeli military response in the occupied territories," it stated. "Canadians need to be free to express their views without fear of being branded as supporting one people over another." However, the controversy didn't abate. In caucus, Robinson was lambasted by colleagues for two hours. While some were completely supportive of his actions, most were terrified that the NDP had lost its credibility as an unbiased observer of Middle East issues and demanded that McDonough fire him as foreign affairs critic.

Privately, Toronto city councillor Jack Layton was supportive of Robinson's actions. "Watched, worried but in TOTAL support as you attempted to reach Arafat's compound," Layton wrote in an email to Robinson. "When will international peacekeeping extend to all rogues? Love, Jack." Libby Davies also defended him vociferously. "I never understood why people were so frigging angry. It was such an overreaction. Was it because it was Svend, or was it because it was the Middle East, or both?" she says. She met privately with McDonough and argued against calls to discipline Robinson.

"Her response was that she had to do something, that the pressure was so great," Davies recalls.

McDonough informed Robinson that she felt she had no choice but to remove him as critic. He was furious. He'd informed her in advance that he would be going to the Middle East. The language he'd used had been similar to language she'd used herself. He was incredibly proud of what he'd achieved as foreign affairs critic and believed that he had espoused a principled and just position on the Middle East. If there was a public outcry against such a stance, he thought a true leader would weather the storm. When it appeared that McDonough wouldn't, he fought back. "I told her that I wouldn't accept that, and that if she fired me as foreign affairs critic, she'd have a battle on her hands," he recalls. However, he also understood the political reality McDonough faced, and he proposed an alternative. Instead of demoting him completely, she could remove responsibility for Middle East issues from his portfolio and become the NDP spokesperson on the Middle East herself. McDonough agreed, and on April 18, 2002, Robinson's partial demotion was announced.

That didn't mean he would keep his mouth shut. In fact, he deliberately sought opportunities to speak out. He spoke at the University of Toronto, at UBC and at a fundraiser for Jews for a Just Peace. Palestinian and Jewish Unity held a dinner in Montreal in his honour. In May he attended a conference in Iraq. There, in the presence of Iraq's Deputy Prime Minister Tariq Aziz, Robinson delivered a scathing condemnation of the Iraqi government's attitude towards the conflict in the Middle East, calling upon Hussein to respect Israel's right to exist within secure, pre-1967 borders and "to stop glorifying the suicide bombers who take the lives of innocent Israeli citizens, both Arab and Jew . . . nothing, I repeat nothing, can justify the mass murder of innocent people who are out at a discotheque, or a restaurant or celebrating a religious holiday." He also pressured McDonough to use more forceful language to describe the conflict.

In Montreal, Concordia University's administration had banned public discussion of Middle East issues after a visit from former

Israeli prime minister Benjamin Netanyahu in 2002 provoked violent scuffles between students. When the Concordia Students' Union defied the ban and invited Robinson, Davies and author Judy Rebick to speak at the university on Middle East issues, the three enthusiastically accepted. Robinson felt that a university was the last place where political debate should be stifled and was happy to participate. The university obtained a court injunction to stop them. Robinson appeared in court to argue against the injunction but was unsuccessful. Undaunted, students hauled a cafeteria table outside and set up a makeshift stage on a sidewalk just off campus, and Robinson, Davies and Rebick addressed the crowd of hundreds with a bullhorn.

Unfortunately, actions like these led a small segment of the public to question Robinson's feelings towards Jews. In the caucus meeting following his trip to the Middle East, some colleagues had accused him of anti-Semitism, and on several occasions over the next months he had that label hurled at him by passers-by in the streets. Many of the people who left furious messages on the voicemail in his office said the same thing. In the fall of 2002, the Jewish Community Centre in Vancouver held an exhibition for painter Jeannie Kamins. The exhibition included portraits of subjects Kamins felt embodied both integrity and controversy. Among them was a portrait of Robinson, which she believed to be one of her best works. After complaints from patrons, the portrait was removed. "I think Kamins showed a total lack of sensitivity by exhibiting that piece, because Svend has proven by his actions and words that he's an enemy of Israel. How would you like it if she painted a portrait of Hitler and showed it there, at the JCC, calling it free expression?" a member of the Vancouver Jewish community told the *Jewish and Israel News*.

Accusations of anti-Semitism were extremely hurtful. Robinson had fought for the rights of Jews on many occasions in his career, including fighting to bring Nazi war criminals to justice in Canada, arguing for changes in divorce legislation to assist Jewish women in obtaining gets from their husbands, and working to help Jews emigrate from the Soviet Union and Syria, where they faced oppression. Furthermore, he had been raised on stories of the heroic Danish resistance to the Nazi occupation, and on the role his own family had played in helping Jews escape the Holocaust. "I deeply regret that some people have suggested that my position and that of my party is in some way motivated by anti-Semitism, does not recognize the pain and anguish of Israeli families who have lost loved ones to suicide bombers, or does not recognize the right of Israel to exist within secure and recognized borders. Nothing could be further from the truth. Indeed, it is painful to me personally to hear these allegations. I have fought anti-Semitism and all forms of discrimination all my life and will continue to do so. Clearly, one can be very critical of the policies of the Israeli government — as I am and indeed many Jews are — without being anti-Semitic," he said. More than the nasty tone of *National Post* articles or the homophobic slurs of political opponents, it was the label of "anti-Semite" that wounded him the most. "It was the most offensive of all the accusations that were levelled against me, on so many different levels," he says, still visibly upset as he recalls what people said.

The label angers his Jewish friends as well. Long-time friend Clayton Ruby strongly disagrees with his analysis of the Middle East conflict. However, when asked about Robinson's feelings towards Jews, Ruby responds gruffly and directly. "Only an idiot would think he's anti-Semitic. He's not," he says. Rebick also bristles at the question. "That's ridiculous and a slander. It's because he stands up for Palestinian rights. Svend is a fighter for human rights, one of the fiercest I've ever known, and that includes Jewish rights. It's a load of crap. Does that put it to rest?" she says. Although they were often political opponents, Frank Dimant of B'nai Brith personally liked Robinson and is dismayed that Robinson was accused of anti-Semitism. "I would never consider him to be anti-Semitic. While we vehemently disagreed with his Middle East views, certainly that is a far cry, in his case, from being anti-Semitic," Dimant says. "I don't think he merited that kind of a response from anybody."

Robinson has no regrets about how he handled the issue. In his view, he had no obligation to refer to suicide bombings in his condemnation of the Israeli occupation. "We didn't make a similar argument with respect to apartheid in South Africa, that whenever we were critical of the racist regime in South Africa, we also had to be equally critical of the ANC," he says. "Overwhelmingly, the issue at that point was the aggression of the Israeli government, in bombing in Jenin and their massive violations of human rights at that time, so it would have been quite inappropriate for me to suggest there was some moral equivalence. I was on record, and I've always been on record, as condemning suicide bombings and targeting civilians. I didn't have to demonstrate my bona fides on that issue." He feels that the anger directed towards him was inevitable once he decided to challenge the Israeli military, and that there was nothing he could have said afterward to assuage that fury. "It wouldn't have made the slightest difference, no," he says. "If I'd uttered the ritual incantation of condemning the suicide bombings as well, do you think people would have said, 'Oh well, that's okay, that was a good balance'? Absolutely not. Out of the question."

Robinson's opponents in the media and on Parliament Hill hoped the public felt that Robinson had crossed the line from being dramatic and fearless to being over-the-top and biased, and would be more likely to dismiss him in the future. When he nominated International Solidarity Movement, a group of peace activists in Palestine, for a Nobel Peace Prize in 2003, the response from certain Jewish groups showed they hoped people now put little stock in Robinson's analysis. "Svend Robinson should not be taken seriously. He is someone who seeks to grab the headlines by doing and saying outrageous things. He's trying to grab the support of Arab Canadians by appearing to promote this group, where any fair-minded, clear-thinking person who understands the situation of the conflict in Israel would never recommend this group for a Nobel Prize. It's an outrageous statement by someone who has proven to be irrelevant to the Canadian political scene," stated Canadian Jewish Congress president Keith Landy.

But what some saw as hyperbole, others saw as pinpoint accuracy. In addressing the situation in the Middle East, Robinson had said what he believed to be true, regardless of how the social and political machinery in Canada might react. It was the same uncompromising approach he always used as foreign affairs critic. If he often came across as dire in his analyses of foreign issues, it was because he thought the situations were dire. He didn't provide a feel-good appraisal of the roles of Canada and Canada's international allies, because in his view there were many things we shouldn't have felt good about. According to Davies, that principled approach has been missing in the years since Robinson's departure from politics. "Some people are concerned that we'll slide, especially on foreign affairs. He was an outstanding voice on foreign affairs when he was critic for so many years. He never shied away from things," she says. "People wanted it. They wanted a party that actually had a real, critical position on foreign affairs — that wasn't the *Time* magazine version . . . and that's, I fear, what we've come around more to now."

SEVENTEEN

Robinson versus God, Round Two

"How do you define any close friendship?" Robinson asks rhetorically. He considers his warm relationship with Libby Davies, the MP whose name was most often associated with his during the latter half of his career. "We share a lot of values in common, we enjoy one another's company, and we've been through a lot of struggles together. Those are things that tend to bind a friendship." Neither can remember when they first met, although Robinson recalls being impressed with her work as a Vancouver city councillor in the 1980s and 1990s. One year younger than him, the British-born Davies developed a reputation as a tireless community activist in Vancouver's poverty-stricken Downtown Eastside and served on council for five straight terms. With Robinson's encouragement, she ran for the NDP in Vancouver East in 1997. She won, and became the MP in the riding next door to Robinson's.

"To me, he was very much a mentor," Davies says. "He worked so hard in the riding, he understood his riding, he was always there for people — to me, that was very much a role that I wanted to follow." As a rookie MP, she watched him in the House, too. She was impressed not only with his skill as a debater, but also with his ability to set aside rhetoric and work constructively across party lines. She recalls him darting back and forth across the aisle in the House, consulting with procedural clerks and with members of other parties. "He was so genuine in his work, and I believe this now today. Everything he did. It wasn't just about political antics or positioning. He really was trying to accomplish things," she says. Behind the scenes, in caucus, Davies usually found herself allied with Robinson. Often she would be the only one. "We had this way of communicating about what was taking place. We were so instantly on the same wavelength," she says. "We're both the same sign — Pisces — and we're meant to be very empathetic," she adds, laughing. Their synchronicity remains today. "I can read him. I know what he's thinking, with just a glance. And it's the same for him."

Where they differed most significantly was in how they related to caucus colleagues. "Svend was more aggressive," Davies says. "I think I had a better sense of when the point had been made. He's relentless." Her ability to co-operate with caucus served her well, but it couldn't bring Robinson into the fold, and he remained an outsider. In fact, during Alexa McDonough's leadership, his relationship with the NDP establishment hit a new low.

Although McDonough feels that her relationship with Robinson was unaffected by the 1995 leadership race, several other MPs and prominent insiders insist that she began to mistrust him after that contest. Robinson, in turn, developed major reservations about McDonough's leadership as early as the 1997 election. He didn't feel connected to the campaign war-room and sensed that when his opinion was solicited by McDonough's inner circle, it was too late to make a difference. His attitude on those occasions probably didn't help. For example, his criticism of the NDP's promise to eliminate the deficit was undiplomatic, to say the least. "I disagree fundamentally and profoundly with the approach on the deficit. We cannot balance the federal budget by 1999/2000, and it is dishonest and stupid for us to say we can," he wrote in a confidential letter to the platform committee. He also complained bitterly about being left out of the strategic planning. "This is an impossible process," he wrote. "What difference this will make, God only knows. Probably as much as my earlier memos."

It turned out that the veteran MP and his leader had very different visions for the NDP. In August 1998, caucus embarked on a five-day retreat to discuss the future of the party, riding the rails from Robinson's Vancouver to McDonough's Halifax. Perhaps the direction the train took was prophetic of the NDP's new direction: after the retreat, McDonough made an announcement that demonstrated a dramatic departure from Robinson's vision for the party. The NDP would be pursuing a more business-friendly approach, part of a concerted effort to court left-leaning Liberal voters in order to finally form a government. Perhaps most indicative of the shift in priorities was the party's proposal regarding budget surpluses. Finance Minister Paul Martin had eliminated the deficit in the 1998 budget, and the NDP now suggested that the government spend one third of the projected surplus on tax cuts, one third on debt reduction, and the final third on restoring funding the Liberals had cut from health and social programs. By contrast, the Liberals themselves were promising to be more generous; they had hinted they might spend half the surplus on reversing their cuts.

"The caucus moved so far to the right that their train almost fell off the tracks," wrote Richard Cleroux in the *Ottawa Sun*. The new NDP worried Stephen Harper, who had left Parliament to become president of the National Citizens Coalition. In Harper's view, the votes of mainstream Canadians were divided between the right-leaning Liberal government and the decidedly right-wing PC and Reform parties, while the NDP was perceived as an unelectable extreme. If the NDP presented itself as a more moderate option, that might result in Canada's first left-wing government. "There is a very real possibility, if the Liberals steer on the right of centre, and the traditional right stumbles along, that eventually there could be a national left-of-centre government," Harper warned in the *National Post*.

For very different reasons, the left flank of the NDP was also distressed by what caucus was proposing. In the left's view, the interests of the business community were already well-served by the other parties. If there was a void for a political party to fill, it was standing up for equality and the environment, not standing up for the economic elite. Shortly after McDonough's announcement, the Provincial Council of the Ontario NDP passed a motion indicating its serious concerns with the party's new direction. Buzz Hargrove, president of the Canadian Auto Workers, mused about permanently cutting ties with the NDP. Predictably, Robinson was also vocal in his opposition. "The idea that somehow business needs another strong voice in Parliament is one that I question," he stated publicly.

Resolutions passed at the 1999 convention ended up placing the NDP somewhere between its traditional spot on the political spectrum and the new centre-left position espoused by McDonough. In the meantime, the debate sparked by the five-day retreat didn't help resolve the tension between McDonough and Robinson. In addition to disagreeing with a move towards the political centre, Robinson felt that caucus was directionless, disorganized and lacking in team spirit. Privately he told his staff he thought the NDP would be lucky to win 18 seats under McDonough's leadership in the next election (in fact, they held on to only 13 in the 2000 election). His staff suggested he try harder to build bridges with her, but he felt that would be fruitless. In his view, he had already reached out to her in the leadership race by publicly supporting her. Now he felt it was her turn to extend an olive branch by giving him a more prominent voice in the direction of the party. He began to wonder if his time on Parliament Hill was running out, and he considered options like working for a non-governmental organization or running for mayor of Vancouver. At the same time, some of his behaviour frustrated caucus colleagues. They felt he was shirking his duties in the House in favour of grassroots work. They complained that he wasn't giving them advance notice when he was about to dissent from a caucus position. A few felt he was undermining McDonough and taking every opportunity to remind people that he would have made a better leader than her. His relationship with Ed Broadbent had been rocky, but his relationship with McDonough was even worse. "It wasn't like he was constantly berating Ed as he was with Alexa. He was always challenging her," says Bill Blaikie.

There is a pause when Davies is asked if she thinks Robinson was actively trying to undermine McDonough. "No," she says finally. "I think he was pushing all the boundaries he could. He was not satisfied by her leadership, in terms of where he thought we should be taking stronger positions, particularly on foreign affairs. I think he pushed her really hard, but he wasn't the only one. I do not believe that he did it to undermine her." In Davies's view, however, many of the other men in caucus did tend to undermine McDonough. "It was awful for her, not because of any one thing, but because of the kind of cumulative impact of how, no matter what she did, it wasn't right, and it wasn't good enough," Davies says. "I believe it's a very gendered thing. If women are seen as too strong or too aggressive, then they're seen as strident. Have you ever heard of a man being called strident? Never. But if they are seen trying to build a consensus — which Jack always did, and that was seen as a strength — in women it is often seen as a weakness." According to Davies, McDonough still perceived Robinson as a threat. Fairly or unfairly, he came to personify the other pressures she experienced as leader. "I always got the sense that he felt kind of bewildered or perplexed about why they couldn't find a common space," Davies says. McDonough is willing to entertain such a hypothesis, although she says she wouldn't necessarily have put it that way herself. "I have to say, Libby Davies is one of my favourite people on earth, and she is more insightful than 99 per cent of the human race. I think that's a very interesting comment," she says.

• • •

When Robinson presented a petition calling on the government to remove the reference to God in the Constitution, the ensuing controversy clearly demonstrated the shortcomings in the working relationship between McDonough and her senior B.C. MP.

In Parliament, MPs present petitions from concerned citizens as often as the snow falls in a Canadian February. In the portion of the day known as "Routine Proceedings," presenting petitions is perhaps the most routine proceeding of them all. In June 1999 the Humanist Association of Canada approached Robinson with a petition signed by about a thousand Canadians who felt that the reference to God in the Constitution was inappropriate in a secular society. Without hesitation he agreed to present the petition to the House. Although he didn't agree with the exact wording of the petition and didn't sign it himself, he was already on record opposing the reference to God in the Constitution, having spoken against it in committee in 1981. Furthermore, as an elected representative, he saw it as his role to present the views of Canadians to the House, regardless of his own personal opinions. For example, he had presented petitions from constituents demanding the recriminalization of abortion. He would never have voted for such a proposal, but he believed that those constituents had the right to be heard. It was part of the promise he often made during election campaigns: he would always present his constituents' views to the House, but he would reserve the right to vote according to his conscience.

On June 8, Robinson presented the Humanists' petition to the House. In accordance with the parliamentary procedures governing the presentation of petitions, he presented it succinctly, without stating his opinion. Next he presented a petition demanding the return of Canadian troops from Yugoslavia. He sat down, and other members continued to present petitions without incident.

"All hell broke loose in caucus the next day," he recalls. Some media reported that Robinson had said "God is offensive to millions of Canadians," which he hadn't. MPs were sent petitions demanding that the reference to God remain. Another round of vicious hate mail, by now mainly e-mails, began filling Robinson's inbox. The Alberta-based Concerned Christian Coalition vowed to defeat him in the next election. However, the strongest opposition came from within caucus. With the exception of Davies and a few others, most of his NDP colleagues were enraged. "This is the most ill-advised thing I have ever seen a politician do," said Pat Martin. Nelson Riis agreed, stating, "It's worse than poor judgement.

I think it's absolutely stupid." When McDonough convened an emergency caucus meeting, many of the MPs demanded that Robinson be fired from his critic portfolios. "Others probably would have been happy to see me drawn and quartered," he recalls.

Under pressure, McDonough felt she had to act. She rose in the House and affirmed that the NDP supported the reference to God in the Constitution. "New Democrats stand together in supporting this clear statement of our most fundamental belief, expressed across the country in a wonderful variety of faiths," she said. To punish Robinson, she had his seat in the House moved to the back bench. "He was advancing a position that was immensely controversial and rejected by the party," McDonough stated. "He did not advise me beforehand, he did not advise his caucus colleagues or the party, and that's precisely why he is being reprimanded."

Robinson's former assistants are still incensed as they recall seeing their boss sitting in the back row, next to the drab orange curtains separating the House from the doors to the opposition lobby. "It was a petition! It was a bloody petition! Talk about being blown out of context. I've always had trouble with this one. He was presenting a petition. That's his job. He's an MP," says Jane Pepper. "The caucus saying they were blindsided by that? What petitions do you inform your colleagues that you're going to be presenting?" Bill Siksay, a theologian by training, was even more upset. As a Christian, he felt strongly that any implication that a human construct like the Constitution had divine endorsement was blasphemous, akin to taking the Lord's name in vain. McDonough's announcement that the supremacy of God was the most fundamental belief of the NDP was appalling to him. "I was just outraged. I mean, that's not why I joined the NDP. I've never seen that anywhere. I thought I'd joined the NDP because of something about economic justice, redistribution of income, that kind of stuff, not the supremacy of God. I cancelled my monthly donation to the party. I felt like I had to do something," he says.

Robinson doesn't believe that his punishment had anything to do with a breakdown in communication prior to presenting the petition. He had little reason to advise his colleagues that he had agreed to present the petition; it wasn't standard practice, and furthermore, he had been on record opposing the reference to God for nearly 20 years. Moreover, not only had he not signed the petition, he hadn't alerted the media (although the Humanists had) and had declined to speak at the rally the Humanists were organizing. "This was not about rational argument. Caucus was terrified of the political implications of this. They thought that this would hurt them politically," he says. In caving in to the pressure to punish him, he feels that McDonough demonstrated inexcusable weakness. "It was a very, very sorry spectacle, and it was caucus at its worst. Caucus as lynch mob."

Many of his colleagues wished that Robinson had taken a quieter, more indirect approach. For example, when MPs are uncomfortable with the subject matter of petitions, they sometimes table them through the "back door" by submitting them to the Clerk of the House, rather than presenting them in the Chamber. This allows a petition to be duly filed with the House without drawing attention to it, but Robinson saw that as a cowardly way to represent constituents' concerns. "Svend was fearless. Sometimes what was a little bit difficult was that his judgment was off, in terms of what the public could cope with. The God thing was like that," McDonough says. "People express their religious beliefs, or their non-religious beliefs or whatever they want to express, and we have freedom of religion in our society. If you can't express your freedom of religious thought in Parliament, that's a bloody big problem. But it was sort of an ill-considered gesture . . . sometimes you need to be a little more nuanced."

After being sent to the back bench, Robinson wrote a furious letter to party headquarters. "Alexa and the federal caucus have made a major political blunder in their totally inept handling of this matter. I have been unfairly and maliciously maligned by some of my caucus colleagues in this shabby affair," he wrote. He pointed out the irony of the fact that, on the same day he presented the petition, three NDP MPs voted in favour of the Reform motion opposing same-sex marriage. "This was a blatant violation of clear party policy, adopted in 1993, calling for equality for gay and lesbian relationships in all areas of federal jurisdiction. Where was Alexa's firm discipline and public humiliation of caucus colleagues then?" he asked. Most of all, he criticized the underlying political fear he saw in McDonough's decision, fear which called into question the NDP's commitment to defend the interests of minorities. "I am appalled by the reference in Alexa's press release to New Democrats 'standing together with the majority of Canadians' on this issue, and referring to a 'small group of Canadians' who seek this change to the Constitution. Is this now to be the basis for our response as a caucus to fundamental human rights and minority rights issues? . . . This is the true political stupidity."

Robinson had done everything in good faith and had still been punished. Even the *National Post* failed to see McDonough's rationale. "By caving in and punishing the atheists' momentary ambassador, Ms. McDonough proved [the atheists] right. Religious Canadians petition the House a dozen times a week, as well they should, for this or that policy based on their beliefs; non-religious Canadians who want to do the same will never find another MP to deliver their message," wrote Paul Wells. "Quite a trick, coming from the leader of a party that claims to care most about minorities." McDonough had made a serious error in judgment. In the end, so did Robinson. After sending his strongly worded letter to the party, he leaked it to the press. "I was just so angry at what had happened, and I wanted people to know what my position was," he says.

McDonough downplays the significance of the petition and of Robinson's 2002 trip to Palestine, the other conflict most often cited as evidence of their poor working relationship. "Those are two incidents of probably about 10,000 that Svend and I shared. Do you know any human beings in life generally, never mind political life, that have 100 per cent approval for everything they've ever done? That's not bad if you can only think of two! You can probably even dredge up a couple of others where he made my life miserable, but I'd have to work at dredging them up," she says. "How could someone be that bigger-than-life, and that driven to affect the future of the world, and not have a bit of turbulence along the way?"

• • •

Poor results in the 2000 election prompted another period of soul-searching for the NDP. With the opposition parties looking weak, Chrétien had called a surprise election, even though he still had a year and a half left in his mandate. The NDP won just 13 seats, barely clinging to official party status. Robinson himself was re-elected by a 4.3 per cent margin, his narrowest since 1979. The Official Opposition Reform Party had rebranded as the Canadian Alliance, and its new leader was Stockwell Day, a former cabinet minister in Alberta. Several reports about Day lead some Canadians to fear that the Alliance harboured a far-right, Christian-fundamentalist agenda. It was reported that Day refused to campaign on Sundays, and that he believed that the world was only 6,000 years old and early man had co-existed with the dinosaurs. That drove some centre-left voters who might have been considering voting NDP to the Liberals, believing they were best placed to keep the Alliance from taking power. It was a phenomenon the NDP campaign was unable to prevent, and the Chrétien Liberals increased their majority. McDonough had focused her campaign almost exclusively on health care, a strategy Robinson (the environmentalist, human rights advocate and constant multi-tasker) saw as ineffective. "I found it incredibly frustrating that the campaign focused so overwhelmingly on this issue," he wrote to McDonough after the election. "Why were the caucus's clear concerns in [other] areas, voiced so strongly before the election, totally ignored?" There was a wide range of activist communities in Canada that shared NDP values, but the campaign hadn't resonated with them. Instead of voting for the NDP, they tended to vote for the Liberals or for fringe parties, or were so disgusted with the political system that they didn't vote at all. Prior to the election, thousands of those activists travelled to Seattle and helped shut down the World Trade Organization conference. "Those kids protesting in Seattle are our people," lamented Robinson. "We're not connecting with them."

The idea that the NDP needed to do a better job of connecting with like-minded social movements wasn't new. When Robinson proposed his rainbow coalition in 1995, it was already a familiar concept. After the disappointing 2000 election, the idea was embraced with renewed urgency. Economist Jim Stanford and Judy Rebick held a meeting in Toronto with a number of energetic young activists, including influential author Naomi Klein. What began as a modest website and a statement of principles about participatory democracy became the New Politics Initiative (NPI), a movement of progressives from inside and outside the NDP dedicated to renewing social democracy in Canada. In the NPI vision, the NDP would disband, and anti-globalization protesters and other grassroots organizations would help form the basis of a new party, one they hoped would engage in political action year-round and be more democratically run than the NDP had been. Although the Green Party issued a statement urging its members not to participate, many activist groups were energized by the proposal. "Politics is too important to be left only to politicians," the NPI website declared.

Robinson joined Stanford, Rebick and Libby Davies on the coordinating committee. His support was based primarily on the belief that this new political entity would be more dedicated to environmentalism and socialism than the NDP had been. However, according to Davies, McDonough thought that Robinson was really using the NPI as a stepping-stone to the leadership. "She was very upset with Svend, and she wasn't so much with me," Davies says. "She seemed to have the sense that what he was doing was that he was up to no good, and what I was doing — although she didn't like it — she didn't feel that it was attacking her or her leadership. She said this to me directly, that she saw our motivations as different things," she says. Publicly McDonough stated that she welcomed the debate, but she made it clear where she stood. "I think it's fundamentally flawed to think one can build a solid electoral social democratic force based just on its connections with social movements," she said. "I think for a variety of reasons, quite understandable reasons, many advocacy and activist groups remain non-aligned in partisan terms. Some of those reasons are associated with their funding sources or with their wanting to be pan-partisan in their efforts," she explained.

At the 2001 party convention in Winnipeg, Robinson gave a speech touting the NPI vision. In his speech, he criticized the traditional approach of the NDP for too often veering toward the political centre. "His speech at the convention was what actually prompted me to get up and give a 'speech of your lifetime' to save the party," Bill Blaikie recalls. "We were constantly by ourselves on issues. All by ourselves — against the Liberals, Reform and the Bloc, to varying degrees — on almost everything. And then he gets up and says we are in the mushy middle. Well, where's the mushy middle? On this, we were alone. On that, we were alone. So where's this coming from?" In response to Robinson, Blaikie gave a stirring speech that may have tipped the balance against the NPI. In the end, most New Democrats preferred to reform the NDP rather than disband it, and Robinson's motion endorsing the principles of the NPI was rejected 684–401. Still, attaining such a high level of support for such a radical idea was a victory in itself. "It was pretty amazing. I was completely astonished by it," says Rebick.

About six months later, McDonough announced her resignation. "In the interests of the party, it's time to move ahead with revitalization. I am confident a new leader can take us to the next level. One of the characteristics of good leadership is knowing when to step aside," she said. The first candidate to declare he was running to replace her was Blaikie. A veteran of 23 years in Parliament, the dignified Manitoba MP immediately garnered the support of nearly every MP in caucus. Naturally pundits wondered if Robinson would run, too. "It's a huge decision. I've got to get a sense of where I'm going, but I have to, of course, consult with my constituents, my party and my partner," he said. In fact, the person he really wanted to talk to was Jack Layton. For the past several years, the Toronto city councillor had been considering an eventual run for the leadership of the NDP. In Toronto, he had successfully promoted curbside recycling, bike lanes and alternative energy sources, and had spearheaded a partnership that retrofitted 467 buildings, cutting 132,000 tons of air pollution a year, while saving $19-million in costs. He was an expert on homelessness, and a founder and co-chair of the White Ribbon Campaign of men against violence against women. Like Robinson, he understood the media and used it to his advantage. He was telegenic and warm, and spoke fluent, colloquial French. He didn't have a seat in the House, but even that wasn't a liability. Known as the "Energizer Bunny" for his seemingly boundless energy when it came to activist causes, Layton would be able to use his time outside the House to engage with social movements and build the bridges the NPI had envisioned for the party.

"We talked it through, and it was clear to me that Jack was the stronger candidate, that he had the potential to build the party," Robinson recalls of his conversation with Layton. "There wasn't a lot of debate or discussion around the issue. To me, it was pretty clear. We had this exciting opportunity to elect a dynamic new leader, and I would do whatever I could to support him." On July 22, 2002, Layton announced his candidacy. Four days later, Robinson and Davies announced that they were endorsing him. They were the only caucus members to do so. In retrospect, it seems surprising — almost inconceivable — that none of the other MPs in caucus saw what Robinson and Davies saw, given the broad-based support Layton would one day earn.

Although their support might have made some New Democrats wary of Layton (the *Globe and Mail* called it "death by endorsement"), it was nevertheless essential. "It gave Jack some credibility in the left," recalls Olivia Chow, Layton's partner. "Svend's endorsement signaled to the activists, especially out on the west coast, that this guy from Toronto had some history." Other NPI supporters also got behind Layton. "Everybody in the NPI was sure that Jack represented what we stood for. Everybody just abandoned ship and began working for the NDP leadership [campaign]," Rebick says. Meanwhile, Layton also secured the support of key players in the party establishment. Most notably, he was endorsed by former leader Ed Broadbent, who had been fervently opposed to the NPI proposal and regularly at loggerheads with Robinson. It was an early demonstration of the capacity to build bridges that became an integral part of Layton's legacy. With support from across the NDP spectrum, and an energetic campaign that signed up thousands of new members, Layton easily defeated Blaikie and the four other candidates vying for the leadership. On January 24, 2003, the man who would come to be nicknamed "Smilin' Jack" ("le bon Jack" in Quebec) took the reins of the NDP, and the party has not been the same since.

Robinson offered to resign his seat to allow Layton to run in a Burnaby–Douglas by-election, but Layton preferred to wait until the next federal election when he could run in Toronto. Layton was an effective leader even without a seat; because he didn't need to be in the House, he could be first in line to greet the reporters swarming in the House foyer waiting for Question Period to end. Under Layton, the caucus united. "I think the party, on all fronts, made a concerted effort to bury the hatchet," says Jamey Heath, the NDP's director of research and communications at the time. Layton gave prominent positions to his former leadership rivals and named Robinson health critic. It wasn't the assignment he wanted. For years he had wanted to be House Leader, the position tasked with navigating the party through the procedural intrigues in the House. With his years of experience as a parliamentarian, and now with a friend as leader, he felt sure he'd be given the job. Although the health portfolio disappointed him, he accepted it and worked diligently. "Svend can be fairly said to have gone out of his way to be quite conciliatory, and caucus did not have the sort of knock-'em-down, drag-'em-out fights. Svend gets some points for being a team player," Heath says.

At the time, public consciousness was dominated by the prospect of war with Iraq, as U.S. President George W. Bush desperately sought international allies to join a planned invasion. The Canadian Alliance, now led by Stephen Harper, who had replaced Stockwell Day, urged Canada to join the Americans. The NDP was fiercely opposed. For months the Liberals refused to say what Canada would do in the event of war. Robinson could have done what some detractors expected him to do: steal the spotlight from Alexa

McDonough, who had been named foreign affairs critic after stepping down as leader. But he didn't. He spoke passionately against the war but kept his focus on health care and let McDonough lead the charge on foreign affairs. "Because Svend supported Jack's campaign, I think he saw himself as part of the team, as opposed to — to some extent — on the outside looking in," Heath says. "That's not to say that Jack and Svend didn't have some conversations. But they were conversations in private, and that did not lead to some of the public instances that were seen in the past."

With Layton at the helm, Robinson was more optimistic about the future of his party than he had ever been. At first glance, such a conclusion seems counter-intuitive. Layton's charisma was undeniable, but the right-wing grip on North American politics seemed unshakeable. Despite the invasion of Iraq, economic difficulties and a gaffe-prone presidency, Republican George W. Bush was still massively popular with roughly half of the U.S. electorate and would win a second term in 2004. The Liberals were set to replace Prime Minister Jean Chrétien with Paul Martin, the popoular right-leaning former finance minister who had presided over the budget cuts of the early 1990s. What worried New Democrats most were the ongoing negotiations between the PCs and the Canadian Alliance. The venerable party of John A. Macdonald was on the verge of being swallowed up by the Canadian Alliance, whose leader made no secret of where he saw himself on the political spectrum. "I would just say to the honourable member [Robinson] that I have known him a long time, and we have a lot to disagree on. I do not know if there are any two members in the House who probably disagree on more items," Harper said to Robinson during one exchange in the House, after Harper had made what Robinson interpreted as a veiled homophobic remark.

Nevertheless, all these factors could leave a lot of room on the left, and Robinson sensed that the NDP was on the verge of a breakthrough. "In my political bones, I feel that something quite profound could be happening in this country," he told staff a few months after Layton's election as party leader.

•   •   •

Although the work had begun years earlier, it was during Layton's leadership that Robinson achieved one of his greatest victories as a legislator. After Stephen Harper's motion to preserve the ban on same-sex marriage was defeated, supportive MPs congratulated Robinson. Liberal Hedy Fry gave him an affectionate hug. After his years of advocacy, Robinson was acknowledged as one of the leaders of the same-sex marriage movement, but it was never his top priority. "There were many other issues touching the lives of gay and lesbian, bisexual and transgendered people that were more important," he says. "In terms of the lives, and the day-to-day reality of gay and lesbian people, marriage was an important symbol, but I never saw it as reaching nirvana when we achieved that victory." During the years in which same-sex marriage was at the forefront of public debate, he was more focused on hate propaganda. It was an issue that had been on his radar since at least the early 1980s. Under Canadian law, it was illegal to incite genocide against members of any racial or religious group, but it was not illegal to incite the extermination of homosexuals. The kind of vicious hatred levelled at Robinson in poorly spelled emails and letters could legally be published on websites, in pamphlets and in books for the entire world to see.

In Robinson's view, hate propaganda and hate crimes were inextricably linked. If violence was encouraged, violence would occur. In Vancouver, a study conducted by the local police showed that there were more violent crimes committed against people on the basis of their sexuality than on the basis of ethnicity and religion combined. Robinson was convinced that adding sexual orientation to hate propaganda legislation would discourage homophobic attacks in the same way that the legislation successfully discouraged racist attacks. In 1999, after a young law student in Fredericton was severely beaten for being gay, Robinson called upon the government to amend the law. "We will be making necessary changes to the Criminal Code in the coming months," responded Justice Minister Anne McLellan. Nearly two years later, no changes had been made. In November 2001 a gay man, Aaron Webster, was beaten to death with a baseball bat in Vancouver's Stanley Park. Within days, Robinson was on his feet in the House. Once more the Liberals insisted that they were preparing a bill, but no bill ever came. On October 24, 2002, Robinson introduced a bill of his own, Bill C-250, which would make hate propaganda targeting homosexuals illegal.

Members of Parliament were three times more likely to die of a stroke than they were to get a private member's bill passed during Chrétien's reign, a time during which some analysts saw power becoming increasingly centralized in the Prime Minister's Office. Of the 285 private members' bills introduced by MPs in the previous session of Parliament, only four (all sponsored by Liberals) had become law. They consisted of a bill to change the names of some ridings, a bill to establish an official parliamentary poet laureate, a bill to designate Sir John A. Macdonald Day and Sir Wilfrid Laurier Day, and a bill to honour the Canadian Horse as our "National Horse." April 30, 2002, was a glorious day of victory for fans of the Canadian Horse, who had been trying to get a Canadian Horse-related private member's bill passed since at least 1995. In that context, for an opposition MP like Robinson to pass a bill of any substance seemed virtually impossible.

Furthermore, opposition to his proposal was fierce. The bill was condemned by powerful organizations such as the Canadian Conference of Catholic Bishops, the Catholic Civil Rights League, the Evangelical Fellowship of Canada, Focus on the Family, and the Canadian Family Action Coalition. Canadian Alliance MP (and future Conservative Minister of Justice) Vic Toews called it "the jackboots of fascism on the necks of our people." Robinson suspected that such strong language was meant to whip opponents of the bill into a frenzy as part of a fundraising drive. (To give opponents of the bill the benefit of the doubt, some believed it could be used to ban the Bible — even though Robinson pointed out that religious beliefs were protected by the Charter, and that his bill would simply make it illegal to advocate the extermination of homosexuals.)

He thought he had the Liberals onside. They agreed to send the bill straight to the justice committee, and after the first three days of public hearings, Robinson began to believe it might actually pass. On May 14, 2003, the day the committee was scheduled to begin detailed clause-by-clause study of the bill, Jack Layton accompanied Robinson to the meeting and stayed throughout, sitting in the public galleries in solidarity with his friend. However, neither of them expected what happened next. Four of the Liberals who usually attended didn't show up that day. Instead, they had been replaced by Tom Wappel, John O'Reilly, Andy Savoy and Paul Steckle — all Liberals who opposed Robinson's proposal. With the Canadian Alliance MPs, the socially conservative Liberals who were already on the committee (such as London–Fanshawe MP Pat O'Brien) and these four additional socially conservative Liberals, opponents to the bill now formed the majority. Vic Toews moved to kill the bill. Already armed with printed and translated copies of a motion, it appeared he had been tipped off in advance about the substitutions, likely by one of the Liberals. In moving his motion, Toews stated that Liberal MP Pat O'Brien was ready to second it, a procedurally unnecessary manoeuvre Toews hoped would indicate bipartisan support.

Robinson was livid. "As I look around the committee table, I have to say that I have seldom felt as great a sense of anger and betrayal as I feel today with respect to this bill. I look at members on the other side of this table, who have never attended a meeting of this committee when it considered this bill on hate propaganda, who showed up today to vote against the bill," he said. In Parliament it is considered a breach of protocol to refer to the presence or absence of members, and his comments provoked indignant points of order, as though parliamentary niceties could hide what the four Liberals were doing. Once again he went on to present the merits of the bill, sharing the story of a teenager who had committed suicide because of the abuse he was subjected to by peers who thought he was gay. As he saw the implacable faces of his opponents, his heart sank. "I thought that was a pretty straightforward concept, to be honest with you, Mr. Chairman. I really did. I didn't think this would be a complicated issue," he said. "I think it puts to shame those members who call themselves 'Liberal' who are not prepared to vote in support of an issue of fundamental justice like this."

"I was really angry," he says. "We'd come that far, and then they send in their God Squad to kill it. It just shocked me." According to Hedy Fry, the four Liberals were acting on their own initiative and had offered to substitute for the regular members of the committee as a personal favour. Ostensibly the offer was meant to give the committee members extra time to catch up on other work, but its real intention was to create an opportunity to defeat Robinson's bill. "What these four people did was they — without us knowing — started a concerted, strategic plan to check with everybody before that meeting," Fry explains. "Everybody was so happy to get somebody [else] to do their duty for them that they didn't stop to think." These socially conservative Liberals had tried to pull a fast one, but they wouldn't get the opportunity again.

When a committee studies a private member's bill, the members are given a deadline. If they haven't voted on the bill by the time the deadline is reached, the bill is automatically returned to the House, where it proceeds through the next steps of the legislative process. If Robinson couldn't ensure that the members voted for his bill, he could at least make sure they missed the deadline. "I pulled out every procedural stop that I could to get that bill through. I had read the rules backwards and forwards in the House and in the Senate. I knew that this was going to be a huge battle, and in order to win it, I had to be one step ahead of them constantly on parliamentary procedures," he recalls. When he saw the four Liberals sitting at the committee table, he filibustered until the end of the meeting and made it clear that if there was another attempt to kill the bill, he wouldn't hesitate to filibuster again. There were enough examples from his career to convince opponents that he was serious, and no further move was made to stop the bill at the committee stage.

The committee missed the deadline, and the bill was returned to the House. There, Liberal MP Derek Lee proposed an amendment adding a specific exemption for religious texts. Even though Robinson was sure it was unnecessary due to the Charter guarantee of freedom of religion, he agreed to Lee's amendment, hoping it would eliminate any ambiguity. The Canadian Alliance, half of the PCs and more than a third of the Liberals still wouldn't support it, but the majority did, and on September 17, 2003, his bill passed the House and was sent to the Senate.

Robinson hadn't had much contact with the Senate in his 25 years on the Hill. The upper chamber rarely sent bills to the House and even more rarely defeated the bills sent to it. Still, senators weren't used to getting private members' bills from opposition MPs, and Robinson wasn't sure how they'd react. More troublingly, time was running out on new Prime Minister Paul Martin. Liberal fortunes were suddenly falling in the wake of allegations they'd paid millions in taxpayer dollars to friends in Quebec in exchange for little or no work, a practice that would come to be known as the sponsorship scandal. Speculation abounded that Martin would call an election before his party's popularity slid any further. It wouldn't take much for an opponent to delay the bill until then. If that happened, all of the work Robinson had done would be for nothing.

But the lone wolf who had infuriated so many colleagues over the years had more friends than people realized. The NDP, the only major party favouring the abolition of the Senate, had no senators, so there would be no natural champion for Robinson's bill in what MPs call "the other place." But a number of his opponents from years past had developed a deep respect for Robinson, and several of them had been appointed to the Senate. With the support of a few key senators, including Serge Joyal, co-chair of the 1981 Constitution committee, PC senator Lowell Murray and Laurier LaPierre, Robinson's former lover, Robinson ensured that the senators understood the importance of his bill. "It's always easier when people like you," says Sonja van Dieen, one of his assistants at the time. Libby Davies also helped marshal support in the Senate. "I made phone calls for him to senators, and I was blown away by the people he knew in the Senate," she says. "The fact is, he had friends in every party, and to me that was his brilliance — his ability to know how the system worked, and to be able to work with people when he needed to get something through. And his bill is an absolute testament to that."

On April 28, 2004, the bill passed by an overwhelming margin. Opponents continued to fume: as the Speaker called the vote, Liberal senator Anne Cools bellowed, "No, never! It is a bad bill!" Later, the Conservatives ran an ad stating, "When Paul Martin and the Liberals supported Svend Robinson's Bill C-250 to restrict your freedom of speech, Stephen Harper said NO." The fight for acceptance was far from over, but Robinson had won a major battle. Today he keeps a framed copy of the bill hanging over his desk at home. In his long career, he has collected gifts from foreign dignitaries and has had his photo taken with presidents, prime ministers, movie stars and the Dalai Lama, but these are not the mementos he shows guests. Instead, he draws their attention to a simple 8.5-by-11-inch frame containing the crowning achievement of an entire career spent fighting for the rights of gays and lesbians — since the days when homosexuals could be fired or evicted just for being gay, when police violently raided their bathhouses, and when a politician didn't dare admit to being gay. "It was my last major parliamentary mission," he says, still immensely proud. "I had to move heaven and earth to get that bill through." At the time, he didn't know it would be his last.

Against prison rules, a guard surreptitiously snapped this photo of Robinson during his incarceration at Ford Mountain Correctional Centre. Robinson had just finished painting the outhouse.

Robinson and Max Riveron in Cuba on August 19, 1994, the night they met.

Robinson with Cuban President Fidel Castro in Havana. Castro jokingly called Robinson "the last surviving socialist MP in Canada."

Surrounded by supporters at the 1995 NDP leadership convention.

Jack Layton supported Robinson's campaign for the leadership.

Ada Yovanovich, Robinson's adoptive Haida mother.

Protesting during the 1997 Asia-Pacific Economic Co-operation (APEC) summit in Vancouver.
PHOTO BY ELAINE BRIÈRE

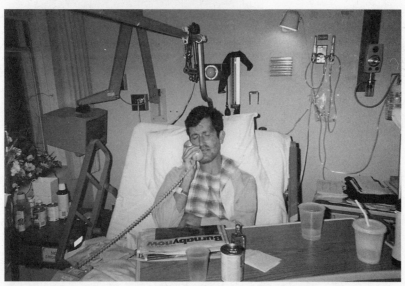

Robinson returned to work within weeks of his fall off an 18-metre cliff on Galiano Island.

Robinson surveys the remains of the Chinese embassy in Belgrade during the Kosovo War in 1999. The embassy was one of several civilian targets reduced to rubble by NATO bombs. Robinson was the first foreign politician to visit Kosovo during the conflict.

Robinson's presence at a picket line usually ensured media attention.

Robinson and a young supporter at Burnaby's Hats Off Day parade.

Robinson's solidarity mission to Israel and Palestine in 2002 provoked a hostile reaction, both at the Israeli military checkpoint and in caucus back home.

Libby Davies and Jack Layton with Robinson on the night of his final nomination as the NDP candidate for Burnaby–Douglas. Davies and Layton were two of Robinson's closest friends and political allies.

Despite the wide range of national and international issues with which he was involved, Robinson's constituents always remained his first priority.

Robinson at work with the Global Fund to Fight AIDS, Tuberculosis and Malaria. PHOTO BY GRAEME TRUELOVE

Svend and Max with Jasmine and Cohiba.

EIGHTEEN

Diamonds are Forever

When the Orpheum opened on Vancouver's Granville Street in 1927, no other theatre in Canada could rival it. Nearly a century later, the opulence of the baroque design and the immensity of the lower orchestra and the balcony above still awe even regular visitors. Usually a casual glance at the line of patrons outside is all it takes to get a sense of what's on offer at each of Granville Street's bars, clubs and concert halls on any given night. But on the evening of March 20, 2004, the strange assortment of people lined up outside the Orpheum was anything but illuminating. There were a few of the middle-aged and well-heeled who make up the Orpheum's usual audience, but they were joined by a remarkably diverse crowd: straight-laced businesspeople, casually dressed trade unionists and hippies of every generation, men and women in their 20s who looked as if they had stepped out of the lineup at the Roxy nightclub down the street by mistake, and behind them, old folks who could easily have been their grandparents. There stood every race, gender and level of flamboyance. That they were all in line to hear a couple of politicians and a linguistics professor would not have been immediately apparent.

To Robinson, peering out from behind the curtain at the packed theatre while Jack Layton strode to the podium, it was like seeing the blood, sweat and tears of his entire career, all in one room. He wasn't ready for this. It was just supposed to be a fundraiser. His constituency association had organized a celebration of his 25 years as an elected MP, but marking that milestone was supposed to be an excuse to get professor Noam Chomsky up to Vancouver, sell some tickets to finance the next election, and hear what the famous linguist, left-leaning political commentator and American icon had to say. But until Robinson saw the sold-out crowd in front of him — so many of them people he knew well, fellow warriors of one political battle or another — the full breadth of his career hadn't hit him.

Twenty-five years. Has it really been that long?

"How a guy who still looks 25 can have accomplished this is beyond me," Layton joked to the crowd. "I chalk it up to his shy, retiring nature."

The crowd laughed, and so did Robinson. Although they were there for Chomsky, they were there for Robinson, too. They knew only too well how far he had pushed the boundaries over the years, and how hard the boundaries had pushed back.

When Robinson took to the stage, more than 2,500 people rose to their feet. He felt a warmth that he hadn't felt in a long time as 25 years' worth of supporters applauded and cheered.

Still dark-haired, still lean, he crossed the stage and reached the podium in a few quick strides. Here, he was in his element. Imperceptibly, except to those who knew him best, he took one more half-second to appreciate the moment. Then he got to work. There was a long list of people to thank, from the volunteers in his first campaign to his current staff, who had flown to Vancouver that morning and were taking the red-eye back to Ottawa that night. Chomsky had to be honoured, of course. With the little time he had left for his remarks, Robinson addressed topical international concerns and then turned the podium over to Chomsky.

Following the famed professor's speech — an indictment of increasing American hegemony and a call to arms to continued resistance — Chomsky and Robinson shared the stage, while Robinson posed questions sent in by audience members. When the curtain fell two and a half hours later, Robinson eagerly headed into the crowd to greet the friends he hadn't seen in so long. The handshakes continued into the evening, and by the time he finally stepped back out into the cool Vancouver night, he was over-whelmed.

•   •   •

"I thought this was just who he was, and that he could keep it up forever," says Dan Fredrick, one of Svend's assistants in his last years in politics. "He always wanted to respond to everyone who wanted him to respond. You can imagine the number of issues over the years. He built up a huge number of supporters. Before I even knew very much about Canadian politics, I used to say — almost like a joke, when I was talking to my friends — if there was any-thing wrong, any injustice that I noticed in the world, I'd say, 'We should get Svend Robinson on this.' Because my understanding of Canadian politics was, Svend Robinson was a fighter for justice. This was before I was even really politically aware. But I think there are a lot of people out there in Canada, and internationally, even, who probably had a similar perception, one way or another — that if something was wrong, let Svend know. And as a result, Svend became almost like this superhero for left-wing activists. And he wanted to, as much as possible, live up to that. It's unsustainable, I guess. He sustained it for a very long time, but I guess, ultimately, it was unsustainable."

On March 20, 2004, Svend stood before the sold-out audience at the Orpheum, chatting with Noam Chomsky and looking every inch a politician in the prime of his influence. But at home, in the first months of 2004, Max knew something was very wrong. Ingrid was in hospital with MS, nearly immobile and in constant pain, and it was devastating for Svend to watch his sister's condition deteriorate, knowing she probably didn't have long to live. Max had seen Svend under stress before, though, and the way he was behaving now wasn't normal. "I was living with somebody differ-

ent," Max recalls. "He was totally hyper. Like, extremely hyper. He
wanted to change things constantly. Which he does, but it was just
at a very high speed ... he was making decisions by the second."
He wasn't sleeping. He wasn't eating. He was travelling almost non-
stop. He and Max were constantly fighting; anything could trigger
an argument. And some of the things he was doing were outlandish to the point of terrifying. On Galiano Island, Svend was fiddling
with the outboard motor to their boat and accidentally dropped it
into the ocean. Max happened to go down to the dock and found
Svend tying one end of a rope around his neck and the other end to
a heavy rock he held, about to jump into the ocean to retrieve the
motor. Svend might sometimes have been foolhardy, but he wasn't
illogical. This was not Svend.

Max told him that enough was enough. He needed to leave politics and start taking care of himself. Svend ignored that advice,
just as he had ignored the advice of his physician to see a psychiatrist after his hiking accident. The manic behaviour continued. On
April 8, 2004, he flew to Kelowna to visit Ingrid. Alone with his
thoughts that day, Max seriously considered leaving him. "Those
days were really bad. I was ready to leave," Max says. "I just couldn't
take it anymore. He was gone. Gone with the wind."

The next day, Good Friday, Svend took the early morning flight
back from Kelowna. He picked up a copy of the *Vancouver Sun*, and
during the flight he scoured the paper for the latest political news.
He happened to notice an ad for a jewellery auction being held near
the Vancouver airport. For some time he'd been thinking of proposing to Max with a diamond engagement ring and had already
started visiting some Burnaby jewellers. Since he'd be at the airport
anyway, he decided to stop by the auction on his way home.

•　　•　　•

After landing in Vancouver, Svend headed directly to the auction.
He signed in, greeted the patrons who recognized him, and wan-
dered over to look at the jewellery.

The RCMP would later value the large diamond ring at $21,500. Momentarily unattended — except by the security cameras — it sat on display on a glass counter, glittering.

Svend picked it up, put it in his pocket, looked up at the video camera and returned to his car. For a moment he just sat there. Then he realized he had left his cell phone on a seat in the auction house. He returned, sat down and watched for a few minutes as the auction continued. He returned to his car.

"And then I realized immediately, 'My God, what is this madness?'"

•　　　•　　　•

He knew he had to return the ring, but in that parking lot he felt something he rarely ever felt: fear. Too afraid to face the embarrassment of going back inside, he drove home. He tried to contact the auction house, but it was too late to reach anyone there. The head office was in Toronto, three time zones away, and it was Good Friday, after all. Still in a manic state, he spent the long weekend working at a frenzied pace. The day after the theft, he spoke at an Indo-Canadian celebration. At home, when he had nothing left to do, he went outside and started chopping wood. He was, by now, in hell. Tortured by shame, he fully understood the possible consequences of what he'd done, but what he couldn't understand was why he'd done it. His actions had gone against every principle he held dear. His identity was crumbling, and there seemed to be no explanation. As a teenager trapped in an abusive home, he had imagined what it would be like to kill himself. In the tormented days after the theft, he thought of suicide once again. But he wasn't a teenager anymore; he was a grown man, and one who had become used to taking responsibility for his actions.

Finally, on Monday morning, he got hold of the auction house and learned that the staff had already contacted the Richmond RCMP. Svend did the same and then spoke with Max.

"He said, 'I did it.' 'Did what?' And then he put his hand in his pocket and pulled out a ring. And I said, 'And what is that?' and then he said, 'I did it.' I said, 'Did what?' again. He said, 'I took it.' I said, 'What, that?' because I thought it was actually a drag queen's ring. It looked really pathetic to me. And then he repeated, 'I took it.' I said, 'You stole a ring? No, you must be kidding.' And he said, 'Yes, I did it. I'm on my way to the RCMP detachment, I've already phoned them,'" Max later recounted to *Maclean's*. "And he just left. And I cried. We spent that whole weekend together, and he never said a word, and I wish he would have."

After being interrogated by police, Svend phoned Clayton Ruby. "He was totally shocked and told me I shouldn't say anything. And I said, 'Well, Clay, I already have,'" Robinson recalls. Eventually the manic behaviour began to subside. In the next days, he sought psychiatric treatment and told the NDP leadership what had happened, so they wouldn't feel blindsided. He also met with his staff. "He took control, told us what happened and sounded sincere about how hard it was for him. We all expressed our surprise and sadness, and we moved on. That hardly took any time, and we all moved on to the next item on the agenda, which was 'What next? How do we deal with this?'" says Sonja van Dieen.

On April 15, flanked by Max, Libby Davies and Burnaby–Douglas riding association president Doug Sigurdson, Svend held a press conference. Just as he had when he came out as a homosexual, he chose to make the news public himself. As he dropped the bombshell, he tried to offer an explanation:

> For some time now, I have been suffering from severe stress and emotional pain . . . The reasons for this are, of course, intensely personal, and I'm not prepared to discuss them, but among others, relate to the cumulative pressures of dealing with the emotional consequences of a nearly fatal hiking accident. The past few months have been particularly difficult and painful. This accumulated stress culminated last Friday, on Good Friday, in my engaging in an act that was totally inexplicable and unthinkable.
>
> . . . I pocketed a piece of expensive jewellery. I did this, despite knowing full well that the employees who were there recognized me, and did so in a context where I'd provided them my full name and contact information in writing, and [knowing] that the entire area

was under electronic surveillance. Something just snapped in this moment of total, utter irrationality . . .

I will not seek to, in any way, avoid full responsibility for my actions . . .

I have sought, and am receiving, professional medical help to understand and deal with these issues . . .

Clearly, at this painful and difficult time, while there are outstanding legal and health issues to be addressed, I must devote my full energy and time to recovery and healing. I will therefore be taking time off for medical leave immediately. My hard-working and experienced staff, who have stood by me like the Rock of Gibraltar in this, will certainly continue to serve the needs of my constituents, and I will remain in close contact with them. I am also stepping down at this time as the federal New Democrat candidate for Burnaby–Douglas while these issues remain unresolved . . .

As you can imagine, this has been a nightmare. I cannot believe that it has happened, but I am human and I have failed.

I have felt such an incredible privilege and honour to serve my constituents here in Burnaby . . . and I feel an equally strong sense of sadness that I have let so many people down.

•　　•　　•

"Our place looked like a flower shop," Max recalls. In the days following Svend's press conference, friends and supporters flooded their home with expressions of sympathy. Davies was as valuable a friend as he could have asked for. Jack Layton flew to Vancouver to be with him. Brian Mulroney and B.C. Premier Gordon Campbell called him personally. "From friends to enemies, they were there for him," Max says.

Svend wrote a letter of apology to the auction company; satisfied, they didn't intend to press charges. However, the opinions of a shocked public were predictably divided. "The 52-year-old New Democrat MP always has had a flair for the dramatic and a penchant for look-at-me stunts. But in my opinion this televised mea culpa topped them all," wrote columnist Ian Mulgrew in the *Vancouver Sun*. "He scheduled a news conference to choke out little more than, 'I won't run again if I'm behind bars.' . . . his judgment was questionable in the past, it now can no longer be trusted in public office." Several letters to the editor referred to Svend's "Academy Award-winning" performance at the press conference. Even Svend's sister Kim logged on to a conservative website, identified herself and urged that her brother be charged. His supporters, meanwhile, hoped for leniency. Their attitude was perhaps best expressed by letter-writer Mitch D'Kugener: "Mr. Robinson made a mistake on Friday, but it only proves what I was beginning to doubt: he is indeed human. I was beginning to think he was Superman."

If the Office of the Attorney-General had announced it was satisfied with Svend's apology, and that he wouldn't be charged, he might have run again. But no such announcement came, and he was left in limbo. With an election call looming, Bill Siksay became the NDP candidate for Burnaby–Douglas, and Svend came to terms with the fact that his political career, for the time being, was over. "Oh, I felt terrible shame. Terrible shame. It was incredibly painful, even though people were so supportive and friendly. Everywhere I went, people would come up to me and say, 'We're really sorry about what happened, and we support you.' And they would tell me stories of something similar that happened to them, or to a member of their family, or a close friend. I mean, I got hundreds and hundreds of letters from people all over the country . . . People were wonderful. But every so often, somebody would say something nasty, like 'Watch out for your jewellery!' or something like that, and that just cut to the quick. It was very, very painful," Robinson says. "The hardest was the people who — in some cases with tears in their eyes — would tell me the sense of loss they felt that I was gone, and that I had been their voice. The Kurdish cab driver at the airport in Ottawa, who was there with his little son, and he said, 'This man was our voice, and we had great hope for him.' Or the Palestinians. I mean, the people for whom I had really been, not the only voice for politically, but certainly a leading and strong voice for — I felt such a sense of loss and betrayal of them, really, that this had happened, and I wasn't able to be there anymore for them. That was the most painful. It really was. It was devastating."

In mid-June an Alberta-based lobby group, run by publisher and former Reform Party activist Link Byfield, ran an ad in *The Province* which read, "Two months ago MP Svend Robinson was caught stealing. Will he be charged with theft?" With one week to go in the election campaign, Svend was charged. On August 6, 2004, he appeared in court and pled guilty to theft over $5000. Many prominent public figures wrote letters to the court attesting to his character. "I hope that one aberration in a truly good life does not compromise his future," wrote Stephen Lewis. David Suzuki wrote, "I believe at this time he deserves our gratitude for what he has done as a politician, our sympathy for the pressures he has lived with, and our compassion in meting out his sentence."

Svend had stood before a judge before, but the verdict delivered by Judge R.D. Fratkin was nothing like the politically charged admonishments he had heard in the past:

I have been sitting here since approximately 9:30 this morning, some two hours and 15 minutes or so, listening to a gut-wrenching tale about a man who has achieved much more than most, and who has taken a fall, probably more than most, all for a bobble [sic], a trinket, a ring. The explanation is that what he did was an aberration, was a one-off, was as a result of enormous amounts of pressure placed on this man — some of it self-imposed — but primarily [by] people seeking his assistance as a member of Parliament, a significant position in this country. He, in his attempt to assist, has run himself ragged. There is evidence to support that proposition by the people who are near and dear to him, who made observations of changes in the man . . . His detractors really say that Mr. Robinson is nothing more, and nothing less, than a common thief who got caught, and who turned himself in, not because of conscience, but because that was the expedient thing to do . . . The sad fact is, there is nobody on this earth who knows what was in Mr. Robinson's mind, save and except Mr. Robinson . . . Shakespeare said that the evil that men do lives after them; the good is oft interred with their bones . . . He has fallen a long way. He has embarrassed himself, lost his opportunity to do that which he does and does well. Further, he is always going to be remembered for this. This is not going to go away. As I say, the public, at least in Canada, I think, has always lived by the sort of guiding principle [that] you don't kick somebody when they're down. Mr. Robinson's down. I do not think we need to kick him.

Fratkin sentenced him to 100 hours of community service and a year's probation, and ordered him to continue his psychiatric treatment. The conditional discharge, common for first-time offenders who had taken steps towards restitution, meant that he wouldn't have a criminal record. Asked today, Svend feels the sentence was fair, although Ruby suggests that the high profile of the case probably resulted in a harsher sentence than what a private citizen in similar circumstances might have faced. Svend chose to perform his community service in Burnaby, taking care of injured animals and building habitats at the Wildlife Rescue Association of B.C. In an interview about a year and a half later, Ken MacQueen of *Maclean's* noted the symbolism of Svend learning to repair the wings of injured birds while he himself grew stronger.

•　　•　　•

Everyone wants to know why. It's the question that keeps coming up, in interviews with Svend's friends, colleagues and supporters, and in casual conversations with political junkies. Few doubt the sincerity of his tears at the press conference. But his explanation of what happened — so lacking in details and a clear cause-and-effect rationale — didn't provide the closure that supporters still crave.

The explanation was unsatisfactory because Svend himself was still grasping at straws, struggling to understand what had happened. "I just went back and forth, and over and over, and up and down, trying to think how this could happen. Two weeks after I'm riding high, celebrating 25 years with Noam Chomsky in a theatre full of people, I'm putting a ring into my pocket. It just didn't make any sense," he says.

Recalling his doctor's suggestion that he seek psychiatric treatment after his hiking accident, in his press conference he had hinted at the possibility of post-traumatic stress related to his fall. It was all he had to go on at the time. It's a reasonable supposition: according to the Canadian Mental Health Association, symptoms of post-traumatic stress disorder (PTSD) may not surface until years after a traumatic event. Svend had shown several symptoms of the disorder, including insomnia and avoidance (evident in his refusal to seriously discuss the accident with a psychiatrist). Although the theft had clearly been preceded by manic behaviour, Svend had recently been displaying an unusual lack of interest in elements of his work, another symptom of PTSD. "I was concerned that Svend wasn't himself for quite some time before the ring incident," recalls Doug Sigurdson. "I found him to be somewhat uninterested in functions of the executive committee, a trait he never showed before." Sonja van Dieen noticed the same thing. "I remember saying to him that I thought he'd been a bit off, that he'd been a bit less interested in the last couple months before the ring thing happened. Like maybe he was tired," she says.

PTSD can easily affect behaviour when triggered by other stressors, psychologist Paul Swingle explained to the *Vancouver Sun* after Svend's press conference. The same is true in the case of a brain injury, which Svend might easily have suffered in his 18-metre fall off a cliff. "Judgement can be affected in a serious way. The kind of behaviour he engaged in sounds like an impulse control issue," stated Swingle. "We get a lot of impulse control problems with patients with traumatic brain injury." Other psychologists interviewed by the *Sun* corroborated Swingle's explanation: PTSD or a brain injury could be responsible for such irrational decision making.

While the lingering effects of the hiking accident probably were factors in what Svend had done, in court Clayton Ruby offered another hypothesis. After decades of extraordinary stress, Svend had finally cracked under the pressure. That explanation, too, makes sense. That he was seriously overworked was no secret. Worse, during his career he had faced a level of vitriol from opponents that few politicians ever experience. He had even endured the wrath of caucus colleagues — those he might have expected to be on his side. Friends suggest that those attacks hurt him far more than he ever let on. He had faced physical danger on the front lines of protests and in war zones. He had even faced it in his own home, due to the ever-present threat of homophobic violence. He had constantly been harangued with messages of obscene hatred and told that he was a sinner and a child-molester, condemned by God to an eternity in hell. On many occasions he'd wanted to leave the job, but something had always compelled him to stay. Unable to make the conscious decision to quit, perhaps he had subconsciously committed an act that would force his resignation and free him from a situation that had become impossible to maintain.

It's an assessment Jane Pepper finds reasonable. Because Svend felt he represented people who had no other voice, the pressures he faced were enormous. "I think the ring was the way to get the hell out when he couldn't get out any other way. To get out on his own — somewhere in there, he would have thought that he was abandoning all those people," she says.

Bill Siksay retained Burnaby–Douglas for the NDP in the 2004 election and served three terms, developing an acute understanding of the pressures Svend faced. Like Svend, Siksay was known for taking positions outside the political mainstream, and he also developed a devoted following. "It's an incredibly hard job to get into, and it's an incredibly hard job to get out of," he says. "When you're somebody like Svend, and to a lesser extent me, when you're taking on things that other people aren't taking on, they're pretty desperate that you stick around to keep the work going. So there really is a lot of pressure to stay in the job, and to make the decision to leave is incredibly hard."

Perhaps Svend couldn't make that decision, so his subconscious made it for him. Such a hypothesis is possible, especially when Svend's troubled childhood is taken into account. According to Janet Woititz in *Adult Children of Alcoholics*, such behaviour is common among people with an alcoholic parent. "Saying no is extraordinarily difficult for you so you do more and more and more. You do not do it because you really have a bloated sense of yourself. You do it because you don't have a realistic sense of your capacity, or because if you say no you are afraid that they will find you out. They will find out that you are incompetent. The quality of the job does not seem to influence your feelings about yourself. So you take on more and more and more and more," Woititz writes. "Many super responsible people, in order to stop, have to get sick. It is the only way out and is very predictable. They give and give and take more upon themselves until they no longer have anything left, and they get sick. In effect, they burn out. They cannot find an acceptable way to stop short of this."

There is yet another possible explanation. After the theft, Svend began taking medication to help prevent the manic behaviour that had preceded his breakdown. His psychiatrist, Dr. Glen Freedman, diagnosed him with cyclothymic disorder, a specific form of what is commonly called bipolar disorder. According to the Canadian Mental Health Association, cyclothymic disorder causes alternating periods of hypomania and depression, which could explain both the frenzied activity in the days leading up to the theft and the suicidal feelings after. In an interview on CBC about a year after Good Friday, Svend revealed that he had a mental illness. He hoped that through this revelation he could help destigmatize mental illness, and at the same time offer his supporters a more complete explanation of what had happened. Still, it wasn't an easy thing for a politician to do. The opponents who had used his sexuality against him in the past would now be able to use his illness as well. "It was challenging, too, because I didn't want to make a direct link between mental illness and criminality either — that mental illness, sort of, 'made me do it.' Maybe it did. I mean, it probably did. I don't know. Because it was irrational, it was ill," he says.

Of course, none of those explanations will satisfy the most cynical. For those inclined to believe the worst about him, the theft simply confirms what they already felt: that he was a self-interested, sleazy politician who, like so many others, was caught with his hands in the cookie jar. It's something Svend knows he has to address, and he is hard on himself. "Maybe, I mean, I saw this ring and thought that I could get away with it somehow. I don't know, right? I mean, I don't want to gild the lily in any way. Maybe there was just an element of bad in it, too. Maybe it wasn't just mental illness or post-traumatic stress or anything else. Maybe this was — who knows? In all of us there's, you know, there's bad and good. Maybe this was bad. Maybe I just, you know — temptation overcame me. I don't know," he says. He still doesn't know what caused him to take the ring on that awful Good Friday in 2004. "It's not an exact science. I don't want to ascribe it to this or that or anything else. We're all incredibly complex as human beings, and there are many different things that drive our behaviour, and maybe that was part of it."

•   •   •

The answer to the question everyone is asking is complex. PTSD, a possible brain injury, a cry for help, mental illness and old-fashioned temptation — all were probably contributing factors. The answer is still unsatisfying to supporters, not because it is incomplete, but because they wish the answer were different. They wish it were clearer, easier to understand. They wish it matched everything else they know about Svend: the selflessness, the bravery, the overwhelming dedication to his principles. Without the benefit of such an answer, supporters must decide between sympathy and condemnation, between focusing on his accomplishments and letting the theft tarnish his legacy.

On April 18, 2004, three days after his press conference, Svend was supposed to receive a lifetime achievement award from the gay and lesbian newspaper *Xtra! West*. Still reeling from the events of the previous week, he didn't attend the ceremony, but organizers presented the award anyway. "Heroes aren't people who are perfect," presenter Aerlyn Weissman said. "Heroes aren't infallible. Heroes aren't unreachable icons who are somehow different from the rest of us. Heroes are people who stand up and speak out, when it's unpopular, when it's dangerous. And they mostly do it with the doubts and fears we all have when we do things that are hard. But they do it anyway. And they sometimes pay a very personal price. Svend Robinson is a hero. He will always be a hero to me. Because it isn't that heroes never fail in their goals, it's that they never fail in trying to achieve them. Heroes are human. They make mistakes, they get scared, and they need support, just as we all do."

NINETEEN

In These Grim and Ominous Days

A week after being sentenced, Robinson went back to work. He was offered a job in the advocacy department of the B.C. Government and Service Employees' Union, the same union he'd belonged to as a young man working as a driving examiner. There he analyzed contracts and presented cases in arbitrations. Several union members criticized their president, George Heyman, for hiring such a controversial figure. Robinson was grateful for the opportunity, particularly during such a difficult period in his life, but he hadn't had a boss in 25 years. "I butted heads with my bosses at the union. I wasn't the easiest of employees," he acknowledges. "I wasn't used to it, to having a boss. And more than once, I suspect, I veered into insubordination. I know that I did. So, it wasn't an easy transition, and I respect the fact that they cut me a lot of slack initially."

"He took a rest, but he never really stopped," Max told *Maclean's*. "He can do so many things in such a short period of time. Probably his mental illness, you could say, makes him more effective in what he does." He wrote editorials and gave talks on mental illness. He corresponded regularly with Bill Siksay, the new MP for Burnaby–Douglas. "I have to say, I was nervous about how Svend would try to influence me," Siksay says. "I did, once in a while, get that from him, and I don't think I did enjoy it very much. I think Svend had a hard time letting go. He read Hansard every night and let people know what he thought of the day's business. I couldn't read Hansard every night." Robinson was an active constituent, and he had high expectations of his MP. "Sometimes he liked what was going on, and sometimes he didn't," Siksay says. It could be frustrating, but it was also valuable. "With Svend, even when you don't like what you're hearing, it's not like it's not important, or well thought out, or probably right."

In October 2004, Robinson spoke at the Burnaby–Douglas annual general meeting. He congratulated Siksay and thanked his friends for the support he'd received after the theft. He also provided a clear hint about what he planned to do next. "In the future, I look forward to continuing to work for equality, for social and economic justice, for respect for our fragile environment, for international human rights, for a better planet," he said. In closing, he echoed Tommy Douglas, who, defeated in 1962, went on to win a by-election and serve six more terms as an MP. As Douglas had in his concession speech, he quoted an old English folk song: "I am hurt, but I am not slain. I will lay me down and bleed awhile, and then I'll rise and fight again."

In late 2003, Stephen Harper's Canadian Alliance merged with the Progressive Conservatives to form the Conservative Party. In the 2004 election, factors such as the united right, the fallout from the sponsorship scandal, and a more popular NDP led by Layton reduced Prime Minister Paul Martin's Liberals to a minority government. It was the first since Joe Clark's in 1979. In that uncertain environment, speculation on when Martin's government would fall was rampant. Anticipating a quick election, media began to ask Robinson if he was ready for a comeback.

It was a question Robinson was asking himself. He felt ready. His psychiatrist told him he had the strength to do it. Max agreed. "I supported it," Max says. "It was too early, yes, absolutely, but he had to do it. Because he had to show some people, 'I'm here, and I still can do things.'" He was certainly still popular in Burnaby. When Siksay had defeated the Liberal candidate, Bill Cunningham, Robinson's enduring popularity had been a significant factor. "His presence was just so powerful," Cunningham says. "He was at every debate, and on every doorstep, even though he wasn't physically at every debate or on every doorstep." Robinson wouldn't usurp Siksay in Burnaby, but another riding was available: Vancouver Centre. It was a wealthier riding than the one he'd represented, and it hadn't elected a socialist since the CCF had won a by-election there in the 1940s. The Liberal incumbent, Hedy Fry, was popular and running again. However, the riding had a substantial gay and lesbian population, and Robinson had a considerable connection to the community. It seemed like a natural fit.

At first, Jack Layton encouraged his candidacy. "I am fully behind your return to the House. We need you," he wrote in a letter to Robinson. However, he also suggested that before deciding to run, Robinson speak to caucus colleagues and commission a poll in the riding to gauge his support. Robinson followed Layton's advice and called his former colleagues. A handful were supportive, but most weren't. Even Libby Davies felt it was too soon. With the Liberals under fire for the sponsorship scandal, the number one issue in the election was expected to be ethics. In that context, the candidacy of a man who had pled guilty to theft wouldn't reflect well on the NDP. "The overwhelming consensus was that the timing was not right, and I conveyed that honestly and directly to Svend," Ed Broadbent says. "It was the real feeling of the caucus that, politically, he would do damage to the party." A few of the conversations were unpleasant, particularly the one Robinson had with Alexa McDonough, who initially, he recalls, hadn't even wanted to take his call. Robinson remembers the call ending with McDonough saying he was medically unstable, while Robinson called her a disgrace. (It is worth noting that McDonough remembers their conversation quite differently. "I don't actually remember that being much of an issue at all," she says.)

Eventually, Robinson came to realize that Layton hadn't wanted him to run but had hoped he would make that decision on his own. Robinson flew to Toronto and the two friends had a frank conversation. "It was terribly, terribly emotional and painful — just the two of us, sitting in his kitchen at his house on Huron Street in

Toronto, and me arguing with him about why I thought I should run, and him equally strongly making the arguments about why I shouldn't," Robinson recalls. His friendship with Layton and Davies was unaffected, but at the time he felt hurt and betrayed. "He didn't like it. But we got through it. I think he now knows that I wasn't doing it to be mean or to prevent him from coming back," Davies says. "He wanted to hear positive things from me, and when he didn't hear that, it upset him . . . It comes back to his single-mindedness. He'd got it in his head that he wanted to run, and that this was the right thing to do."

He didn't have the support of most of his former colleagues, but the results of the poll he'd commissioned showed that he had a shot. The NDP trailed the Liberals in Vancouver Centre by 18 percentage points, but once pollsters identified Robinson as the candidate, the gap narrowed to 6 percentage points, which was within the margin of error. If he had a great campaign, and if the Liberals' popularity continued to falter while Layton's continued to climb, anything could happen.

Furthermore, he felt that his experience over the past year and a half had made him a better man. He wrote to his caucus colleagues, hoping to convince them that he had become an easier person to work with. "All of you were incredibly supportive last year and since then, and I will never forget that. I know it was not an easy thing for you to have to deal with, and I still wince when I think of it. But you cannot go through something like that and not come out a changed person, hopefully a better person," he wrote. In an interview with the *Globe and Mail*, he admitted that humility hadn't come easily. "That was a legitimate criticism of me. I was always so certain of what I took on, and if you didn't agree, it was, 'Get out of my way.' I know this is going to sound hokey, but the experience I went through was not only painful but transformational. When I look at people I can't be quite as judgmental as I was. Before, it was black and white and right and wrong. I'd be a hypocrite if I approached things that way now," he said.

With the glimmer of hope that the poll had provided, on October 21, 2005, at the Sylvia Hotel, where he'd worked as a night-time desk clerk during university, he announced he was seeking the NDP nomination in Vancouver Centre. "Svend Robinson's candidacy in Vancouver for the federal elections is very welcome news. Particularly in these grim and often ominous days, his courage and dedication to human rights are sorely needed," wrote Noam Chomsky in support. Robinson's Haida brother, David Suzuki, once again was at his side. "I am filled with admiration for Svend's integrity, his total commitment to social justice and the environment, and his fearlessness in speaking out on controversial issues," stated Suzuki. Hedy Fry looked forward to running against an opponent of Robinson's calibre. "I looked forward to it because Svend is a good debater, and I love debate. It was very challenging, but stimulating, for me to go up against somebody who was worthy of debating, as opposed to somebody who just read word for word what their party put on the page," Fry says. Facing Robinson made her nervous. "I wasn't sure how it would turn out."

The reaction from the mainstream media had a markedly different tone. Even before Robinson announced his comeback, the media seemed to be looking for an opportunity to put a final nail in his coffin. In July 2004, Robinson offered them one. According to House of Commons regulations, after leaving office a former MP is allowed a brief grace period to wrap up certain outstanding work. Robinson joined a delegation of Canadian MPs at a conference of the Organization for Security and Co-operation in Europe in Edinburgh, where he resumed his role as chair of the human rights committee for three days until members could elect a new chair. To ensure that his trip didn't cost the taxpayers anything extra, the NDP allowed Robinson to take the place of its delegate. The Liberals did the same thing, choosing to send recently retired MP Clifford Lincoln rather than a sitting member of caucus.

But Robinson's participation in the conference proved to be a mistake that caused unnecessary grief for his former colleagues, a fact he now readily acknowledges. "I wanted to have one final opportunity to say goodbye to my friends and former colleagues in that body in which I had been so active, and to chair the committee, but I never should have gone. Dumb, dumb, dumb," he says.

His participation was heavily criticized by the Canadian Taxpayers Federation and various media outlets. A political cartoon in the *Vancouver Sun* depicted a giant wild boar (labelled "boondoggle") reading a newspaper with the headline "NDP send ex-MP Svend Robinson on taxpayer-funded junket," while a smiling Jack Layton looked on. In such a context, Robinson expected the media to react even more savagely when he announced he was running again, and he was certain references to the ring would feature prominently in their attacks.

"The reinvented New Democrats have a very familiar ring," wrote Don Martin in *The Province*, in a not-so-subtle allusion. He also took a dig at Robinson's mental illness, calling him a "bipolarizing retread." Predictably, the *National Post* also opposed his candidacy. "Ordinarily, the last thing we would do is encourage voters to embrace Hedy Fry . . . but if Svend Robinson is the main alternative . . . she will likely prove the lesser of two evils," pronounced an editorial. Another *National Post* article during the campaign quoted Judge Fratkin's remarks during Robinson's sentencing out of context, giving the impression that Fratkin saw Robinson as nothing but a common thief. (The *Post* printed a correction the next day.)

Most vicious of all was *Maclean's*, which had recently appointed a new editor: Kenneth Whyte, former editor of the *National Post*. "Svend him packing! Will the voters of Vancouver Centre please do the rest of Canada a favour?" urged the cover of *Maclean's*, in a supposedly witty play on words. "Now Robinson is back, once again seeking a seat in the House of Commons. It's our turn to cry for help," proclaimed the editorial. "He's a self-aggrandizing lout with a disdain for parliamentary and judicial institutions . . . The presence of Svend Robinson in an election that has government ethics as a key issue is a blight on the New Democratic Party and an insult to the public at large. The voters of Vancouver Centre are obviously free to elect whomever they please. We trust them to see Svend Robinson's opportunism for what it is and make a stand for higher standards of political, ethical, and legal behaviour. In other words, to send him packing." Ken MacQueen's feature article compared Robinson's theft to two other recent B.C. scandals: Premier Gordon Campbell's dangerous drunk driving in Hawaii, and Vancouver Canucks winger Todd Bertuzzi's violent on-ice attack that left another player with three fractured vertebrae in his neck. That Robinson's transgression involved stealing and then returning a piece of property, rather than endangering the lives of others, didn't stop *Maclean's* from suggesting that his quest for redemption "may be the toughest test yet of the capacity of British Columbians to forgive, forget and move on."

Such attacks were unsurprising. "I mean, why wouldn't they take full advantage of this? It was red meat for them, right? I gave them a gift on a platter, and naturally they're going to take advantage of that," Robinson says. "All the people whose agendas I had challenged — this was just manna from heaven for them. And the right-wing media? Of course they're going to do that. So no, I wasn't surprised in the slightest. It was to be expected."

Layton defended Robinson's candidacy but kept his distance and didn't visit the riding during the campaign. "That was understandable," Robinson says, without any hint of bitterness. It would be more difficult to close the gap with Fry without Layton joining him on the campaign trail, but if Vancouver Centre's sizeable gay and lesbian community backed him, he could still win. In his first campaign in 1979 he couldn't tell the public he was gay. In 2006 both his Liberal and Conservative opponents supported same-sex marriage. Rather than fearing a backlash for supporting equal rights, the candidates in this campaign needed to actively court the gay and lesbian community in order to win. Although one Liberal candidate in Surrey publicly referred to Robinson as "Mrs. Robinson," it was undeniable that the political landscape had changed dramatically since 1979. It is difficult to believe that such progress would have been possible without him. However, the gay and lesbian community felt that they had a difficult decision to make. Hedy Fry had also been a valuable advocate for them, and many resented Robinson for forcing them to choose between the two instead of running in another riding against an incumbent who had been less supportive of their cause.

"What blew my mind was for the last two and a half weeks of the campaign, we didn't have a [lawn] sign [left]," Fry says, recalling the momentum in her campaign. She remembers a gay man who entered her office and told her he wouldn't vote for the NDP because Robinson was "a racist — he thinks gays vote gay." According to Davies, the demographics in the riding weren't an asset to Robinson at all. "It was probably the worst decision to run in Vancouver Centre, because the whole gay community was still hugely mad at him," she says. "People can be the most unforgiving of their own."

• • •

"By the time election day came around, I knew I was going to lose," Robinson says. "All candidates harbour the illusion that there'll be some kind of miraculous victory, but realistically the numbers just weren't there, and I knew that." The NDP's numbers were up nationally, and their B.C. seat count doubled, but that success didn't translate into more support in Vancouver, where the NDP vote either stayed the same or fell. In Vancouver Centre, the NDP vote fell by about the same amount that the Liberal vote rose, and Fry was re-elected. After seven straight election victories, on the day that Stephen Harper became prime minister of a minority government, Robinson lost by a considerable margin — well over 8,000 votes.

That he hadn't been overwhelmingly endorsed by the gay and lesbian community didn't surprise him. "They're pretty conservative. And they judged me pretty harshly, too," he says. "It was a combination of things. It was kind of a perfect storm, because they loved Hedy. Hedy had really cultivated the gay community, and rightly so — she worked hard for the community. She was visible, she attended events, she's outspoken and supportive of equality issues. So they liked her. And a lot of them just felt that I was too radical to start with. I mean, I was never a favourite of the more conservative west-end gay bankers, as I called them. So the assumption that they would [all] vote for me I always knew was totally unrealistic. So I wasn't surprised. But disappointed? Sure."

With the well-oiled campaign team he had used in the past now working to re-elect Siksay in Burnaby–Douglas, Robinson had to adjust to a new riding association and a new way of doing things. "Instead of being surrounded by people you had known for almost 30 years, you're surrounded by people you might have known for only three weeks. It didn't feel like he was at home," recalls Jan Taylor, who volunteered on the campaign. Some of the team felt that the party hadn't given Robinson the kind of support he needed to win, a defensible assessment considering Layton didn't visit the riding. "Svend had been a tremendous asset to the party," Taylor says. "It would seem to me that the party would then bring every force it could to make that a successful campaign, and I don't think they did that . . . I think he deserved better than he got."

In retrospect, Robinson acknowledges that Layton and Davies were right in trying to dissuade him from running. "I refer to it now as my kamikaze mission in Vancouver Centre. I wasn't listening to anybody. A big part of it was just showing the world that I could do this. And it was too much about me, and not enough about the party," he says. "It was a mistake. I shouldn't have run. It really was too early."

On election night, Robinson watched the results with Max, Coro Strandberg and Joan Sawicki. "It was just such a difficult night. I was up in the hotel room with Svend, and he was trying to work on his speech. He'd never written a defeat speech. And that was a big thing. He'd never had to deliver one," Sawicki recalls. Once a volunteer in Robinson's riding association, Sawicki went on to become Speaker of the Legislative Assembly during Mike Harcourt's B.C. NDP government, and a cabinet minister under later NDP Premier Glen Clark. Throughout her political journey, Robinson had been both ally and mentor, but that night she was the one helping him. "In our careers together, it was the only time that he really allowed me to give back for him a little bit of what I felt Svend had done for me. Although it was a difficult night, a sad time, it was also a little bit special for me because I could do that. There weren't many times that Svend would allow you to get that close to him in a personal way."

His concession speech was gracious — "Magnanimous as always, vintage Svend," recalls Sawicki — and when it was over, he made his way to the Conservative and Liberal campaign headquarters to offer his congratulations. "That's class," said Conservative campaign manager Gary Mitchell. But even in the last act of Robinson's public life, he was a polarizing force. Instead of appreciating the gesture, the local Liberals had the same reaction some thought Alexa McDonough had when Robinson withdrew from the 1995 leadership race: they felt Robinson was trying to upstage his opponent. "Everybody else thought that it was not kosher for him to do it, that it was kind of trying to steal my thunder," Fry says. "It didn't upset me or anything, but it upset a lot of people."

• • •

There was one final way in which Robinson helped to make a difference in the period leading up to the 2006 election. For nine months, Dr. Julio Montaner and six men with AIDS had lobbied Health Canada to approve certain drugs that had been shown to be effective in clinical trials. Media attention was an essential part of their campaign. Facing public pressure, federal Health Minister Ujjal Dosanjh had indicated his personal support for Dr. Montaner and his patients but was unwilling to interfere with the bureaucrats making the decision. Health Canada rejected the application, suggesting the men wait to participate in another clinical trial a year later. But a patient with AIDS couldn't count on surviving a year; one of the men had already died waiting.

On December 2, 2005, two days before being acclaimed as the NDP candidate, Robinson held a press conference with two of the men, Tiko Kerr and Paul Lewand. "Who is running the department? Why are bureaucrats telling [Dosanjh] what to do?" he asked. "Hedy is Tiko's member of Parliament and Paul's member of Parliament, and nothing has happened. Nothing has happened on this issue." Three days later, activists bearing coffins demonstrated outside Dosanjh's campaign office. That day, the government indicated that a change in policy might be forthcoming. "Things are only moving because we're applying pressure, and they're only moving because we've gone public," said Kerr. On December 20, the drugs were approved through a "compassionate use protocol." In gratitude, Kerr, a popular Vancouver artist, donated a painting for Robinson to use as a campaign poster.

For one final time, Robinson had used his privileged position as a public figure to help bring additional media attention to a cause. "You can actually make a difference," Libby Davies says, reflecting on her former colleague's effectiveness as an advocate for change. "Sometimes people are very cynical about that. Even MPs can be cynical. And he showed that you can actually change something . . . He raised the bar on how an MP can work."

• • •

In conversation with New Democrats and those on the left, there is a common belief that, as Noam Chomsky said, we live in grim and ominous times. But equally common is the belief that Svend Robinson has done his part to illuminate the darkness. If anyone has earned the right to rest on his laurels, to ride off into the sunset, to enjoy a pension-funded life of leisure, he has. Asked if he considered retiring after his defeat, Robinson's response is immediate and unsurprising. "Never even for a microsecond," he says.

TWENTY

Chemin de Blandonnet 8

It's not quite Parliament Hill. Unlike the majestic neo-Gothic legislature dominating the Ottawa skyline, the glass office building that serves as the headquarters of the Global Fund to Fight AIDS, Tuberculosis and Malaria is monolithic but otherwise entirely nondescript. It's in Geneva, Switzerland, but not quaint, cobblestoned Geneva. It's near-the-airport Geneva, which could be near-the-airport anywhere. With a little imagination, it could even be on Kingsway, the main thoroughfare in south Burnaby. The L'Oréal corporate offices are across the street from the Global Fund, and it would be easy to mistake the two buildings for each other. But of the various organizations headquartered in the area, only one has invested over $22-billion since 2002 to fight diseases among the world's most vulnerable populations.

Inside, Svend Robinson is working the phones. As the senior advisor for parliamentary relations, he uses his influence with contacts in legislatures throughout the world to secure more funding for Global Fund initiatives. He follows budgets and parliamentary calendars, and tracks the fortunes of each political party, knowing that governments can be replaced and, with them, commitments to the world's poor. Usually he's travelling, attending conferences and meetings, but today he's catching up on his work in the office.

He has Australia on the phone right now, and he's promoting a recent Global Fund initiative in which wealthy countries agree to forgive half the debt owed to them by a developing country if the Global Fund promises to spend an equivalent amount fighting disease in the developing country. It's an arrangement that helps developing countries escape the crippling debt they owe to the world's wealthy, while allowing the Global Fund to do what it does best: finance effective programs that save lives.

It may not be Parliament Hill, but Svend Robinson is still Svend Robinson. He was instrumental in a 2010 lobbying effort to convince the Canadian government to increase funding to the Global Fund, which it did by 20 per cent that year. "He's effective," says Hedy Fry, who continues to encounter him in her work as a parliamentarian. "Svend is always effective in what he does. He doesn't let go." In Geneva he's respected by colleagues, who elected him to serve on the staff council, representing the interests of staff in talks with management, and also chose him to serve as a trustee of the multi-million-dollar staff pension fund. It's no surprise that his relationship with his superiors is sometimes testy. Neither is it surprising that, when there is tension, he usually has a good reason for the position he's taking. His uncompromising standard of ethics intact, Svend still has battles to fight, even in a respected international organization like the Global Fund.

Although shades of his former life permeate his work, the only reminder of his colourful political past on the walls of his office is a poster from a 1988 World AIDS Day church service in Halifax, at which he was the guest speaker. Otherwise, his walls are sparsely decorated. A photo of Max (now his spouse, after a private wedding ceremony in Burnaby in 2007 that escaped the media's attention) is taped to the printer on his desk. When he's not on the phone, he listens to classical music while he works. Casually dressed yet professional colleagues with an array of international accents pop into his office with questions. He sends few emails, preferring to get up and visit colleagues at their desks when he has questions of his own. He eats lunch at his desk. It's always the same: a sandwich, yogurt and fruit.

His work day over, Svend takes the elevator to the parking level and crosses the lot to his reserved spot, number 1007. The "1" has been partially obscured by recent repairs, leaving 007, a wonderfully ironic number for one of the chief critics of CSIS. He gets into his blue 2004 BMW 320d station wagon and begins the drive home. Max has rigged it to beep whenever he goes over the 120-kilometre-an-hour speed limit. It beeps. He slows as he approaches the French border, but he doesn't have to stop. Seeing his diplomatic plates, the border guards wave him through. Like many Swiss, he and Max do most of their grocery shopping in France, where food is cheaper. He picks up bread, cheese and pâté, and he's on the road again.

In contrast with near-the-airport Geneva, the small Swiss village of Prangins, situated on Lake Geneva between Geneva and Lausanne, is almost deliberately quaint. The old part of town, which a visitor can thoroughly explore in minutes, is nearly deserted. Eventually the lonely visitor will encounter a passer-by who will offer a friendly "Bonjour!" Many of the buildings are from the 1700s or earlier. As in any proper European village, there is a castle. The castle in Prangins was once owned by Napoleon's brother, and for a time the French philosopher Voltaire stayed in it as a guest. Svend pulls up in front of the townhouse where he and Max now live. It is a short walk from Lake Geneva, and an even shorter walk from a renowned Swiss psychiatric hospital, a fact Max loves to share with guests.

Immediately upon opening the door to their home, Svend is noisily accosted by two small, fluffy, white Havanese dogs, their long hair pulled up on top of their heads like 1980s ponytails. Svend and Max brought both dogs (named Jasmine and Cohiba) from Cuba when they were puppies almost a decade ago. In the presence of these dogs, the tall, robust man who thundered at Canada's prime ministers for a quarter of a century becomes a completely different person. He's instantly on all fours, hugging and kissing them as though he hasn't seen them in weeks. Whether the day is good or bad, when he gets home from work, the same spontaneous showering of affection is repeated.

• • •

After being defeated in 2006, Svend returned to work with the B.C. Government and Service Employees' Union. In 2007, Canadians active in Public Services International, a global federation of public sector unions representing workers in 140 countries, suggested he consider a position as an advocacy officer with the French-based organization. "As someone who believes strongly in the public sector, it was a great opportunity to speak out on behalf of the rights of working people, and for a stronger public sector," Svend says. Furthermore, in the wake of his defeat, the anonymity that life in Europe would provide was appealing. "In part, one of the reasons why I left the country — why I feel so comfortable in Switzerland — is that here, nobody knows who I am. I can just be totally anonymous and go about my life, and not be thinking, 'Jeez, what lens are they looking at me through?' And that's comforting," he says.

In 2008, Max encouraged Svend to attend an International AIDS Society conference in Mexico. A chance encounter at the conference with Stephen Lewis, and a brief meeting with Michel Kazatchkine, then the executive director of the Global Fund, led Svend to his current work. Svend credits Lewis with urging him to work on AIDS issues, recalling the distinguished activist and former leader of the Ontario NDP saying, "Why aren't you doing this work? You could really make a difference." Svend had always had tremendous respect for Lewis, and when he made that suggestion, Svend paid attention. He was initially hired to produce a report on how the Global Fund could engage more effectively with elected officials. Impressed with his recommendations, the Global Fund hired him full-time. Walking his dogs in a lakeside park with a view of the Alps, he reflects on his decision to stay. The work he does is challenging and makes good use of his unique skill set. He knows there aren't many people with the contacts and experience to do what he does. He enjoys the pace of life in Prangins, he adds, and could see staying in Switzerland indefinitely.

Despite the distance from B.C., Svend has maintained his friendships with those closest to him. Libby Davies and her partner, Kim, see Svend and Max several times a year, and Davies actually feels closer to him now that they are no longer colleagues. "It's just been growing," she says. "We've seen him in difficult circumstances. We've seen the side of Svend that many people don't see, and we're very respectful of that. I think that helped cement a friendship." Without knowing it, Davies uses almost the same words Svend uses himself to describe their friendship. She laughs, describing her trips to visit him. "I always say to him, 'Man, you have another career as a travel planner,'" she says. "We basically say, 'Okay, Svend, we want to come to Geneva,' and the next thing you know, he's told us what flights to come on, with the best stops . . . When we went the last time to Geneva, he booked the trains for us! And then we just paid him back." She still marvels at how he finds the time to be so involved in everything he does. "They're terrible cooks, though. They live out of a Costco frozen foods section. That's one thing that we've done on occasion is cook for them. They buy terrible things." What Davies describes wouldn't surprise guests who have seen Svend puzzle over how to turn on his own oven.

Svend and Max are able to spend about a month a year in B.C. and are treated like locals in the Gulf Islands. They have a place on Parker Island, which is accessible only by private boat. Jack Layton and Olivia Chow spent so much time there that when Svend and Max built a hot tub, the Toronto power couple chipped in to help cover the costs. Displaying a hint of Wayne Robinson's insatiable appetite for relocation, Svend and Max have moved regularly, even within the Gulf Islands. They are in the process of moving from Parker back to Galiano Island, to a comfortable place overlooking Montague Harbour and the sailboats dotting the bay. Svend is still drawn to natural settings, and although he is now, more than ever, a truly global citizen, he is very much at home on the west coast.

He still pushes boundaries, both metaphorical and physical. When he had a half day off during a conference in Zambia, he visited the mighty Victoria Falls and went bungee jumping. "I don't know what that says about him," Davies says. "Is he trying to prove something to himself? I don't know. Is he trying to prove that he can survive no matter what? That whatever bad things will happen, he will survive, and he'll be stronger? I don't know if it's like a never-ending test of himself." In the years since the theft, he has learned to recognize the warning signs of manic behaviour. Max and friends like Clayton Ruby have learned as well. "Clay has this little mantra. He says, 'Manic, manic, manic!' if I'm getting too rushed and approaching the precipice again," Svend says. His time management skills have improved, allowing him to maintain an emotional balance while dedicating himself fully to his work. "He does as much, or more," Max says. "I don't see it as an issue . . . So far, it's under control."

Svend appears to be at peace with the way his political career ended. "I had 25 amazing years in public life as an elected representative, and now I'm in a position where I can do some important work internationally. Personally, I have to say . . ." Here he pauses, then sighs. "I mean, probably having that incident happen was a good thing for me, because it forced me to confront the mental health challenges that I wasn't confronting, that I was just denying. And had I not done that, the consequences could have been fatal. And I'm still standing . . . It was horrendous. It was a nightmare. But it probably was also life-saving." He has come to see his mental illness as a gift that allowed him to accomplish as much as he did. "Part of that was that it was ultimately manic behaviour. Some of the most amazing artists, as well, have struggled with mental illness — Van Gogh and others, a lot of others, actually — and it's been a gift to them, too. So I look at it through that lens as well. While it's obviously had lots of destructive impact, it's also been a gift."

"It's really hard for him not to be working, not to be on the phone," Max says, considering the question of whether Svend might actually retire some day. It's a serious question, given Svend's history of overwork, but Max lightens the mood with a joke. "But if he retires, he might get something part-time as a telephone operator with Telus. That would make him happy."

•   •   •

In Burnaby, Svend still makes the little gestures that inspired such loyalty from the community. Del Lowe (formerly Del Carrell), one of the volunteers who helped him secure his first nomination as the local NDP candidate in 1977, is now in her late 80s. She recalls Robinson visiting during the 2011 election. Just as she'd remembered him, he was in a rush and only able to stay for a few minutes, but he took the time to make her feel valued. During his quick visit, he told her that people like her were the "backbone of the party." As she recounts the story, her elderly frame seems to grow a little taller. It's the sort of compliment a politician running for office gives, but Robinson isn't running for office. He simply wants to let people who helped him know that what they contributed mattered.

Now officially a non-resident of Canada, and therefore not entitled to vote in Canadian elections, Robinson has nevertheless maintained an active interest in Canadian politics since moving to Switzerland. After the 2011 election, he visited Ottawa to meet the new NDP caucus, now the Official Opposition. "I think he wanted to get the feel of all the Quebec MPs," suggests Olivia Chow, referring to the youthful Quebec contingent of the NDP caucus that she believes best represents Robinson's brand of politics in Parliament today. "It was wonderful. He's one of the elders. Imagine Svend being the elder!" she says, laughing. She considers the future of these young MPs. "Will they be as passionate as Svend? I don't know. It's too early. I've only worked with them for a few months, but some of these young guys are just — fire in their belly," she says. "There's never another Svend, but it's just good to see that there's a new generation of political activists up here. Passionate and very committed. Will they be as brilliant? Well, remember Svend became really experienced. He started very young."

The 2011 election brought a sense of rejuvenation, validation and empowerment to a party that had become used to being a disregarded also-ran. Finally, after decades of scrounging for occasional victories on isolated policies, the NDP would have the muscle to truly shift public discourse. Official Opposition status brought increased research funding, greater representation on parliamentary committees, more question time in the House and, most importantly, credibility. With a leader who had united caucus and who appeared to inspire Canadians perhaps more than any other politician of his generation, the NDP seemed poised for an even greater breakthrough. That promise was dealt a serious blow when Jack Layton was diagnosed with cancer for a second time, after already receiving treatment for prostate cancer. When the news broke that Layton was ill again, Robinson flew to Toronto to be with his friend. "He visited Jack when Jack was sick. He flew in, visited Jack and then flew out. He flew in specifically. It was very sweet of him," Chow says. When Layton died in August 2011, Robinson was devastated, not only by the loss of a good friend, but by what he saw as a lost opportunity for the NDP as well. "I had said to Jack that I was absolutely convinced that he would be prime minister. And I am. I remain to this day convinced that, had he lived, he would have been prime minister of this country. I have no doubt about that," he says.

Robinson hasn't felt as connected to the NDP since Layton's death. He wasn't present at the leadership convention that elected Tom Mulcair, Quebec's former Environment Minister, over Brian Topp, the party organizer backed by Ed Broadbent and much of the establishment. Notably, Robinson remained neutral in the race to succeed Layton. He encourages the NDP to carry on Layton's goal of forming the government. "When Jack first spoke of the importance of running, not to be the conscience of the nation but to be the government, and for him to be the prime minister, many in the party, including myself, were incredulous," Robinson recalls. "This was totally unrealistic, we thought. But Jack understood that this mind shift, both internal and external, was absolutely critical."

Robinson is open to strategic alliances with other opposition parties if it proves necessary, but draws the line at a merger with the Liberals. "Our core values and principles are too distinct," he says. He also cautions the NDP not to become so awed by the prospect of forming a government that it is afraid to take stances that could be perceived as radical. While he understood Layton's desire for the NDP to be seen as a party of "proposition, not just opposition," one criticism he makes of Layton's tenure is that on too many occasions during Stephen Harper's minority governments, the NDP supported Conservative bills in principle at second reading, hoping to make amendments in committee. "It led to support for a number of bills that were in my view profoundly flawed," he says, referring to several criminal justice bills, such as the bill imposing certain mandatory minimum sentences and raising the age of consent for sexual activity. In areas such as these, Robinson believes the NDP should have demonstrated its unequivocal opposition, instead of waiting for amendments that too often never came. Still, Robinson believes that the NDP can modernize its language and approach to draw in new constituencies, without sacrificing principles. "It is essential that the NDP speak to Canadians in language that resonates with them and their families," he says. "Effective communication is so important. If you have wonderful policies, but nobody knows what they are or understands them, you will never move people to support you."

Along with gains for the NDP, the 2011 election also resulted in a Conservative majority government. As an employee of the Global Fund, Robinson doesn't see it as his role to delve into an analysis of Stephen Harper's administration. He'd prefer to leave that job to current parliamentarians, a policy he'd adhere to no matter who was in power. When asked to offer general advice to today's MPs, he is more obliging. He draws upon his experiences in the constituency, advising MPs to serve all their constituents, not just those who voted for them. "Be the best MP you can be for them — responsive to their concerns, visible and active in the community — so they know that you have their back when they need you. And at the same time, don't be afraid to take a strong stand on the issues. Time and again my constituents in Burnaby and Vancouver would tell me that while they didn't always agree with my stands, they valued and respected the fact that they knew where I stood," he says. "And don't get 'Parliament-itis' — so caught up in the magic of being an MP that you forget who put you there and how to serve them." Just as crucially, though, he reminds MPs to look beyond their constituencies and make decisions as global citizens, considering the impact on the most vulnerable on the planet. "The oil sands and asbestos exports are classic examples," he explains. "They don't just impact Canadians or Albertans or Quebeckers, but have an impact far beyond our borders."

He also urges parliamentarians to pay closer attention to aboriginal issues. "If there is one overriding issue of injustice that we must as Canadians address, it's aboriginal justice," he says. "These are people who too often don't have clean drinking water, for God's sake, who have levels of infant mortality that are at Third World levels, whose kids still die of tuberculosis, who live in appalling poverty in cities like Winnipeg, Vancouver and Edmonton. I just think it's Canada's shame. I'm not involved anymore in Canadian politics, but if there's one important issue I can identify, that's it," he continues, becoming visibly upset. The passion that drove Robinson throughout his career rises to the surface. "If people knew that aboriginal people were jammed in some cases into absolutely inhumane housing conditions, and that their homes are sometimes firetraps — I mean, how many Indian people have died because of house fires? It's an untold story. It just makes me angry to even talk about it. It's a bloody — I don't swear, but it's a bloody outrage."

Robinson still has a nose for new ideas that are both heretical and compelling. One idea he'd like to see gain traction is that of a publicly owned financial institution that would compete alongside the big banks. Such an institution would bring some of the positive social values of a credit union; what he irreverently calls the "Left Bank" could offer better financial products to underprivileged citizens and more readily invest in small and medium-sized businesses. But because of its size, it would be far more powerful than a credit union. Another benefit of a publicly owned bank would be that the profits could be returned to Canadians in the form of social services. Mortgage profits, for example, could be returned to the housing sector. "Instead of a small group of wealthy shareholders benefiting, why shouldn't those profits be plowed back into affordable housing?" Robinson asks. In response to the inevitable argument from the right wing that governments are inherently inefficient and cannot successfully run a business as large and complex as a bank, he scoffs. "That's an ideological argument. There's not one shred of evidence that that's true," he says. "They said the same thing about public auto insurance."

The idea of a publicly owned financial institution is one Robinson has proposed before, in caucus and to the NDP's platform committee prior to elections, but the party wasn't willing to put it forward. Robinson sees such changes to the financial sector as part of a broader debate about the role of government and the public sector that should be taking place in the wake of the 2008 global financial crisis, a massive recession spurred in part by deregulation and predatory lending practices by powerful financial institutions. "This is a historic moment, with the demonstrable failure of global capitalism, when the left could be putting forward a vision of a very different world," he says. "I fear that the NDP and other social democratic parties are missing this opportunity, where they could be calling for truly revolutionary, transformational politics. Why not a publicly owned financial institution in Canada? Why not a publicly owned pharmaceutical company to challenge the power of big pharma, and make affordable drugs available, both in Canada and in Africa and other poor parts of the world? Why shouldn't the Canadian people own their own natural resources?" he asks. "With the exposure of the obscene profits and abuses of so many of the leaders of financial institutions globally, what a great opportunity for us to learn to do things differently. But we're letting it slip."

•   •   •

"Whatever fears he had, you would not see them. What you saw was utter commitment to principle," says Clayton Ruby. "He was the best MP to have ever existed. There is no one even remotely like him." Libby Davies is just as complimentary, saying, "I really believe that, politically, he's been the most important element in the NDP. He helped make the NDP what it is."

His influence on our legal landscape is undeniable, but the battles he fought to have that impact made him one of the most polarizing figures in Canadian political history. For thousands of Canadians who struggled for representation in mainstream politics, Robinson articulated their vision of Canada with an unflinching precision unmatched by any other political figure. For others, he provoked a visceral loathing, not just because of the positions he took, but also because of the audacious manner in which he sometimes presented his point of view. But what is most gratifying and beautiful about social evolution — and about a democracy in which people can freely express their views — is that, in many cases, positions for which Robinson was vilified when he first espoused them eventually became mainstream. Even now, in the interviews conducted to prepare this biography, he expresses opinions that in some cases are diametrically opposed to the status quo mantras of what is wrong and right with the world. One wonders how many of those opinions — so daring today — will one day represent the common wisdom.

Robinson's style made him more effective than perhaps any other opposition MP of his generation, but it was a style that may have had a shelf life. Arguably, it was less effective in his later years in Parliament, when opponents in the media were able to redefine his image, casting him as a self-interested showman. It wasn't true, but it made Robinson seem more predictable and, in so doing, dulled the interest of mainstream Canadians, whose opinions so often define public policy. But what he may have lost in his ability to galvanize popular opinion, he gained in credibility with people on the non-mainstream left. He became their voice and their link to the corridors of power on Parliament Hill. At the same time, the relationships he built across the political spectrum and his growing expertise in parliamentary procedure helped him maintain his effectiveness.

The audacity of his political vision ensured that conflict remained a dominant feature in his life. He was often the victim of bullies: the child of an abusive alcoholic, the new kid in school tormented by his classmates, the lonely gay man in a House of Commons where homophobia was rampant, the laughingstock of a vindictive media. Rather than succumbing to such victimization, he rose above it, choosing to use his own experiences to educate the public about discrimination and injustice. But rejecting victimization often meant embracing conflict, both with opponents and allies. He was a team player, in his own way, and was hurt when his colleagues refused to support positions he felt they should be fighting for together. He took the disagreements he had with leaders like Ed Broadbent and Alexa McDonough hard — harder, it seems, than the leaders themselves did. While some of his NDP colleagues occasionally earned Robinson's ire for what he saw as political fear and a lack of vision, perhaps their conflicts with him were exacerbated by Robinson's expectations of victimhood, and by his understandable need to fight back.

There are prominent New Democrats who feel that Robinson was a detriment to the NDP. They suggest that for decades they had to handle an unpredictable maverick who foisted unnecessary controversies upon them, and that it wasn't until his departure from politics that the NDP could finally contend for government. Others argue that, without him, the left flank of the NDP would have abandoned the party long ago, leaving it a hollow and superfluous imitation of the Liberal Party. But the supposed dichotomy between electoral pragmatism and steadfast principles must be rejected. There must be room for dissent in a successful, democratic party, and surely there is value in being able to tell the fearless, uncompromising truth, regardless of the political consequences. As Davies said, Robinson raised the bar on what an MP can do. Perhaps we should demand more from our politicians who walk the same marble hallways of Parliament that he once did. But we must also demand more from ourselves. We must learn not to punish politicians for presenting facts we don't want to hear but that are essential before we can achieve the dramatic change we need. When renowned scientists warn that human industry is causing fatal damage to the environment, and when every day tens of thousands of our brothers and sisters die of preventable disease, malnutrition or starvation — one child every four seconds — while untold billions are spent on weapons, and while the world's richest just keep getting richer while the gap between them and the poorest grows ever wider, dramatic change is an immediate moral necessity.

•   •   •

In the backyard of a modest townhouse in Prangins, on a flagpole that the owner discovered couldn't accommodate the rectangular Canadian flag, the square Swiss flag flutters in the wind. In the fridge are a variety of Swiss cheeses, the owner's favourite cheddar being more difficult to find in Switzerland. Though Gallic icons abound in the shadow of the Alps, *British Columbia Magazine* is on the coffee table, and Svend Robinson is upstairs, at his desk, on the phone, still working. There are no veterans of wars that never end.

Acknowledgements & Sources

I was washing the dishes one evening, in Kitchenuhmaykoosib Inninuwug First Nation where I was working in 2009, when I decided I wanted to write this book. I finally proposed the idea to Svend Robinson in 2010, and he agreed to provide me with a series of interviews, access to his personal archives and permission to contact his family, friends and colleagues for further interviews. The biography was written in Ottawa, Vancouver and Delta between 2011 and 2013.

There are many to thank, many more than this list will allow. Dennis Gruending provided mentorship during the early stages of the book. Rolf Maurer of New Star Books took a chance on an unknown writer. I am grateful to the many politicians, activists and parliamentary staff who agreed to be interviewed and to the colleagues and friends who gave me the benefit of their knowledge, experience and encouragement: Alexandre Audet, Brian Bell, Gaye Bell, Bill Blaikie, Patrick Boyer, Ed Broadbent, Pat Carney, Patrick Casey, Olivia Chow, Nick Ciavarella, Chris Considine, Bill Cunningham, Libby Davies, Allan Dawe, Frank Dimant, Sean Fewster, Dennis Foon, Dan Frederick, Hedy Fry, Terry Glavin, Bill Graham, Herb Gray, Maria Gruending, Thomas Hall, Meagan Hatch, Michael Hatch, Jamey Heath, Janice Hilchie, Brett Kenworthy, Ijab Khanafer, Phil Larocque, David LeDrew, Catharine Leggatt, Brian Lim, Sandra Loewen, Del Lowe, Alexa McDonough, Brendan McGivern, Audrey McLaughlin, Brian Mulroney, Alexis Normand, Lorne Nystrom, Jane Pepper, Abby Pollonetsky, Judy Rebick, Miles Richardson, Jason Richter, Max Riveron, Gretchen Robinson-Trollinger, Clayton Ruby, Joan Sawicki, Doug Sigurdson, Bill Siksay, Coro Strandberg, Peter Suedfeld, John Syrtash, Jan Taylor, Jamie Trepanier, Dana Truelove, Sonja van Dieen, Ian Waddell, Meg Wilcox, Lila Wing and Johan Wouterloot.

Philippe Boisvert and Laurence Brunet-Baldwin provided helpful legal insights. Michael MacDonald at Library and Archives Canada helped compile Robinson's massive archives kept there. The talented and lovely staff at Intuition Photography provided headshots and somehow made me look good. Elaine Brière, Sean Griffin and Philip Hannan generously allowed me to use their photos of Robinson, and Dennis Foon allowed me to borrow the phrase "Diamonds are Forever" from his screenplay on Robinson's life.

I would like to thank my mother, Judy, my father, Patrick, and my sister, Dana, for a million things, and for a lifetime of political education that led to this moment. I'd like to thank my wife, Janine Truelove, for another million things, and for putting up with me now. (I love you all, and any achievement of mine can be traced to the love and support you've shown me.)

The first four drafts were edited by Judy Truelove, who was my first editor when I was an elementary school student and is still the perfect writing teammate. The book is immeasurably better for her precise and insightful analysis and advice, and I am immensely grateful for the hours she spent poring over the text. The final drafts were edited by Audrey McClellan, who was as informed, professional and understanding as I could have asked for. Finally, I would like to thank Max Riveron and Svend Robinson. They opened their lives to me — at first, a near stranger — and were always available to provide interviews, documents and anything else I needed. No biographer ever had it so good.

WORKS CITED

Sources of research for this book include books, academic texts, and newspaper and magazine articles from major and minor Canadian and international publications. The official records of the House of Commons were also an invaluable resource. While other publications may distort, spin or revise, these public documents are the indisputably neutral record of what actually occurred in Parliament. Sources, therefore, include *Debates* (the transcript of speeches in the House, often known as Hansard), *Journals* (the record of decisions made in the House, including voting records) and similar publications produced by the Senate and parliamentary committees. Svend Robinson also provided a wealth of personal correspondence, campaign materials, notes, photos and journals.

Extensive interviews were conducted with Robinson, his family, friends and former colleagues, as well as with other parliamentary staff and experts in a variety of fields. In all cases, quotes from interviews conducted by the author are attributed in the present tense.

Below is a selection of sources, organized by chapter, topic and general chronology in the text.

INTRODUCTION

"Protester-in-chief": Clyde H. Farnsworth, "Canada's chief protester picks new cause: Suicide," *New York Times*, July 31, 1996.

"The knight of the vanishing left": Lisa Hobbs Birnie, *Western Lights: Fourteen Distinctive British Columbians* (Vancouver: Raincoast, 1996).

Length of service: Information on members of Parliament is available at the Parliament of Canada website, http://www.parl.gc.ca. (The two British Columbians with longer continuous service were Howard Charles Green and Angus MacInnis, and the three New Democrats were Les Benjamin, David Orlikow and Bill Blaikie.)

Stephen Harper disagreed: *Debates*, October 24, 2002.

1. THE YEAR OF THE DRAGON

Wayne Robinson's "wandering spirit": Phil Kinsman, "Svend Robinson, at 28, has the NDP's high-profile position as justice critic," *Ottawa Journal*, June 13, 1980.

Robinson's need for control: John Lownsbrough, "Canada's gay MP: How Svend Robinson survived his own honesty," *Saturday Night*, May 1989.

2. DIRECTIONS

Transient young people occupied the Student Union Building: "16-hour SUB occupation had its tense moments," *UBC Reports*, October 22, 1970.

Northern Ontario in the 1970s: Alvin Finkel and Margaret Conrad, *History of the Canadian Peoples: 1867 to the Present* (Toronto: Addison, Wesley, Longman, 2002).

Robinson's grievance: Svend Robinson's United Steelworkers of America grievance #352.

Sherwood Lett Memorial Scholarship: UBC press release, October 18, 1972.

Trudeau "bollixed": Allan Fotheringham column, *Vancouver Sun*, October 4, 1977.

End of marriage: "Robinson: Portrait of the MP as a young man," *Vancouver Sun*, February 5, 1981.

3. THE GIANT-KILLER

Barrett by-election: Interview with Robinson.

Broadbent's popularity: Nick Taylor-Vaisey, "Broadbent crusades against inequality," *Maclean's*, December 27, 2012, http://www2.macleans.ca/2012/12/27/ed-broadbent-crusades-against-inequality/.

Miscalculating Robinson: Allan Fotheringham column, *Vancouver Sun*, October 4, 1977.

Robinson's career as lawyer: Phil Kinsman, "Svend Robinson, at 28, has the NDP's high-profile position as justice critic," *Ottawa Journal*, June 13, 1980; Robert Matas, "There's no stopping Svend," *Globe and Mail*, June 19, 1999.

4. TOMORROW STARTS TODAY

1979 election: Roy Wood, "Readers' survey points to NDP strength in Burnaby," *Columbian* (New Westminster, B.C.), May 18, 1979; "Law student defeats SFU head Jewett for NDP nomination in Burnaby riding," *Vancouver Sun*, October 3, 1977; "CLC, NDP will keep up good work," *Columbian*, June 28, 1979; Lee Rankin, "Barrett hams it up," *Boundary Road*, April 18, 1979; "Lewarne challenges Robinson claim," *Boundary Road News* (Burnaby, B.C.), May 2, 1979.

"Rookie who hardly needs any seasoning": Douglas Fisher, "How the House shapes up," *Vancouver Sun*, October 19, 1979.

Early activities in the House: *Debates*, October 12, 16 and 19, and November 5 and 30, 1979; *Journals*, October 24, 1979.

Galindo Madrid: Jane Gilbert, "A man without a country" (thesis in Svend Robinson collection, Library and Archives Canada); Doug Collins, "Silly Symphony turned ship-jumper into a refugee," *Columbian*, November 27, 1979; *Debates*, November 19, 1979; correspondence from Ron Atkey, December 3, 1979.

1980 election: Jeffrey Simpson and Robert Sheppard, "Tories fall 139–133," *Globe and Mail*, December 14, 1979; Allan MacEachen, "Behind the fall of Joe Clark," *Toronto Star*, December 11, 2009, http://www.thestar.com/opinion/2009/12/11/behind_the_fall_of_joe_clark.html; "Robinson: Portrait of the MP as a young man," *Vancouver Sun*, February 5, 1981.

"Politics is like an addiction": Allan Saunderson, "All work and no play," *Burnaby Times*, July 5, 1979.

Political staff: Interviews with Del Carrell, Sandra Loewen, Coro Strandberg and Jane Pepper.

5. THE JUST SOCIETY

Social life: "Robinson: Portrait of the MP as a young man," *Vancouver Sun*, February 5, 1981.

Nazi war criminals: "Canada and war criminals: a timeline," *CBC News Online*, June 28, 2005, http://www.cbc.ca/news/background/warcrimes/timeline.html; *Debates*, April 15, 1981, and April 1, 1982; *Evidence of the Standing Committee on Justice and Legal Affairs*, December 1, 1981.

"Full-time Minister of Justice": George Brimwell, "Sex crime curbs needed now: MP," *Toronto Sun*, October 16, 1980.

Prison issues: Various correspondence to Robinson from inmates; *Debates*, November 14, 1980, June 3, 1981, and January 24, 1983; "Sharing cell in prisons 'dangerous,'" *Globe and Mail*, August 4, 1982; Jane Taber, "Repentant Robinson vows to stay thorn in side of government," *Ottawa Citizen*, December 8, 1984.

Sued for defamation: Judgments of the Supreme Court of British Columbia and Court of Appeal of British Columbia in *Parlett v. Robinson*; *Opinions of the Lords of Appeal for judgment in the cause Turkington and others (practising as McCartan Turkington Breen) v. Times Newspapers Limited*.

Thrown out of the House: *Debates*, May 6 and June 8, 1982 (in the clamour of Question Period, the Speaker missed what was said; after checking the record, on June 16 she offered Robinson the opportunity to retract his remarks. Robinson refused and was ejected); "Chrétien 'lied about report on Berger,'" *Ottawa Citizen*, June 9, 1982; Bruce Ward, "New Democrat ejected for saying Chrétien lied," *Toronto Star*, June 17, 1982; *Debates*, October 19, 1983 (criticizing the Speaker).

Glass bottles: Robinson's householder, Fall 1983; *Debates*, October 17, 1983.

Young offenders: *Debates*, April 15 and May 17, 1981; *Evidence of the Standing Committee on Justice and Legal Affairs*, April 20, 1982.

Freedom of information: *Debates*, January 29 and December 10, 1981, and June 28,

1982; "NDP says concessions enough to end information bill filibuster," *Globe and Mail*, July 1, 1981.

CSIS: Philip Rosen, "The Canadian Security Intelligence Service," Parliamentary Information and Research Service, Library of Parliament, January 24, 2000, http://www.parl.gc.ca/Content/LOP/researchpublications/8427-e.htm; *Debates*, February 10 and June 5, 12 and 19, 1984; "Kaplan says security law in jeopardy," *Globe and Mail*, June 6, 1984; "Limits placed on security bill debate in effort to end committee impasse," *Globe and Mail*, June 7, 1984; "MPs applaud Kaplan as security bill passes," *Globe and Mail*, June 22, 1984.

Maher Arar: "Harper's apology 'means the world': Arar," *CBC News*, January 26, 2007, http://www.cbc.ca/news/canada/story/2007/01/26/harper-apology.html; Commission of Inquiry into the Actions of Canadian Officials in Relation to Maher Arar, *Report of the Events Relating to Maher Arar* (Ottawa: Public Works and Government Services Canada, 2006); Neil Macdonald, "Canadians secretly added to U.S. security list: WikiLeaks," *CBC News*, May 18, 2011, http://www.cbc.ca/news/world/story/2011/05/15/rfa-macdonald-csis.html.

6. LOVE WITHOUT FEAR

Bathhouse riots and the Human Rights Act: Gerald Hannon, "Rage! The 1981 Toronto bathhouse riots," *Xtra!* February 17, 2011; Peter Bochove, "A deliberate campaign against gay sexuality," *Xtra!* February 17, 2011; *Debates*, May 9, 1980, June 19, 1981, and May 11, 1983; *Evidence of the Special Joint Committee on the Constitution of Canada*, January 28, 1981; call log book from Robinson's constituency office; "Tory MPs scuttle new gay rights bill," *Globe and Mail*, May 12, 1983.

John Lewis: Interviews with Robinson and Ian Waddell; Daniel Gawthrop, "Jumping to conclusions," *Canadian Forum*, December 1998.

Solicitation: *Debates*, December 17, 1981, and June 17, 1982.

"Information impresario": From the Jack Webster Foundation website, http://www.jackwebster.com/foundation/index.php?page=jack.

Airline charter cancellations: Correspondence from Robinson to Ed Broadbent; "Airlines overcharge on cancellations: MP," *Toronto Star*, November 15, 1982.

Robinson's Webster! appearance: Daniel Gawthrop, "Svend the survivor beats the odds," *Georgia Straight*, August 26–September 2, 1994; *Debates*, December 7, 1982; Robinson's personal journal (quote from PC convention).

NDP position on solicitation: Iain Hunter, "Ex-NDP justice critic to push policy on soliciting," *Ottawa Citizen*, February 21, 1983; Robinson's personal journal.

Dropped as justice critic: Jim Robb, "Outspoken MP 'disappointed' at being axed," *Ottawa Citizen*, January 20, 1983.

Later movement on solicitation: Tanya Gulliver, "Solicitation laws bad, say Young Liberals," *Xtra!* March 17, 2005; Report of the Subcommittee on Solicitation Laws, "The Challenge of Change: A Study of Canada's Criminal Prostitution Laws," December 2006; Sam Pazzano, "Ontario top court legalizes brothels, soliciting stays illegal," *Toronto Sun*, March 26, 2012.

Burnaby: Various Robinson householders and meeting minutes of Burnaby

NDP riding associations; George Brimwell, "What your MP can do for you," *Reader's Digest*, March 1988.

7. BARNACLES AND EAVESTROUGHS

Constitution Act, 1982, background: Michael Valpy, "A charter of equivocal rights," *Vancouver Sun*, November 3, 1980.

The Constitution in committee: *Evidence of the Special Joint Committee on the Constitution of Canada*, January 12, 21, 22, 27, 28, 29 and 30, 1981; Douglas Todd, "Should we render the Canadian Constitution unto God?" *Vancouver Sun*, June 19, 1999; Chapter 2 of the Constitution of South Africa (environmental protection as a constitutional right); Alvin Finkel and Margaret Conrad, *History of the Canadian Peoples: 1867 to the Present* (Toronto: Addison, Wesley, Longman, 2002) (lobbying from women's groups); *Debates*, May 9, 1980.

The Constitution back in the House: *Debates*, February 23 and November 20, 1981; call log book from Robinson's constituency office; *Journals*, November 26 and December 2, 1981.

Vindications: Terry Romaniuk, "The Oakes Test," Centre for Constitutional Studies, August 20, 2007, http://www.law.ualberta.ca/centres/ccs/rulings/theoakestest.php; Graham Fraser, "What the framers of the Charter intended," *Options politiques*, October 2003; Judgment of the Supreme Court of Canada in *Health Services and Support v. British Columbia*.

Property rights background: David Johansen, "Property Rights and the Constitution," Law and Government Division, Library of Parliament, October 1991, http://publications.gc.ca/Collection-R/LoPBdP/BP/bp268-e.htm.

Property rights in committee: *Evidence of the Special Joint Committee on the Constitution of Canada*, January 23 and 27, 1981.

Property rights in the U.S.: Carl J. Mayer, "Personalizing the impersonal: Corporations and the Bill of Rights," *Hastings Law Journal*, March 1990; Judgment of the Supreme Court of the United States in *Kelo v. City of New London*.

Property rights in the House: *Debates*, April 18, 21 and 29, 1983; interviews with Robinson and Ian Waddell; *Journals*, May 2, 1983.

8. WHATEVER MEASURES ARE NECESSARY

1984 election: Alvin Finkel and Margaret Conrad, *History of the Canadian Peoples: 1867 to the Present* (Toronto: Addison, Wesley, Longman, 2002); Peter Maser, "Gallup be damned — Mulroney marching ahead full steam," *Ottawa Citizen*, May 5, 1984.

MPs' attitudes towards homosexuality: Interview with Patrick Boyer; Nicole Parton, "A shameful omission from the Rights Act," *Vancouver Sun*, March 1, 1988; *Debates*, October 20 and December 1, 1986.

Subcommittee on Equality Rights: Interviews with Robinson and Patrick Boyer; *Debates*, March 26, 1985, and May 7, 1996; David Rayside, *On the Fringe: Gays and Lesbians in Politics* (Ithaca, NY: Cornell University Press, 1998); *Report of the Subcommittee on Equality Rights*, 1985; "Toward Equality," Government response to the *Report of the Subcommittee on Equality Rights*, March 4, 1986.

Justice issues: Debates, November 29, 1984, October 28, 1985, November 20, 1985, October 7, 1986, and April 28, 1987; "NDP MP forces delay in study on capital punishment," *Ottawa Citizen*, December 19, 1986; "Red-light area backed," *Vancouver Sun*, October 11, 1985; "Bill on prostitution 'threat to freedom,'" *Globe and Mail*, September 10, 1985.

Foreign affairs: Robinson's householder, Fall 1986; *Debates*, January 21, 1985, and April 15, 1986; correspondence from Robinson to Speaker John Fraser, 1987.

Chile under Pinochet: "Hinchey Report on CIA Activities in Chile," U.S. Department of State, September 18, 2000, http://foia.state.gov/reports/hincheyreport.asp; "Flashback: Caravan of death," *BBC News*, July 25, 2000, http://news.bbc.co.uk/2/hi/americas/850932.stm; "Chile recognises 9,800 more victims of Pinochet's rule," *BBC News*, August 18, 2011, http://www.bbc.co.uk/news/world-latin-america-14584095.

Robinson's trip: Correspondence from the Chilean Community Association of British Columbia; trip report written by Barbara Jackman; "Diputado Canadisense justifica el terrorismo," *El Mercurio*, September 9, 1987; "Church Report on Covert Action in Chile 1963–1973," U.S. Department of State, December 18, 1975, http://foia.state.gov/reports/churchreport.asp (funding of *El Mercurio*).

9. WHITE SWAN

Haida blockade: Statement of Claim by the Council of the Haida Nation at the Supreme Court of British Columbia; "Logjam," *Vancouver Sun*, November 23, 1985; "Island in the storm," *Globe and Mail*, November 26, 1985; David Spaner, "From mouthy kid to high-profile MP," *Burnaby Now*, February 5, 1986.

Aftermath of blockade: Robinson's statement to the court; Judgment of the Supreme Court of British Columbia in *Western Forest Products v. Skidegate Indian Band*; "History of the establishment of Gwaii Haanas," Parks Canada, December 21, 2012, http://www.pc.gc.ca/pn-np/bc/gwaiihaanas/plan/plan1/Plan1C.aspx.

Tension with the NDP: Handwritten notes from a meeting of Robinson's riding association executive; Robinson's letter to the editor, *Globe and Mail*, June 21, 1999; Robinson's personal journal; Daniel Gawthrop, "Svend the survivor beats the odds," *Georgia Straight*, August 26–September 2, 1994.

Friendships with NDP MPs: Ian Mulgrew, "Svend should do the right thing: resign," *Vancouver Sun*, April 16, 2004; Brad Evenson, "A lone wolf joins the pack," *Ottawa Citizen*, October 15, 1995.

Heckling Ronald Reagan: "Nicaragua," in *Human Rights Watch World Report, 1989* (New York: Human Rights Watch, 1990), http://www.hrw.org/reports/1989/WR89/Nicaragu.htm; Robert Lee, "Commons cringes as MP heckles U.S. president," *Ottawa Citizen*, April 7, 1987; Svend Robinson, "Svend replies," *Burnaby Now*, May 6, 1987; Tim Harper, "Bush might not address House," *Toronto Star*, November 20, 2004.

10. LEAP DAY

AIDS: David Beers, "A very political prisoner," *Vancouver Magazine*, September 1994; Kate Dunn, "Bishops who oppose explicit AIDS-prevention programs are immoral: MP," *Montreal Gazette*, April 6, 1990.

Other gay politicians: John Lownsbrough, "Canada's gay MP: How Svend Robinson survived his own honesty," *Saturday Night*, May 1989.

Support from New Democrats: "Svend to say he's gay," *Vancouver Province*, February 25, 1988; handwritten notes from a meeting of Robinson's riding association executive.

Media speculation: David Myers, "Baring heart on Parliament Hill," *Angles*, April 1988; Dave Haynes, "Gay MP condemns media attitudes," *Calgary Herald*, June 11, 1988; "Laws needed to protect homosexuals from violence, MP says after incident," *Vancouver Sun*, February 29, 1988 (after office vandalized).

Coming out: Stephen Bindman, "'I'm proud to be gay,' MP Robinson declares," *Ottawa Citizen*, March 1, 1988.

Reactions: Stan Persky, "Svend Robinson speaks with Stan Persky," *Q Magazine*, April 1988; Dave Haynes, "Gay MP condemns media attitudes," *Calgary Herald*, June 11, 1988; "Robinson calls Devine a bigot for remarks on homosexuals," *Globe and Mail*, March 4, 1988; Susan Riley, "Svend is a liberal hero," View from the Hill column, *Ottawa Citizen*, March 1988; Keith Baldrey, "Vander Zalm worried by gays' declarations," *Vancouver Sun*, March 5, 1988; Barbara McLintock, "Zalm attacks gays," *Vancouver Province*, March 1988; Hilary McKenzie, "Homosexual relations," *Maclean's*, March 14, 1988; Svend Robinson, "When it comes to immorality, look who's talking!" *Globe and Mail*, August 7, 2003; Orland French, "Coming out of the closet to crusade," *Globe and Mail*, March 3, 1988.

Hate mail: Christine Harminc, "Robinson stars in campy parade to mark Toronto's gay pride day," *Globe and Mail*, June 27, 1988; descriptions of the hate mail are based on examples kept in the National Archives and in Robinson's personal archives.

Robinson as role model: Doug Ward, "Lone wolf back in the spotlight," *Vancouver Sun*, April 16, 2004; David Beers, "A very political prisoner," *Vancouver Magazine*, September 1994.

"Not a one-issue politician": Tom Barrett and Ellen Saenger, "Controversial Burnaby MP nominated by acclamation," *Vancouver Sun*, March 7, 1988.

Criticism from opponents during the campaign: Joanne MacDonald, "Gay candidate sparks muted debate," *Vancouver Sun*, October 6, 1988; John Lownsbrough, "Canada's gay MP: How Svend Robinson survived his own honesty," *Saturday Night*, May 1989; Larry Pynn, "Burnaby–Kingsway battle shapes up," *Vancouver Sun*, November 12, 1988; Robert Matas, "Robinson fighting phantoms in re-election bid," *Globe and Mail*, November 9, 1988; Michael Smythe, "The end of Svend?" *Life Gazette*; "Waxing offensive," *Globe and Mail*, November 4, 1988.

Robinson's campaign: Notes from a meeting of Robinson's riding association; David Rayside, *On the Fringe: Gays and Lesbians in Politics* (Ithaca, NY: Cornell University Press, 1998).

"Canada lost in this one": Larry Pynn, "Backers cheer Robinson: It's a win for gays, he tells rally," *Vancouver Sun*, November 22, 1988.

Robinson's new syntax: *Debates*, April 12, 1989, June 19, 1991, and June 12, 1992; Bill Andriette, "Svend! Canada's gay MP celebrates one year of being out," *Guide to the Gay Northeast*, June 1989.

Michelle Douglas: "Forces firm on ban of homosexuals," *Globe and Mail*, March 6, 1985; interview with Clayton Ruby; correspondence from Michelle Douglas to Robinson.

11. THE FRONT LINES

"We set out in this campaign": "Last words on a hard-fought campaign," *Vancouver Sun*, November 22, 1988.

Corporate donations: Correspondence between Robinson and various NDP officials.

Iraq hostages: Frederick Harris, "Thanks to Ottawa's heavy-handed diplomacy, Saddam Hussein might tell the three federal politicians trying to free Canadians detained in Iraq and Kuwait to go jump in the Gulf," *Globe and Mail*, November 13, 1990; "The price Iraq extracts for letting hostages go," *Globe and Mail*, November 9, 1990; Paula Kulig, "Svend Robinson: rebel with a cause," *Canadian Lawyer*, March 1995; Colin MacKenzie, "UN backs use of force in Gulf," *Globe and Mail*, November 30, 1990.

Sanctions and wars in Iraq: *Debates*, January 15, 1991; Michael Powell, "The deaths he cannot sanction; Ex-UN worker details harm to Iraqi children," *Washington Post*, December 17, 1998; Mike Trickey, "Revenge is only motive for attack on Iraq, says former UN inspector," *Ottawa Citizen*, June 6, 2002; Iraq Body Count website, http://www.iraqbodycount.org.

Sheila Copps and Robinson: Allan Fotheringham, "The way of the world," *Globe and Mail*, January 12, 2002.

China-Canada relations: "No slow boat from China," *Halifax Chronicle-Herald*, January 9, 1992; Julian Beltrame, "Should be catalyst for review of Canada's policy of aid, human rights," *Ottawa Citizen*, January 8, 1992.

Robinson's trip to China: Jan Wong, "Canadian MPs defy Beijing officials," *Globe and Mail*, January 6, 1992; Beryl Gaffney, "How we were kicked out of China," *Ottawa Citizen*, January 8, 1992; "MPs assaulted; Ottawa outraged," *Halifax Chronicle-Herald*, January 8, 1992; Ben Tierney, "Tape shows Chinese held diplomat against will," *Vancouver Sun*, January 13, 1992; "Short trip to China," *Montreal Gazette*, January 8, 1992; Angus Foster, "Canadian MPs expelled from China," *Financial Times*, January 8, 1992; Ben Tierney, "MPs say belongings stuffed into plastic bags," *Vancouver Sun*, January 8, 1992; "No slow boat from China," *Halifax Chronicle-Herald*, January 9, 1992.

Reaction to the expulsion from China: "MPs assaulted; Ottawa outraged," *Halifax Chronicle-Herald*, January 8, 1992; E. Kaye Fulton, "Forbidden excursions," *Maclean's*, January 20, 1992; Daniel Gawthrop, "Svend the survivor beats the odds," *Georgia Straight*, August 26–September 2, 1994.

Logging in Malaysia: David Suzuki, "The buzz saw of 'progress' hits Sarawak,"

Toronto Star, March 12, 1994; *Debates*, April 7 and May 7, 1992; payment vouchers given to the Penan by the logging companies.

Reaction to Robinson's visit: "Malaysia charge a 'desperate lie,'" *Ottawa Sun*, February 25, 1992; correspondence from Mahathir bin Mohamad to activist Ramena Tibando, February 21, 1992; transcript of press conference with Robinson and David Suzuki, February 14, 1992.

Mulroney's policy on foreign aid: Julian Beltrame, "Expulsion from China," *Ottawa Citizen*, January 8, 1992.

Robinson's trip to India: "Canadian MP's visit a mockery, says détenu," *World Sikh News*, February 7, 1992.

Clayoquot background: "Biodiversity in jeopardy," *Ottawa Citizen*, April 12, 1994; "Clayoquot decision balances environmental, economic and social values," Office of the Premier of British Columbia press release, April 13, 1993; Robert Matas, "Robinson joins protest against logging in Clayoquot Sound," *Globe and Mail*, April 17, 1993.

Clayoquot blockade: "Greens block road to protest B.C. logging," *Toronto Star*, July 6, 1993; Greenpeace handout entitled "Chronology of events in Clayoquot Sound," in Robinson's personal archives; correspondence between Robinson and members of the Tla-o-qui-aht Nation; Valerie Langer, "Clayoquot heroes — Honouring protest alumni's 10th anniversary," *Common Ground*, July 2003; "Woodworkers oppose Kennedy's visit," Industrial, Wood and Allied Workers of Canada press release, July 30, 1993.

Robinson only blocking trucks for an hour and a half: Proceedings at sentence of the Supreme Court of British Columbia in *MacMillan Bloedel Limited v. Sheila Simpson et al.*

Harcourt announces accord: Valerie Langer, "1993's Clayoquot Summer was a game-changer," April 13, 2013, http://focs.ca/2013/04/comment-1993s-clayoquot-summer-was-a-game-changer/; William Boei, "Clayoquot Indians join forest fight," *Vancouver Sun*, August 26, 1993.

Logging in Clayoquot Sound reduced: Valerie Langer, "Clayoquot heroes — honouring protest alumni's 10th anniversary," *Common Ground*, July 2003.

Reaction to Robinson's involvement from NDP and allies: "Clayoquot decision justified: MacWilliam," Lyle MacWilliam press release, July 6, 1993; Peter O'Neil and Doug Ward, "Robinson will admit contempt, colleague says," *Vancouver Sun*, May 12, 1994.

Possible charges: Greenpeace handout entitled "Chronology of events in Clayoquot Sound" and Bernie Johnstone's report to Crown Counsel, in Robinson's personal archives; Barbara McLintock, "Svend may face criminal charges," *Vancouver Province*, February 4, 1994; Larry Still, "MP admits criminal contempt," *Vancouver Sun*, July 7, 1994; David Beers, "A 'very political prisoner,'" *Vancouver Magazine*, September 1994; "For the record," *Vancouver Province*, July 8, 1994.

Charges and proceedings in court: Office of the Attorney General of British Columbia press release, May 10, 1994; Clare Ogilvie, "Svend ready to pay," *Vancouver Province*, July 7, 1994; "Robinson pleads guilty in blockade trial," *Globe and Mail*, July 7, 1994; Proceedings at sentence of the Supreme Court of British Columbia in *MacMillan Bloedel Limited v. Sheila Simpson et al.*; Robert Matas, "Reform urges more punishment for Robinson," *Globe and Mail*, July 27, 1994.

Experiences in prison: Paul Chapman, "Svend paints jail outhouse," July 28, 1994; "MP released from jail," *Globe and Mail*, August 4, 1994; Kate Malloy, "Svend Robinson released from prison on good behavior," *Hill Times* (Ottawa), August 4, 1994; Steve Mertl, "No more anti-logging protests," *Montreal Gazette*, August 4, 1994; Daniel Gawthrop, "Svend the survivor beats the odds," *Georgia Straight*, August 26–September 2, 1994 (media mob outside of prison).

Reform Party on Robinson's imprisonment: Robert Matas, "Reform urges more punishment for Robinson," *Globe and Mail*, July 27, 1994.

Robinson's salary during his imprisonment: Correspondence between Robinson and House of Commons Pay and Benefits.

Merits of civil disobedience: "Disobedience, and the just law," *Globe and Mail*, July 8, 1994; Gareth Kirkby, "Robinson — a hero for our times," *Burnaby News*, July 10, 1994; Frank Bucholtz, "Robinson — can't have it both ways," *Burnaby News*, July 10, 1994; Guido Marziali, "Robin Hood or just hood?" *Burnaby News*, July 30, 1994.

12. THE LAST WORD

Mitch Jacobson: *Debates*, September 24, 1991.

Sue Rodriguez: "Sue Rodriguez and the right-to-die debate," CBC Digital Archives, http://www.cbc.ca/archives/categories/politics/rights-freedoms/sue-rodriguez-and-the-right-to-die-debate/topic-sue-rodriguez-and-the-right-to-die-debate.html.

Considine's arguments in the B.C. Court of Appeal: Rand Dyck, *Canadian Politics: Critical Approaches*, 4th ed. (Scarborough, ON: Nelson, 2004).

Support from a majority of Canadians: "Robinson not afraid to speak his mind," *Burnaby Now*, May 29, 1994.

Decision of the Supreme Court: Judgment of the Supreme Court of Canada in *Rodriguez v. British Columbia*.

Rodriguez's friendship with Robinson: Interview with Chris Considine.

"Two Christian fundamentalists": Interview with Robinson.

Robinson not charged: Special Prosecutor Robert Johnston's report to the Crown, in Robinson's personal archives.

"I will work hard": Transcript of Robinson's statement to the press, June 28, 1995.

Legislative developments: *Debates*, February 15, 1994, September 21, 1994, and March 6, 1997; *Journals*, February 16, 1994, March 25, 1998, and April 21, 2010; archival material from the Standing Committee on Procedure and House Affairs, http://www.parl.gc.ca/CommitteeBusiness/CommitteeArchive.aspx?Language=E&Mode=1&Parl=35&Ses=1; "Assisted-suicide ban struck down by B.C. court," *CBC News*, June 15, 2012, http://www.cbc.ca/news/canada/montreal/story/2012/06/15/bc-assisted-suicide-ruling.html; "Assisted-suicide crusader Gloria Taylor dies in B.C.," *CBC News*, October 5, 2012, http://www.

cbc.ca/news/canada/british-columbia/story/2012/10/05/bc-gloria-taylor-dies.
html; Chantal Hébert, "Quebec gives life to idea of doctor-assisted death," *Halifax Chronicle-Herald*, January 20, 2013.

13. THE SILENCE OF OUR FRIENDS

Mulroney's legacy: "Hounded by low ratings, Canada's Mulroney resigns," *Spokane Spokesman-Review*, February 25, 1993; Robert Walker, "Albertans well rewarded with patronage plums," *Calgary Herald*, August 25, 1985; "Chrétien vows new manner of leadership," *Lakeland* (FL) *Ledger*, November 7, 1993; "Canada's deficits and surpluses, 1963–2012," *CBC News*, March 25, 2013, http://www.cbc.ca/news/interactives/canada-deficit/.

1993 election and Peck flyer: Guido Marziali, "Peck gets heck; apologizes," *Burnaby News*, October 20, 1993; Guido Marziali, "Peck smears secure Robinson victory," *Burnaby News*, October 27, 1993.

Liberal policies: Alvin Finkel and Margaret Conrad, *History of the Canadian Peoples: 1867 to the Present* (Toronto: Addison, Wesley, Longman, 2002); *National Magazine*, CBC-TV, September 11, 1995, videotape in Robinson's personal archives; Alex Ballingall, "Canada sinks lower on the list of foreign aid donor nations," *Maclean's*, April 25, 2012; Jennifer Paul and Marcus Pistor, "Official development assistance spending," *In Brief* (publication of the Parliamentary Information and Research Service, Library of Parliament), May 13, 2009; R. Douglas Francis and Donald B. Smith, *Readings in Canadian History: Post Confederation* (Scarborough, ON: Nelson Thomson Learning, 2002); Assembly of First Nations, "Fact Sheet on First Nations Education Funding," n.d., http://www.afn.ca/uploads/files/education/fact_sheet_-_fn_education_funding_final.pdf; Terrance Wills, "Liberal MP charges Martin budget breaks Red Book promises," *Montreal Gazette*, March 2, 1995; Bill Robinson, "Canadian military spending 2010–2011," *Foreign Policy Series*, March 9, 2011; Office of the Auditor General of Canada, "Canada's policies on chrysotile asbestos exports" (government response to Environment Petition No. 179 — Chrysotile asbestos), October 30, 2006, http://www.oag-bvg.gc.ca/internet/english/pet_179_e_28915.html.

"What the Liberals fought": Unidentified clipping from the *Globe and Mail*, May 1, 1995, in Robinson's personal archives.

"The current Liberal government": James Bickerton and Alain-G. Gagnon, *Canadian Politics* (Peterborough, ON: Broadview Press, 1999).

"The Reform Party represents": Matthew Hays, "Party line," *The Advocate*, June 27, 1995.

Liberal legislation on sexual orientation and Roseanne Skoke: *Journals*, June 15, 1995, and May 9, 1996; *Debates*, September 20, 1994, and May 9, 1996; Bill Pegler, "Interview with Svend Robinson: A man of the people," *Briarpatch*, November 1994.

Gun control: David Vienneau, "NDP stunned as 8 MPs aim to oppose gun law," *Toronto Star*, March 14, 1995; *Journals*, June 13, 1995.

1994 South African election: Correspondence from the Department of Foreign Affairs to Robinson, March 24, 1994; Robinson's personal journal.

Kurdish rights: *Debates*, April 6, 1995; correspondence between Robinson and officials with the Department of Foreign Affairs until 2004.

Burnaby firefighters: "Burnaby cleared for 'Operation Respond,'" *Burnaby News-Leader*, December 8, 1996; *Debates*, October 10, 1996; *Journals*, December 4, 1996.

Unpasteurized cheeses: Robinson's householder, Fall 1996.

Best local politician: Robinson's householder, Fall 1996.

Media attacks: Scott Feschuk, "Canada's hungriest publicity hounds," *Globe and Mail*, May 9, 1998; Daniel Gawthrop, "Svend the survivor beats the odds," *Georgia Straight*, August 26–September 2, 1994; David Beers, "A very political prisoner," *Vancouver Magazine*, September 1994.

Conservative media: Debbie Millward, "The *Vancouver Sun*: A corporate chronology," *Vancouver Sun*, December 19, 2011; "Conrad Black at the Huffington Post: Lord Of Crossharbour answers your questions," *Huffington Post Canada*, July 24, 2012, http://www.huffingtonpost.ca/2012/07/24/conrad-black-huffington-post-questions_n_1699566.html.

Personal life: Janet G. Woititz, *Adult Children of Alcoholics* (Deerfield Beach, FL: Health Communications, 1983); E. Kaye Fulton, "Gay and proud," *Maclean's*, May 16, 1994.

14. THE RAINBOW COALITION

NDP poll numbers: Doug Fischer, "NDP chooses between ideology or power," *Ottawa Citizen*, October 12, 1995; Matthew Hays, "Party line," *The Advocate*, June 27, 1995; Vicki Barnett, "Hopefuls assail right's 'ugly, divisive' agenda," *Calgary Herald*, October 2, 1995; Norm Ovenden, "Race to replace NDP leader attracts little interest, even among party faithful," *Ottawa Citizen*, August 21, 1995.

Media dismissals: "The New Democrats offer little new," *Globe and Mail*, September 13, 1995; Rick Gibbons, "Party with little to celebrate," *Ottawa Sun*, October 12, 1995; editorial cartoon, *Globe and Mail*, September 28, 1995; editorial cartoon, *Calgary Sun*, May 1, 1995.

"The party may be over" and "Robinson would bring": Daniel Gawthrop, "Svend the survivor beats the odds," *Georgia Straight*, August 26–September 2, 1994.

"Central doctrinal schism": Mark Kingwell, "Who's left?" *Saturday Night*, April 1995.

"We're doomed": Ian McLeod, "Under the rainbow," *Canadian Forum*, March 1995.

Robinson's candidacy: Gareth Kirkby, "Robinson goes for power," *Burnaby News*, April 30, 1995; Svend Robinson, *Economics for People and a Planet*, leadership campaign materials, September 1995; *National Magazine*, CBC-TV, September 11, 1995, videotape in Robinson's personal archives.

Robinson's supporters: Robinson's NDP leadership campaign materials and campaign team lists.

Lorne Nystrom: Norm Ovenden, "Race to replace NDP leader attracts little interest, even among party faithful," *Ottawa Citizen*, August 21, 1995; Hugh Winsor, "Are the New Democrats renewable?" *Globe and Mail*, September 23, 1995.

Herschel Hardin: Hubert Bauch, "You have the right to choose, NDP candidates tell Quebecers," *Montreal Gazette*, June 12, 1995.

Alexa McDonough: Hugh Winsor, "Second fiddle leads NDP," *Globe and Mail*, October 16, 1995; Robert Fife, "NDP chooses between the firebrand and the bore," *Ottawa Sun*, October 13, 1995.

"The fears or prejudices of others": Robinson's NDP leadership campaign materials.

Team player issue: Doug Ward, "'Maverick' runs for leadership," *Vancouver Sun*, April 28, 1995; Hugh Winsor, "Feisty McDonough raises solidarity issue," *Globe and Mail*, October 13, 1995.

Robinson's support from youth, Quebec and McDonough delegates: "The NDP must change its ways to make the left relevant again," *Saint John Telegraph-Journal*, October 7, 1995; Tim Naumetz, "Political press pan NDP dress rehearsal in Hull," *Hill Times* (Ottawa), August 31, 1995; Hubert Bauch, "You have the right to choose, NDP candidates tell Quebecers," *Montreal Gazette*, June 12, 1995; Gareth Kirkby, "Robinson did Burnaby proud," *Burnaby News*, October 18, 1995; Glenn Wheeler, "Radical overthrow of the NDP," *Now Magazine* (Toronto), October 19–25, 1995.

Robinson's convention speech: Transcript of Robinson's speech to the 1995 NDP leadership convention.

McDonough's convention strategy: Warren Caragata, "Stunning ending," *Maclean's*, October 23, 1995; Gareth Kirkby, "No home advantage," *Burnaby News*, September 27, 1995; Geoff Bickerton, "Labour at the NDP convention," *Canadian Dimension*, December 1995–January 1996; David Rayside, *On the Fringe: Gays and Lesbians in Politics* (Ithaca, NY: Cornell University Press, 1998); Alex Munter, "Outlook from inside Svend's campaign," *Capital Xtra!* November 17, 1995.

Robinson's support for McDonough: Shawn McCarthy, "New Democrats pick McDonough," *Toronto Star*, October 15, 1995; Alex Munter, "Outlook from inside Svend's campaign," *Capital Xtra!* November 17, 1995; Robinson's personal notes.

Reaction to Robinson's withdrawal: Peter O'Neil, "Labour boss rejects NDP's Robinson," *Vancouver Sun*, June 6, 2002; Gareth Kirkby, "Robinson did Burnaby proud," *Burnaby News*, October 18, 1995; Hugh Winsor, "Second fiddle leads NDP," *Globe and Mail*, October 16, 1995; David Rayside, *On the Fringe: Gays and Lesbians in Politics* (Ithaca, NY: Cornell University Press, 1998).

Media reaction to McDonough's victory: "Electing Audrey II," *Winnipeg Free Press*, October 15, 1995; "Aléxa qui?" *La Presse* (Montreal), October 17, 1995.

15. FALLING

Reunification of same-sex couples: "The man from Havana," *Globe and Mail*, January 19, 1998.

Condition in hospital: Confidential patient file, provided courtesy of Robinson; correspondence from Vancouver Hospital President and CEO Murray T. Martin to *Vancouver Province*, January 7, 1998.

Back at work: Doug Ward, "Lone wolf back in the spotlight," *Vancouver Sun*, April 16, 2004; *Debates*, February 2, 1998; notes from Robinson's staff retreat, 1998.

Max and the media: Gareth Kirkby, "Side by each," *Xtra! West*, March 5, 1998; Robert Matas, "MP battered but not beaten," *Globe and Mail*, January 19, 1998; Doug Ward, "MP says love for his partner kept him alive after cliff fall," *Vancouver Sun*, January 13, 1998.

16. THE EXCLUSION OF ALL OTHERS

1997 election: Dan Hilborn, "Robinson joins NDP resurgence," *Burnaby Now*, June 4, 1997; Robert Sheppard, "The Battle for Burnaby," *Globe and Mail*, May 21, 1997; David Rayside, *On the Fringe: Gays and Lesbians in Politics* (Ithaca, NY: Cornell University Press, 1998).

Same-sex marriage: *Debates*, March 16, 1993, June 8, 1999, and October 29, 2001; *Journals*, March 25, 1998, April 10 and October 5, 2000, February 14, 2001, and September 16, 2003; Judgment of the Court of Appeal for Ontario in *Rosenberg v. Canada*; Judgment of the Supreme Court of Canada in *M. v. H.*; *Second Report of the Standing Committee on Justice and Human Rights*, March 24, 2000; Rand Dyck, *Canadian Politics: Critical Approaches*, 4th edition (Scarborough, ON: Nelson, 2004).

Kosovo War and the NDP position: *Debates*, March 24, 1999, and June 13, 2000; Lawrence Martin, "Robinson turns against both sides," *Ottawa Citizen*, May 27, 1999; Human Rights Watch, "The Crisis in Kosovo," February 2000, http://www.hrw.org/reports/2000/nato/Natbm200-01.htm; Richard Norton-Taylor, "MoD leak reveals Kosovo failure," *Guardian* (London), August 15, 2000; Svend Robinson, "Report of Fact-Finding Mission to Belgrade, Kosovo and Macedonia," copy in Robinson's personal archives; Vincent Marissal, "Un désastre complet," *La Presse* (Montreal), May 27, 1999.

Robinson's trip to Kosovo: Patrick Graham, "Lone walk out of Kosovo ends Robinson's odyssey," *National Post*, May 21, 1999; Svend Robinson, "Report of Fact-Finding Mission to Belgrade, Kosovo and Macedonia," copy in Robinson's personal archives; Pat Bell, "Stop the bombing, MP begs after visit to Balkan ghost towns," *Ottawa Citizen*, May 27, 1999; Christopher Michael, "Robinson peace mission heading into Kosovo," *National Post*, May 18, 1999.

Robinson and East Timor, before the referendum: *Debates*, October 7, 1998; "MP Svend Robinson demands Canadian government finally act on East Timor," Robinson press release, September 7, 1999; "Canadian Labour Congress delegation to East Timor," Canadian Labour Congress press release, August 10, 1999.

East Timor after the referendum: "Militias exact murderous revenge in East Timor," East Timor Alert Network press release, September 4, 1999; "Canada's meagre response: too little, too late," *East Timor Alert Network Newsletter*, Summer 1999; East Timor Alert Network strategy notes; *Evidence of the Standing Committee on Foreign Affairs and International Trade*, September 17, 1999.

Order of Timor-Leste: Presidential decree of April 24, 2012, *Jornal da República*, http://www.jornal.gov.tl/?mod=artigo&id=4022.

2001 Summit of the Americas background: Naomi Klein, *Fences and Windows: Dispatches from the Front Lines of the Globalization Debate* (Toronto: Vintage Canada, 2002); Alvin Finkel and Margaret Conrad, *History of the Canadian Peoples: 1867 to the Present* (Toronto: Addison, Wesley, Longman, 2002); *Debates*, February 28, 2001.

Police brutality: "Quebec police used 5,148 canisters of tear gas at Summit of Americas," *Ottawa Citizen*, May 4, 2001; Naomi Klein, *Fences and Windows: Dispatches from the Front Lines of the Globalization Debate* (Toronto: Vintage Canada, 2002); Tooker Gomberg, "Silenced by a plastic bullet," *Now Magazine* (Toronto), June 1–15, 2001; Shirly Heafy, "Chair's Interim Report of Commission for Public Complaints Against the RCMP," October 29, 2003, and Shirly Heafy, "Chair's Final Report After Commissioner's Notice," February 18, 2004, in Robinson's personal archives; "RCMP pay Svend $10,000," *Vancouver Province*, September 30, 2005 (Robinson's lawsuit); "Canada: Amnesty International calls for public enquiry into alleged police brutality," Amnesty International press release, May 22, 2001.

"I don't want to exaggerate": Robinson's response to a question asked by Tom Parry of CBC Radio, as noted in the *Statement of Claim* in Robinson's action against the *National Post*.

Focus on pants: Justine Hunter, "Plastic bullet ruined my pants at Quebec Summit, NDP MP says," *National Post*, April 24, 2001; "Montreal firm offers Svend year's supply of pants," *National Post*, April 28, 2001; "Chinos for Svend sent in, along with $81.69 more," *National Post*, May 1, 2001; *Statement of Claim* in Robinson's action against the *National Post*; *Debates*, April 25, 2001; Michael Higgins, "Cabinet minister donates $10 to Svend pants fund," *National Post*, April 26, 2001; *Evidence of the Standing Committee on Foreign Affairs and International Trade*, June 7, 2001.

Legal proceedings with the National Post: Transcript of examination for discovery; settlement agreement between Robinson and the *National Post*; "Corrigendum," *National Post*, September 13, 2003.

Trip to Iraq and National Post editorials: Christopher Michael, "Robinson's adventure: a one-man trip to a war zone," *National Post*, May 15, 1999; Michael Powell, "The deaths he cannot sanction; Ex-UN worker details harm to Iraqi children," *Washington Post*, December 17, 1998; *Debates*, April 6, 2000; Alexander Rose, "Svend goes to Iraq," *National Post*, January 20, 2000.

Response to September 11, 2001: *Debates*, September 20, October 16, 18 and 29, and November 28, 2001; Government of Canada, "History of Canada's Engagement in Afghanistan 2001–2012," June 7, 2012, http://www.afghanistan.gc.ca/canada-afghanistan/progress-progres/timeline-chrono.aspx?lang=eng.

Omar Khadr: Aaron Wherry, "This young man in an unfortunate situation," *Maclean's*, September 30, 2012, http://www2.macleans.ca/2012/09/30/this-young-man-in-an-unfortunate-situation/; "Omar Khadr returns to Canada," *CBC News*, September 29, 2012, http://www.cbc.ca/news/canada/story/2012/09/29/omar-khadr-repatriation.html.

Conflict in Jenin: Report of the Secretary-General prepared pursuant to General Assembly resolution ES-10/10, https://www.un.org/peace/jenin/; Hilary Mackenzie, "UN envoy urges probe into Israeli army actions," *Vancouver Sun*, April 19, 2002; "UN: 'End the horror in the camps,'" United Nations press release, April 7, 2002.

Robinson's position on the Middle East: "Svend Robinson calls for Canada to stand firm on Middle East," Robinson press release, March 18, 2002.

Robinson's trip to the Middle East: Correspondence from Robinson, July 19, 2002; statement by Robinson, April 18, 2002; comments by Jack Layton during the 2003 NDP leadership debate, *CBC Newsworld*, January 7, 2003.

"I plead guilty": Peter O'Neil, "Israel 'appears' guilty of war crime: Robinson," *Vancouver Sun*, April 19, 2002.

McDonough on "state terrorism": Campbell Clark, "Canadian MP heading to Ramallah, hoping to meet Arafat," *Globe and Mail*, April 4, 2002.

"Racist, humiliating, destructive": Comments by Noam Chomsky on the Australian Broadcasting Corporation's *Lateline* program, April 8, 2002.

"Staining the Star of David": Nicholas Watt, "MP accuses Sharon of 'barbarism,'" *Guardian* (London), April 17, 2002.

Reaction to Robinson's trip: Steven Chase, "NDP relieves Robinson of Mideast responsibilities," *Globe and Mail*, April 19, 2002; Bob Rae, "Parting ways with the NDP," *National Post*, April 16, 2002; "The position of the New Democratic Party of Canada on the crisis in the Middle East," Alexa McDonough press release, April 16, 2002; Peter O'Neil, "Israel 'appears' guilty of war crime: Robinson," *Vancouver Sun*, April 19, 2002; e-mail from Jack Layton to Robinson, April 11, 2002.

Robinson informed McDonough in advance: Statement by Robinson, April 18, 2002.

Continued engagement in Middle East issues: Correspondence from Palestinian and Jewish Unity to Robinson, June 17, 2002; correspondence from Jews for a Just Peace to Robinson, October 31, 2002; correspondence from Robinson, June 3, 2002; Catherine MacLeod, "Canadian shocks summit with anti-Saddam speech," *The Herald* (U.K.), May 8, 2002; correspondence between Robinson and Alexa McDonough.

Speaking at Concordia: Svend Robinson, "Shame on Concordia University," *Globe and Mail*, November 25, 2002; Judy Rebick, "Panellists threatened with legal action," *Rabble.ca*, November 14, 2002, http://rabble.ca/news/panel-lists-threatened-legal-action.

Anti-semitism: Lauren Kramer, "Spat over painting sparks debate on free speech for Vancouver Jews," *Jewish and Israel News*, December 19, 2002; statement by Robinson, April 18, 2002.

Jews in the Soviet Union and Syria: Robinson's householders, 1987 and 1989; *Debates*, December 4, 1991.

International Solidarity Movement: Jenny Hazan, "Canadian MP comes under fire for pro-Palestinian Nobel nomination," *Jerusalem Post*, May 21, 2003.

17. ROBINSON VERSUS GOD, ROUND TWO

NDP's business-friendly approach: Jane Taber, "Socialist realism," *Ottawa Citizen*, September 26, 1998; Robinson's caucus retreat notes; correspondence from Gary Evans, one of Robinson's assistants.

Reactions to the NDP's new approach: Richard Cleroux, "Steamy stuff on the Hill," *Ottawa Sun*, September 4, 1998; Robert Fife, "NDP's McDonough hopes to be like Blair," *National Post*, December 21, 1998; notes from meetings of the Ontario NDP Provincial Council on September 19 and 29, 1998; Valerie Lawton, "NDP troops split on new 'alternative,'" *Toronto Star*, August 30, 1999.

Conflicts with McDonough: Notes from Robinson's staff retreats in 1997, 1998 and 1999.

God petition background: Jane Tibetts, "Atheists want 'God' removed from Charter," *National Post*, June 4, 1999; Douglas Todd, "Petition aims to take God out of Charter," *Vancouver Sun*, June 4, 1999; *Debates*, June 30, 1988 (petition to recriminalize abortion); *Debates*, June 8, 1999 (presenting the God petition).

"God is offensive to millions": "Correction," *Ottawa Sun*, June 9, 1999; Joel-Denis Bellavance, "NDP's Robinson accuses leader of 'stupidity,'" *National Post*, June 16, 1999.

Reaction to petition: Robert Matas, "Embattled Robinson leaps back into fray," *Globe and Mail*, June 12, 1999; Daniel Leblanc, "Bid to drop God from Charter fuels storm," *Globe and Mail*, June 9, 1999; Ian Austin, "Svend doesn't have a prayer, is demoted," *Vancouver Province*, June 10, 1999; Joel-Denis Bellavance, "NDP's Robinson accuses leader of 'stupidity,'" *National Post*, June 16, 1999; Art Babych, "'God petition' draws NDP fire for maverick MP," *Catholic Register*, July 5, 1999.

"Our most fundamental belief": *Debates*, June 9, 1999.

NDP MPs in favour of Reform motion: *Journals*, June 8, 1999.

"The true political stupidity": Correspondence from Robinson to NDP President Dave MacKinnon, June 12, 1999.

"By caving in": Paul Wells, "McDonough proved petitioners right," *National Post*, June 17, 1999.

Stockwell Day: "Stockwell Day: Preaching politician," *BBC News*, November 28, 2000, http://news.bbc.co.uk/2/hi/americas/1042814.stm.

NDP electoral strategy: Correspondence from Robinson to Alexa McDonough and NDP MP Dick Proctor, January 17, 2001.

New Politics Initiative background: Interview with Judy Rebick; New Politics Initiative website http://www.newpolitics.ca (no longer active).

Green Party: "New Politics Initiative and the Green Party," Green Party Interim Leader Chris Bradshaw press release, September 20, 2001.

"I think it's fundamentally flawed": Terry McDonald, "NDP gearing up for clash of ideologies," *Hill Times* (Ottawa), August 13, 2001.

NPI motion defeated: Jeffrey Simpson, "Here's to you, Mr. Robinson," *Globe and Mail*, November 26, 2001.

2003 NDP leadership race: "McDonough continues NDP revitalization —

launches leadership race," NDP press release, May 5, 2002; Bill Blaikie's NDP leadership campaign materials; Peter O'Neil, "Labour boss rejects NDP's Robinson," *Vancouver Sun*, June 6, 2002; Robert Sheppard, "Champion of the far left," *Maclean's*, October 7, 2002; Jack Layton's NDP leadership campaign materials; Doug Ward, "Low-profile New Democrat seeks top job," *Vancouver Sun*, July 27, 2002; Paul Sullivan, "And now heeere's death by endorsement," *Globe and Mail*, July 31, 2002.

Debate on war in Iraq: *Debates*, March 17 and 20, 2003.

Robinson and Stephen Harper: *Debates*, October 24, 2002; Campbell Clark and Brian Laghi, "Harper remark homophobic, MPs charge," *Globe and Mail*, October 24, 2002.

"In my political bones": Notes from Robinson's staff retreat, 2003.

Sexual orientation and hate propaganda background: *Debates*, May 11, 1983, December 13, 1999, November 21 and December 11, 2001; Kate Adach and Sam Eifling, "Ten years after Aaron Webster's death: What's changed?" *The Tyee*, November 17, 2011, http://thetyee.ca/News/2011/11/17/Homophobic-Hate-Crimes/.

Private members' bills and power in the Prime Minister's Office: Robert Roy Britt, "The odds of dying," January 6, 2005, *LiveScience.com*, http://www.livescience.com/3780-odds-dying.html (odds of dying of a stroke); Jeffrey Simpson, *The Friendly Dictatorship* (Toronto: McClelland and Stewart, 2001); *Journals*, June 2, 1995, and April 30, 2002; Status of House Business for the 1st Session of the 37th Parliament, September 16, 2002, http://www.parl.gc.ca/HousePublications/Publication.aspx?Pub=status&Language=E&Mode=1&Parl=37&Ses=1.

Bill C-250 introduced: *Journals*, October 24, 2002.

Opponents to Bill C-250: Laureen McMahon, "CCCB silent after passage of C-250," *B.C. Catholic*, May 3, 2004; Julia Garro, "Look who's waiting in the wings," *Xtra! West*, January 19, 2006; Douglas Todd, "Robinson defends his bill, labels foes 'fearmongers,'" *Vancouver Sun*, December 24, 2001.

Bill C-250 in committee: *Journals*, October 24, 2002; *Evidence of the Standing Committee on Justice and Human Rights*, February 25, May 6 and 13, 2003; *Minutes of Proceedings* and *Evidence of the Standing Committee on Justice and Human Rights*, May 14, 2003; Status of House Business for the 2nd Session of the 37th Parliament, November 12, 2003, http://www.parl.gc.ca/HousePublications/Publication.aspx?Pub=status&Language=E&Mode=1&Parl=37&Ses=2.

Bill C-250 back in the House: *Journals*, June 11 and September 17, 2003.

Bill C-250 in the Senate: *Journals of the Senate* and *Debates of the Senate*, April 28, 2004.

Conservative ad: Conservative Party of Canada print advertisement entitled "Conservative Values, Your Values," in Robinson's personal archives.

19. DIAMONDS ARE FOREVER

RCMP valuation of the ring: "No jail time for Svend Robinson," *CBC News*, August 6, 2004, http://www.cbc.ca/news/canada/story/2004/08/06/svend_plea040806.html.

"He said, 'I did it'": Ken MacQueen, "Svend Robinson running in election," *Maclean's*, December 19, 2005.

Robinson's press conference: Kim Pemberton and Neal Hall, "'I have failed': Tearful NDP MP Robinson stole jewellery, seeks help," *Vancouver Sun*, April 16, 2004.

Letter of apology: Allan Woods, "Svend Robinson charged with theft," *National Post*, June 22, 2004.

Reactions to the theft: Ian Mulgrew, "Svend should do the right thing: resign," *Vancouver Sun*, April 16, 2004; letter to the editor, *Surrey/North Delta Leader*, April 21, 2004; "Citizens Centre 'Charge Svend' ad creates media frenzy," *Life Site News*, June 14, 2004, http://www.lifesitenews.com/news/archive/ldn/2004/jun/04061408; Mitch D'Kugener, letter to the editor [newspaper unknown; clipping in Robinson's personal archive]; Allan Woods, "Svend Robinson charged with theft," *National Post*, June 22, 2004; Link Byfield's group was the Citizens Centre for Freedom and Democracy.

Court proceedings: "In Depth: Svend Robinson Profile," *CBC News*, October 21, 2005, http://www.cbc.ca/news/background/robinson_svend/; correspondence from Robinson to supporters, October 17, 2004; Reasons for Sentence in *Regina v. Svend Johannes Robinson*; Ken MacQueen, "Svend Robinson running in election," *Maclean's*, December 19, 2005; Allan Woods, "Svend Robinson charged with theft," *National Post*, June 22, 2004.

Post-traumatic stress or a brain injury: "Post-Traumatic Stress Disorder," Canadian Mental Health Association website, 2013, http://www.cmha.ca/mental_health/post-traumatic-stress-disorder/#.UcPDFhZSW18; Janet Steffenhagen, "Possible post-traumatic stress disorder, psychologist says," *Vancouver Sun*, April 16, 2004; Kim Pemberton and Neal Hall, "'I have failed': Tearful NDP MP Robinson stole jewellery, seeks help," *Vancouver Sun*, April 16, 2004.

Adult children of alcoholics: Janet G. Woititz, *Adult Children of Alcoholics* (Deerfield Beach, FL: Health Communications, 1983).

Medication and cyclothymic disorder: Ken MacQueen, "Svend Robinson running in election," *Maclean's*, December 19, 2005; correspondence from Robinson to supporters, October 17, 2004; "Bipolar Disorder," Canadian Mental Health Association Vancouver-Burnaby Branch website, 2010, http://vancouver-burnaby.cmha.bc.ca/get-informed/mental-health-information/bipolar-disorder.

Xtra! West Hero Award: Notes from speech made by Aerlyn Weissman at the *Xtra! West* 2003 Heroes Awards, April 18, 2004.

19. IN THESE GRIM AND OMINOUS DAYS

Robinson's return to work: Correspondence from Robinson to supporters, October 17, 2004; Ken MacQueen, "Svend Robinson running in election," *Maclean's*, December 19, 2005.

Hints of a comeback: Notes from Robinson's speech at the October 29, 2004, Burnaby–Douglas NDP riding association meeting; Gary Mason, "Robinson contemplating a return to political life," *Globe and Mail*, October 1, 2005.

Reaction from former colleagues: Robinson's personal notes.

Polling in Vancouver Centre: Correspondence from Robinson to the NDP caucus.

"That was a legitimate criticism": Gary Mason, "Robinson contemplating a return to political life," *Globe and Mail*, October 1, 2005.

2006 election supporters: Correspondence from Noam Chomsky to Robinson; Robinson's campaign materials.

Participation in OSCE conference and media criticism: Notes from Robinson's speech at the 2004 annual general meeting of the Burnaby–Douglas NDP riding association, October 29, 2004; correspondence from the Canada-Europe Parliamentary Association, June 25, 2004; "Robinson's Scottish trip defended," Canadian Press, July 16, 2004; Roy Peterson, editorial cartoon, *Vancouver Sun*, July 17, 2004.

Media reaction to Robinson's candidacy: Don Martin, "Federal NDP far from enamoured by Svend Robinson resurgence," *Vancouver Province*, October 23, 2005; "Svend and Hedy," *National Post*, October 22, 2005; Brian Hutchinson, "Who to believe in Vancouver Centre," *National Post*, December 9, 2005; "Corrigendum," *National Post*, December 10, 2005.

Criticism in Maclean's: Ken Whyte biography, Rogers Publishing website, http://www.rogerspublishing.ca/about_us/management/bio.shtml#Whyte; cover and editorial, *Maclean's*, December 19, 2005; Ken MacQueen, "Svend Robinson running in election," *Maclean's*, December 19, 2005.

Liberal and Conservative opponents support same-sex marriage: Gary Mason, "Claws are out as Fry takes on Robinson," *Globe and Mail*, December 3, 2005.

"Mrs. Robinson": Vaughn Palmer, "Killjoy Conservatives force fun-seekers to find humour elsewhere," *Vancouver Sun*, January 21, 2006.

Forced to choose between Robinson and Fry: Robin Perelle, "Torn between two allies," *Xtra! West*, January 19, 2006.

AIDS drugs: Peter O'Neil, "Svend Robinson on the comeback trail: Fighting his opponents and his past," *Vancouver Sun*, December 24, 2005; Peter O'Neil, "Priest dying of AIDS pleads for new drug," *Vancouver Sun*, December 3, 2005; Matt Kieltyka, "Release AIDS drugs: Svend," *24 hrs* (Vancouver), December 2, 2005.

20. CHEMIN DE BLANDONNET 8

Global Fund investments: "Fund the Global Fund to Fight AIDS, Tuberculosis and Malaria," Make Poverty History website, http://www.makepovertyhistory.ca/act/fund-the-global-fund-to-fight-aids-tuberculosis-and-malaria.

Canadian funding: Mitchell Raphael, "Why Svend Robinson speaks so well of Harper," *Maclean's*, March 7, 2011, http://www2.macleans.ca/2011/03/07/mitchel-raphael-on-why-svend-robinson-speaks-so-well-of-harper/.

Index

eign travel as "junkets," 143, 285–86;
Summit of the Americas, 224–26; SR
comes out, 126–30; SR uses for environmental issues, 112–13, 151, 154;
SR uses for foreign affairs, 100–101,
119, 147, 151, 230; SR uses for prison
reform, 48; SR uses to gain approval
for AIDS drugs, 290–91; SR uses to
speak against homophobia, 127, 128,
213–14; SR's 2005–6 campaign, 285–
87; SR's Chinese fact-finding mission, 146, 147; SR's sexuality, 61–62,
123; SR's theft of ring, 272–73, 275;
SR's use of, 40–41, 101, 182–83, 245,
262, 303 (*see also* Rodriguez, Sue);
SR's view of attacks, 183, 287; value
of access to, 40–41, 182–83, 273–74.
See also BCTV; CBC; Fotheringham,
Allan; *Globe and Mail*; *National Post*; ·
Province, The; Southam Inc.; *Toronto
Star*; *Vancouver Sun*; Webster, Jack;
Xtra!West
Medicare, 19, 29
Ménard, Réal, second MP to affirm
homosexuality, 137
mental illness, 276, 278, 279, 281. See
also bipolar disorder; post-trau-
matic stress disorder
Michael, Christopher, 226
Middle East: controversy over SR's
statements and visit to Israel, 229–
36; SR's 2002 visit, 263. *See also* Iraq;
Israel; Palestinians
Midnight Oil, 155
Milen, Robert, 99–100
Mitchell, Gary, 290
Mitchell, Margaret, 38
Montaner, Julio, 290
Morgentaler, Henry, 97
Mulcair, Thomas, 299
Mulroney, Brian: 1988 federal election,
134; calls SR after fall from cliff, 209;
death penalty, 97; Mulroneymania,
89; relationship with SR, 174–75;
retires, 175; "Svend as Minister of

Defence," 133; SR heckling Ronald
Reagan, 119; SR's theft of diamond
ring, 272; ties foreign aid to human
rights, 151–52; view of Ed Broadbent,
174; views on discrimination, 91–92;
views on sexuality, 94–95; vindi-
cated by Liberal cuts, 177
Mulroney, Gary, 95
Munro, Jack, 189
Murphy, Rod, 86
Murray, Lowell, 256
Mutang Urd, Anderson, 151

National Action Committee on the
Status of Women, 187
National Archives (Ottawa), SR's hate
mail, 130–31
National Citizens Coalition, 239
National Post: coverage of SR's 2005–6
campaign, 286; defines SR as self-interested publicity hound, 183; ideological vendetta against SR, 224–27;
not legitimate news source, 227; SR
sues for libel, 225–26
Nazi war criminals, 46–47
Netanyahu, Benjamin, 233
New Democratic Party of Canada
(NDP), 14; 1975 federal leadership,
28; 1979 federal election results, 36;
1984 federal election, 90; 1988 federal election results, 134, 139; 1989
federal leadership race, 139–40, 193;
1993 federal election, 175–76; 1995
leadership race, 185–98; 1997 federal
election, 215; 2000 federal election,
246; 2003 leadership race, 248–50;
2004 election, 282; 2006 federal
election, 288; 2011 federal election,
298; acrimony of leadership races,
192–93; "barren years" (1993–97),
178; Burnaby, 26; Charter of Rights
and Freedoms, 58, 72; co-operating
with Liberals, 27; convention policy
vs pragmatic politics, 64–67; debt
and deficit reduction, 188, 238, 239;